FUNDAMENTALS OF HISTORICAL MATERIALISM

The Marxist View of History and Politics

Doug Lorimer

Fundamentals of Historical Materialism
Doug Lorimer

Published in agreement with the author for sale only in South Asia.

First Published in India 2006
Reprinted 2009
Reprinted 2013
Reprinted 2025

ISBN 978-81-87879-90-9

Published by
AAKAR BOOKS
28 E Pocket IV, Mayur Vihar Phase I
Delhi 110 091, India
www.aakarbooks.com

Printed at
D.K. Fine Art Press, Delhi

Contents

Introduction

The purpose of this book is to provide the reader with a general introduction to the fundamental ideas of historical materialism — the Marxist theory of human history and society.

For Marxists the study of human history is inseparable from the study of society. Human beings, Karl Marx and Frederick Engels noted, "can be distinguished from animals by consciousness, by religion or anything else you like. They themselves begin to distinguish themselves from animals as soon as they begin to *produce* their means of subsistence".[1] That is, what distinguishes humans from other animals is that they consciously produce their means of subsistence through the use and fabrication of tools. But in order to do this, they must consciously cooperate with others of their kind. Society, which involves living and working together as an integrated group, is the result of labouring to produce food, clothing and shelter. How human beings have related to each to produce their means of life is the foundation of society and of human history. The fundamental laws of *social life* are identical, in the Marxist conception, with the fundamental laws that govern human *history*.

This approach stands in sharp contrast to the dominant approach of bourgeois social "science", as studied and taught in bourgeois academic institutions. The latter compartmentalises the study of social life into a number of unconnected disciplines such as archaeology, social anthropology, economics, political science, history, and sociology. Within these disciplines further compartmentalisation occurs. Thus "history" is divided into ancient, medieval and modern and into all kinds of history, for example, political history, economic history, cultural history, urban history, agrarian history, etc. Sociology, defined by bourgeois academics as the "study of the origin, development, organisation, and functioning of human society" and as "the science of the fundamental laws of social relations",[2] is divided into dozens of specialised branches none of which is concerned with actually uncovering the fundamental laws which govern the origin, development and organisation of human society.

1. Bourgeois Science and Reductionism

Bourgeois social "science" is incapable of fulfilling the task of a genuine science of society, i.e., to provide an integral theory of society by revealing the general laws that govern its origin, organisation and development. Indeed, the dominant schools of bourgeois social theory since the beginning of the 20th century have argued that it is fruitless to even attempt to create such a general theory of social development because, they claim, society is simply an accidental collection of atomic individuals and history is nothing more than a record of accidental, unique events. If everything in social life and history is individual and unique then, of course, it would be pointless to even conceive of a *science* of society and history. The bourgeois atomistic view of society inevitably leads not to scientific explanation, but to *mere description*, to the ordering and classification of empirical facts on the basis of the subjective likes and dislikes of the individual historian or social commentator.

Contemporary bourgeois thought has lost its earlier confidence in the capacity of human reason to uncover the objective, material causes of social phenomena. Such agnosticism in social theory has an inner connection with the irrationalism that is generated in bourgeois thought by the decay of the capitalist social system, with its deepening spiral of economic chaos, wars and social crises.

The atomistic view of society arises from one side of the contradictory nature of the capitalist social system. Capitalism separates and pits people against one another through the generalised commodification of the means of production and labour-power. Frederick Engels noted this when he described the crowds in the London streets in his first major work, *The Condition of the Working Class in England*:

> This isolation of the individual, this narrow self-seeking, is the fundamental principle of our society everywhere ... The dissolution of mankind into monads, of which each one has a separate principle and separate purpose, the world of atoms, is here carried out to its utmost extreme.[3]

This atomisation of social life under capitalism gives rise among its intellectual elite to a reductionist approach to the conception of all phenomena, both natural and social. This reductionist approach is characterised by four basic assumptions:

1. There is a natural set of units or parts of which any object of study is made.

2. These units are homogeneous within themselves, at least as they affect the object of which they are the parts.

3. The parts are ontologically prior to the whole. That is, the parts exist in isolation and come together to make wholes. The parts have intrinsic properties, which they

possess in isolation and which they lend to the whole. In the simplest cases the whole is nothing but the sum of its parts; more complex cases allow for interactions of the parts to produce added properties of the whole.

4. Causes are separate from effects, causes being the properties of subjects, and effects the properties of objects. While causes may respond to information coming from effects (so-called "feedback loops"), there is no ambiguity about which is the causing subject and which is the caused object.

This is the conception of the natural world and social life which permeates bourgeois science. It views parts as separate from wholes and reifies parts as isolated things in themselves, as causes separated from effects, as subjects separated from objects. It is an intellectual conception that has been generated by bourgeois social relations.

Beginning with the first stirrings of merchant entrepreneurship in 13th century Europe, and culminating in the bourgeois revolutions of the 17th and 18th centuries, bourgeois social relations have emphasised the isolated, commodity-owning individual as the primary social actor. By successive acts of enclosure, the mass of the population was separated from the means of production of life's necessities and reduced to "social atoms", colliding in the marketplace, each with his or her special interests and properties intrinsic to their role in society.

No individual person, however, is confined to a single role in bourgeois society. The same people are both consumers and producers, both owners and renters. Yet bourgeois social theory sees society as constructed of homogeneous individual parts, each with only one particular interest. The mass of "consumers" have their interest, "labour" its interest, "capital" its interest, with the whole of capitalist society taking a shape determined by the action of these categories on each other.

The claim that the capitalist social order is the "natural" result of the adjustment of demands and interests of competing interest groups is an ideological formulation meant to make the structure seem inevitable, but it also reflects the social reality that has been constructed. Workers as individuals do compete with each other to sell the only commodity they own, their labour-power, in a market whose terms have been made by struggles between workers and capitalist employers. Consumers do have an interest in the commodities offered to them that is antagonistic to the interest of the producers. But these interest groups have been *created* by the very system of social relations of which they are said to be the basis.

The reductionist method views the properties of any object of study as reducible to the individual properties of its structural elements, which are regarded as at base homogeneous. Hence an attempt is made to isolate these parts as completely as possible and to study these parts. This underestimates the importance of *interaction* not only of the parts of the object of study, but of the object of study with all other objects.

The faith in the atomistic nature of the world that lies at the basis of the reductionist approach of bourgeois science makes the allocation of relative weights to separate causes the main aim of science, making it more difficult to study the nature of interconnections. Where simple behaviours emerge out of complex interactions, reductionism takes that simplicity to deny complexity; where the behaviour is bewilderingly complex, it reifies its own confusion into a denial of lawful regularity.

The fundamental error of reductionism as a general point of view is that it supposes that the complex object is somehow "composed" of simple, homogeneous "natural" parts, which exist *prior to* and in *isolation from* the object. From this conception of the world, the aim of science is to find those smallest units that are internally homogeneous, the "natural" units of which the world is "composed".

The history of classical chemistry and physics is the epitome of this bourgeois, atomistic view of the world. In classical chemistry microscopic objects were composed of molecules, each of which was homogeneous within itself. With the development of the atomic theory of matter, these molecules were seen as composed of atoms of different kinds, so the molecules were then seen as internally heterogeneous. Then it appeared that the very atoms defied their name (*atomos*, indivisible), because they too were internally heterogeneous, being composed of elementary particles — neutrons, protons and elections. But even that homogeneity has disappeared, and the number of "elementary" particles has multiplied with each creation of a more powerful particle accelerator.

2. Dialectics and Reductionism

In contrast to the reductionist conception of bourgeois science, Marxism takes a dialectical approach to the study of the natural world and social life. It assumes from the beginning that all things are *internally heterogeneous* at *every level*. This heterogeneity does not mean that the object or system is composed of fixed, immutable natural units. Rather, the correct division of the whole into parts must vary, depending upon the particular aspect of the whole that we wish to understand.

It is a matter of simple logic that parts can be parts only when there is a whole for them to be parts of. Part implies whole, and whole implies part. Yet reductionism ignores this relationship, isolating parts as pre-existing units of which wholes are composed. In the real world, however, the two aspects cannot be separated. Indeed, all parts of the physical world are in interaction with each other to some degree, constituting a whole — the material universe.

The first principle of a dialectical view is that whole is a relation of heterogeneous parts that have no prior independent existence *as parts*. The second principle, which flows from the first, is that, in general, the *properties of parts* have no prior alienated existence but are acquired by *being parts of a particular whole*. In the atomistic conception of the world, the intrinsic properties of the alienated parts confer properties on the whole, which may in addition take on new properties that are not characteristic of the parts, i.e., the whole may be more than the sum of the parts. In the dialectical view, the parts have properties that are characteristic of them *only* as they are parts of wholes: the properties come into existence in the interaction that makes the whole. A person cannot fly by flapping their arms, no matter how much they try. Nor can a group of people fly by flapping their arms simultaneously. But people do fly, as a consequence of a particular socioeconomic formation that has enabled the creation of aircraft, pilots and fuel. It is not the society that flies, however, but individual members of that society, who have acquired a property that they did not have outside of that particular socioeconomic formation. The limitations of individual humans are negated by social interactions. The whole, thus, is not simply the *object* of interaction of the parts but is the *subject* of action of the parts.

A third dialectical principle is that wholes are *not inherently balanced or harmonious*. Their identity is not fixed. Rather they are the loci of internal *opposing* processes, and the outcome of these opposing processes is balanced only temporarily. The interpenetration of parts and wholes (parts *make* wholes, and wholes *make* parts) is a consequence of the interchangibility of subject and object, of cause and effect.

In the atomistic world of the reductionist, objects are the passive, caused elements of other active, causal subjects. In the bourgeois theory of the evolution of living organisms (the Darwinian and neo-Darwinian theory of evolution of species by means of natural selection), organisms are usually seen as the objects of the environment: through natural selection, autonomous changes in the environment cause adaptive alterations in the passive organism. In reality, organisms are both subjects and objects of evolution. They both make and are made by their environments (the physical world and other organisms that they interact with) and are thus actors in their own evolutionary history. For example, nearly every present-day terrestrial organism is under strong selection pressure to live in an atmosphere rich in oxygen and poor in carbon dioxide. But this metabolic problem has been posed by the activity of living organisms themselves over three billion years of evolution. Without the activity of living organisms

— producing oxygen by photosynthesis and depleting carbon dioxide by fixing it in the form of carbonates in sedimentary rock — the present-day terrestrial atmosphere would be nearly all carbon dioxide, as is the case with Mars and Venus.

Because elements recreate each other by interacting and are recreated by the wholes of which they are parts, *change is a characteristic of all objects and all aspects of objects*. This is a fourth dialectical principle.

In bourgeois thought change occupies an apparently contradictory position that follows from the history of the "classical" bourgeois revolutions of the 16th, 17th and 18th centuries. The triumph of capitalist social relations over feudalism was accompanied by an exuberant, arrogant, and liberating iconoclasm: what was, need not be; ideas do not have to endure. People could change their social position; success came by innovation. But with the consolidation of the dominance of bourgeois social institutions, capitalist society itself was seen as the culmination of social development, the final release of the "intrinsic property" of humanity — the pursuit of private gain through "free trade" — from the fetters of "artificial" feudal restraints. From that point on, change was to be restricted within narrow bounds: making technical innovations, gradual improvement of laws, balancing, adjusting, compromising competing interests.

Legitimation of capitalist society as the "end of history" meant denial of both the need and possibility for fundamental social change. Stability, balance, equilibrium and continuity became positive virtues in society and therefore also the objects of intellectual interest. Change was increasingly seen as superficial, as only appearance, masking some underlying stasis. Even where deep-going change cannot be ignored, it is acknowledged reluctantly and denied with the world-weary aphorism, "The more things change, the more they are the same".

In the reductionist world outlook, there are constants and variables — those things that are fixed and those that change as a consequence of fixed laws operating with fixed parameter values. In the dialectical world outlook, since all elements (being both subject and object) are changing, constants and variables are *not fixed, distinct* categories, but *relative* categories. The time scales of change of different elements may be very different, so that one element has the appearance of being a fixed parameter for the other. Furthermore, the laws and parameters of change *themselves change* in relation to changes in the object of which they are a part.

In the reductionist world view, entities may change as a consequence of developmental forces, but the forces themselves remain constant or change autonomously as a result of intrinsic developmental properties. In fact, however, the systems that are the *objects* of laws of transformation become *subjects* that change these laws. Systems destroy the conditions that brought them about in the first place and create the possibilities of new transformations that did not previously exist. The law that all living things arise from other living things only came into terrestrial existence about one billion years ago. Biotic systems originally arose from inanimate matter, but that origination made its continued occurrence impossible, because the living organisms consumed the complex organic molecules out of which biotic systems could arise from inanimate matter. Moreover, the terrestrial atmosphere that existed before the emergence of living organisms has been "polluted" with reactive oxygen to such an extent that these complex organic molecules rapidly disintegrate outside of living organisms.

The change that is characteristic of all material systems arises from both internal and external relations. The internal heterogeneity of a system may produce a dynamic instability that results in internal development. At the same time the system as a whole is developing in relation to the external world, which changes and is changed by that development. Thus internal and external processes of change affect each other and the system, which is the nexus of these processes.

The dialectical recognition that all objects are internally heterogeneous leads us in two directions. The first is the claim that there are *no ultimate units* out of which the world is built up — no fixed, homogeneous, primary "building blocks". This is not a preconception imposed by Marxists on nature but a generalisation from experience: all previously proposed homogeneous "basic units" have so far turned out to be heterogeneous and the recognition of this fact has opened up new fields for study and practical use. Therefore, the assertion that there are no homogeneous "basic units" points science in the direction of investigating each level of the organisation of matter without having to search for such illusory primary units.

A second consequence of the recognition of the heterogeneity of all systems, whether natural or social, is that it directs us toward an explanation of change in terms of *opposing processes united within that system*. Heterogeneity is not merely diversity; the parts or processes confront each other as *opposites*, conditional on the whole of which they are parts.

3. Motion and Contradiction

What characterises the dialectical world outlook of Marxism is its recognition that the world, in all its aspects, is constantly in motion. Constants become variables, causes become effects, and systems develop, destroying the conditions that gave rise to them. Even elements that appear to be stable are in a dynamic equilibrium of opposing forces that can suddenly become radically unstable, as when a dull grey lump of metal of a critical mass becomes a fireball brighter than a thousand suns. Yet the motion is not unconstrained and uniform. Organisms develop and differentiate, then die and disintegrate. Species arise but inevitably become extinct (the diversity of species that exist today constitute less than one percent of all those that have ever existed). Even in the less complex physical world there is no evidence of uniform motion.

Motion, change and development are the consequences of the interaction of opposing forces and processes which characterise all things. This central concept of dialectical thought, the *principle of contradiction*, is the most contentious and difficult of its principles. For the reductionist, contradictions can only exist in our understanding of things or between things, but not as an intrinsic character of things themselves. In the dialectical view, things move, change and develop because of the actions of *opposing forces within and upon them*, and things are the way they are because of the *temporary balance* of these opposing forces.

The principle that all things are internally heterogeneous directs our attention to the opposing processes at work *within* the object. The opposing forces are seen as contradictory in the sense that each *taken separately* would have *opposite effects*, and their joint action may be different from the result of either acting alone. But the object is not simply a passive victim of these opposing forces.

The dialectical view insists that persistence and equilibrium are not the normal state of things but require explanation, which must be sought in the actions of opposing forces. The conditions under which the opposing forces balance and the system as a whole is in stable equilibrium are quite special and depend upon the variables within the system not exceeding the parameters of the system. In this case, external events producing small shifts among the variables will be erased by the self-regulating processes of the system.

These opposing processes can now be seen as part of the *self-regulation and development* of the object. The relations among the stabilising and destabilising processes become themselves the object of interest, and the original object is seen as a system, *a network of positive and negative feedback.*

The negative feedbacks are the more familiar ones. If the blood pressure of an animal rises, sensors in its kidneys detect the rise and set in motion the processes which reduce blood pressure. If more of a commodity is produced than can be sold, the price of the commodity falls, and the surplus is sold cheaply while production is cut back; if there is a shortage, the price rises, and that stimulates production. In each case a particular state of the system is self-negating in that within the context of the system an increase in something initiates processes that lead to its decrease and maintain the system's integrity. But systems also contain positive (destabilising) feedback: high blood pressure may damage the pressure-measuring structures, so that blood pressure is underestimated and the homeostatic mechanisms themselves increase the pressure; overproduction may lead to cutbacks in employment, which reduce purchasing power and therefore increase the relative surplus.

Real systems include pathways for both positive and negative feedback. Negative feedbacks are a prerequisite for stability; the persistence of a system requires self-negating pathways. But negative feedback is no guarantee of stability and under some circumstances — a preponderance of positive feedback or if the indirect negative feedbacks by way of intervening variables are strong enough — the system will become unstable. That is, its own condition is sufficient cause of its negation. Thus systems are either self-negating (state A leads to some state not-A) or depend for their persistence on self-negating processes.

The stability or persistence of a system depends upon a particular *balance* of positive and negative feedbacks, on parameters governing the rate of processes falling within certain limits. But these parameters, although treated in mathematical models as constants, are *real-world objects* that are themselves *subject to change*. Eventually some of these parameters will cross the threshold beyond which the original system can no longer persist as it was. The equilibrium is broken. The system may go into wider and wider fluctuations and break down, or the parts themselves, which have meaning only within a particular whole, may lose their identity *as parts* and give rise to a qualitatively new system. Further, the changes in the parameters may be a consequence of the *stable behaviour* of the system that they condition in the first place.

The dialectical world view is that no system is really completely static, although some aspects of a system may be in dynamic equilibrium. The *quantitative changes* that take place within the apparent stability cross thresholds beyond which the *qualitative behaviour* is transformed. All systems are in the long run self-negating, while their short-term persistence depends on internal self-negating states.

Self-negation is not simply an abstract possibility derived from arguments about the universality of change. We observe it regularly in nature and society. Monopoly arises not as a result of the thwarting of "free enterprise" but as a consequence of its success; hence the futility of anti-trust and pro-competitive legislation. The freeing of serfs from feudal ties to the land also meant the possibility of their eviction from the land; freedom of the press from the political control of the feudal oligarchy has increasingly meant freedom for the oligarchy of capitalist press barons to control political information and debate. The self-negating processes of capitalism are often expressed as ironic commentaries, as the realisation of ideal goals turns out to thwart their original intent and produce their opposites.

A second aspect of contradiction is the *interpenetration of seemingly mutually exclusive categories*. A necessary step in theoretical work is to make distinctions. But whenever we divide something into mutually exclusive and jointly all-encompassing categories, it turns out on further examination that these opposites interpenetrate. Thus at first glance, "deterministic" (necessary) and "random" (chance) processes seem to exemplify mutually exclusive categories. The first implies order and regularity, when the second implies their absence. But processes that seem to be completely deterministic can generate apparently random processes. In fact, the random numbers used for computer simulation of random processes are generated by deterministic processes (algebraic operations). In the last decade, mathematicians have become interested in so-called chaotic motion, which leads neither to equilibrium nor to regular periodic motion but rather to patterns that look random. In systems of high complexity the likelihood of stable equilibrium may be quite small unless the system was explicitly designed for stability. The more common outcome is chaotic motion (turbulence) or periodic motion with periods so long as never to repeat during even long intervals of observation, thus appearing as random.

Second, random processes may have deterministic results. This is actually the basis for predictions about the number of traffic accidents or for actuarial tables. A random process results in some frequency distribution of outcomes. The frequency distribution itself is determined by some parameters, and changes in these parameters have completely determined effects on the distribution. Thus the distribution as an object of study is deterministic even though it is the product of random events.

Third, near thresholds separating domains of very different qualitative phenomena, a small displacement can have a big effect. If these small displacements arise from lower, i.e., less complex, levels of the organisation of matter, they will be unpredictable from the perspective of the higher, more complex, organisations. And in general the intrusion of events from one level to another appears as randomness.

Contradiction also means the coexistence of *opposing principles* (rather than opposing *processes*) which, taken together, have very different implications or consequences than they would have if taken separately. Commodities, for example, embody the contradiction between use-value and exchange-value (reflected indirectly in price, in "monetary values"). If objects were produced simply because they met human needs, we would expect the more useful things to be produced before less useful ones, and we would expect objects and methods of production to be designed to minimise any harm or danger and maximise durability or repairability. The amounts produced would correspond to the levels of need; any decline in need would allow either more leisure for those directly engaged in their production or the production of other objects. If objects had no use-value at all, of course, they couldn't be sold; use-value makes exchange-value possible. But the prospect of exchange-value leads to results that often contradict the human needs that called forth the commodities in the first place. Commodities will be produced, for example, only for those who can pay for them, and priority will be given to the production of those commodities with the highest profit margins. Productive innovations which make commodities easier and cheaper to make may create unemployment or ill health for workers and consumers. Thus the process of satisfying human needs by the creation of commodities whose exchange-value is paramount actually leads to the lack of satisfaction of human needs.

4. Human History and Natural History

The contrast between the dialectical materialist and the reductionist world views is most sharply seen in their radically different approaches to the question of the relation between human history and natural history. The reductionist view makes the continuity between prehuman and human evolution absolute. The reductionists, as biological determinists, see human affairs as the direct result of biological patterns that evolved in the past, which have created a fixed human nature (supposedly located in our genes) that determines our behaviour and social organisation — with the patterns of behaviour and social organisation that are characteristic of bourgeois society being presented as corresponding to this fixed human nature.

For Marxists the evolution of humans from prehumans presupposes *both* continuity and discontinuity. Marx insisted that human history was part of natural history. By this he meant that the human species is part of nature and, like other animals, humans have to interact with nature to survive. But humans differ from all other animals by the way in which they go about interacting with nature to sustain themselves. They do this by engaging in *labour*, i.e., consciously cooperating together to produce their means of subsistence. In doing so, they introduce a discontinuity in natural history — the emergence of a new level of the organisation of matter which is qualitatively different from other forms of animal life, i.e., social life. Labour expresses both humanity's *discontinuity* with nature and its *continuity* with nature.

> Labour [Marx observed] is, first of all, a process between man and nature, a process by which man, through his own actions, mediates, regulates and controls the metabolism between himself and nature. He confronts the materials of nature as a force of nature. He sets in motion the natural forces which belong to his own body, his arms, legs, head and hands, in order to appropriate the materials of nature in a form adapted to his needs. Through this movement he acts upon external nature and changes it, and in this way he simultaneously changes his own nature.[5]

Here is the answer to the *basic problem* that Marx and Engels began with in their study of human society: *how is change in general possible in human society?* They found the solution in the actual, practical *productive* interrelation between humans and nature, in the indisputable fact the very life-process of humanity, individually and collectively, involves a constant interaction by humans with nature to *produce* their means of life.

In the act and fact of production Marx and Engels saw, as all people may, that humanity not only can, but does, take a hand in the universal process of the redistribution of matter and motion. Thereby humanity demonstrates its material connection and dependence upon nature — but also, and thereby, humans alter nature, and that more or less in accordance with their own will and desires. This not only demonstrated humanity's "one-ness" *with* nature, but its dialectical distinction *from* nature, in the act and fact of their productive opposition of themselves to nature as one of nature's own forces. More: it demonstrated that nature's production of change, alteration, and new material formations was no more magical and mysterious than humanity's productive activity; and, also, that humanity's power of production was no less "miraculous" than nature's own.

This approach, applied to the long celebrated "world-riddles" — the origin of humanity, of thought — gave a conception so revolutionary and of such far-reaching profundity that its discovery is easy to miss — and all the critics of Marx and Engels, and 99 percent of the "simplifiers" of Marxism, miss it completely.

Natural science has established that the sum-total of the matter and motion in the universe is a constant quantity. But the fact of the indestructibility of the sum-total of matter and motion in the universe is only the conservative side of a truth which has another and a *revolutionary* side — the fact that *forms* of matter, and of motion — *including humanity itself* — are convertible, capable of *radical transformation*, and that, given the necessary preconditions, by humans. The "one-ness" of the universe is proved not by its abstract existence, but by this concrete and specific *convertibility*.

The recognition of the *material unity* of the universe is not reached by ignoring the multiple differences in the forms of matter and motion: it is demonstrated by the *practice* of both nature and humanity — which shows these differences to be not "ultimates" but mutable, conditional products of specific material interactions. Nor is it reached in the abstract evolutionism of bourgeois reductionism which first of all resolves all change into an infinity of alterations so minute that they can be ignored and treated as nonexistent. It is reached through the recognition that everything in the universe is the *product of an infinite process of dialectical interaction*. Only through this conception could humanity, and its thought processes and their historical progression, be brought within the scope of a unitary conception of the universe.

That the self (every person's consciousness of their own existence) and the not-self (the recognition of the existence of a world outside one's individual consciousness) are "ultimates" is true — in the sense that they and their oppositional relation are presupposed in all human experience. But equally true, and far more revolutionary in significance, is the fact that every act of human practice produces not only *objective change*, but the *subjective alteration* of "experience". And here lies the fact which shatters the agnosticism that today permeates bourgeois philosophy concerning the question of whether our thinking correctly reflects objective reality, wherein it is alleged that the former can at best only "represent" and "symbolise" the latter. Practice, and particularly social cooperation in *production-practice*, is the generating source of the consciousness of self, and also of the inseparable interrelation between the self and the not-self. People do not need to "prove" by logic the existence of either; both are proved simultaneously and in conjunction by the act and fact of practice — particularly production-practice.

Not that the universe is "ultimately" one whole, but that its immediate, concrete multiplicities show a capacity for being changed and transformed; not that humanity is, being material, one with the universe, but that humanity, *because it is material in a material universe*, can participate in the universal process of change and transformation, and in doing so can in social combinations *use* the universe more or less in accordance with human will — this was the revolutionary fact upon which Marx and Engels based their conception of human history.

Marx and Engels did not fall into the error of the "objectivist" (really: *contemplationist*) error of starting with humanity as a biological species and tracing its evolution from this starting-point to today by means of a string of conjectures. Just as in his analysis of capitalist economy, Marx started with its *existing* essential relation — that of the commodity — and found therein, on analysis, all the basic relations of bourgeois society, Marx and Engels also found the logical starting point for a scientific analysis of human society and its development, not by conjuring conjectures drawn from the past, but by examining the essential relation of society in the *present*.

Human beings (as biological specimens) can be "explained" — more or less — with the aid of the fact that humans were evolved as a distinct species by nature. But that of itself will not explain why they advanced beyond that stage. To find an indisputable fact upon which to base not only the theory that society can be changed, but a practical technique for bringing that change about, it was hopelessly irrelevant to look to the fact that what are now humans were once (in the persons of their ancient ancestors) *not yet humans*. A fact adequate to change the present had to be found actually available in the present. A fact sufficient to account for the *existence* of society throughout all its stages of development had to be found operating in *all stages of human history*. Moreover, this had to be such a fact as would from *its own nature* undergo sufficient changes to account, as well as for the existence of human society, for the sequences of changes, in all their historical multiplicity, which society had undergone.

What fact is there which is actively operating *at all periods* of human history? A fact sufficiently powerful to keep people in permanent interrelation even when their differences of desire set them flying at each other's throats? There is only one such fact — *the fact of common dependence upon material production*.

But Marx and Engels were not concerned only with society as a simple continuity. They were concerned, and that specifically and practically, with its *discontinuity*, its sudden jumps from one stage of existence to another. These jumps, which so baffle the "evolutionists" and "gradualists" that they attempt to argue them out of existence, were not only the very things that had to be explained; they were the outward and visible signs that *real* progress had in fact been achieved, that *new* forms of society could, and did, actually come into being — that the *will* to change the world had an *objective* justification.

That Marx and Engels propounded a conception of history that ascribed the fundamental cause of social evolution to production is well known. What is not so well known, nor appreciated, is that their *dialectical* materialist conception of history is not so much a theory of social evolution as it is a theory of *social revolution*, of how people can *change* their social life to progressively satisfy their material and cultural needs.

* * *

All things that are distinctive about humans, from tool-making, speech and thinking to the latest triumphs of art, science and technology, are products of our collective activity over the past several million years. What humans are is the product of human history, of *what* humans have made and *how* they have made it. This is what Marx meant when he wrote that the "human essence is no abstraction inherent in each single individual" but the "ensemble of social relations", i.e., the totality of social practice.[6]

Never before in history have human beings been so interdependent upon each other, upon their collective labour activities. Capitalism has socialised the labour process and welded the whole world into one interdependent productive system. This has been the progressive side of capitalism. It has laid the material social foundations for the free association of all humanity, while at the same time accentuating "dog-eat-dog" competition of each against all by making every human need a commodity in a worldwide market dominated by the drive for private enrichment by a tiny minority of super-rich families.

The social environment is the product of *collective human action*. It can therefore be *changed* by the collective action of the working people in order to create a social environment suited to the fundamentally cooperative nature of human social life, a social environment suited to the full satisfaction of the material needs and unhampered cultivation of the physical and mental capabilities of every person. But in order to do this, working people need a scientific understanding of the laws that govern and shape social life. That is what historical materialism provides. ❦

Chapter 1

Historical Materialism as a Science

Historical materialism is a science concerned with the general laws and motive forces of the development of human society. Like all other sciences, historical materialism seeks to reveal the essence of the object of its study by uncovering the *material relations* that are at the foundation of the surface phenomena of its object of study.

The great 20th century physicist Albert Einstein observed: "The belief in an external world independent of the perceiving subject is the basis of all natural science."[1] This belief is the cornerstone of the materialist world outlook. But pre-Marxist materialists were inconsistent and limited. They were unable to apply the principles of philosophical materialism to the study of social life and history and in this field held idealist views.[2] The great contribution of Marx and Engels to the development of scientific thought was that they completed the half-built edifice of materialism, that is, extended it to the study of society, thanks to which the materialist world outlook became for the first time comprehensive and fully consistent and effective.

1. The Emergence of Historical Materialism

Certain social and theoretical preconditions were required before historical materialism could come into being. It was ushered in by the logical development of progressive social, political and philosophical thought. But social conditions also played their part in revealing the possibility of discovering the laws of social life.

The acceleration of social development, the kaleidoscopic events following the English, and especially the French, bourgeois revolutions; the extreme aggravation of class contradictions and collisions; the emergence on the historical scene of the working class — such in general were the social preconditions that favoured the appearance of historical materialism.

When historical progress was extremely slow, as in the age of feudalism, it was difficult to perceive any particular laws of progressive social development, to understand the supplanting of one social system by another.

The great events that took place at the end of the 18th and in the first half of the 19th centuries showed that society was a living social organism subject to change and obeying in its existence and development certain objective laws that were independent of the human will and consciousness.

This was the conclusion reached by Hegel,[3] for example, in his philosophy of history. Despite his idealism and mysticism, Hegel attempted to consider world history from the standpoint of the internal necessity of its development. He made brilliant conjectures concerning the law-governed nature of social development and the correlation of freedom and necessity in social life.

The discovery of the laws of social development was also prepared by the studies of the English bourgeois economists William Petty, Adam Smith and David Ricardo, by their views of labour as the source of wealth, and their contribution to the labour theory of value. The English economists, Karl Marx said, gave us the economic anatomy of classes. Although they saw the basis of the existence of the three great classes of bourgeois society (landowners, bourgeoisie and proletariat) in the different sources of their income (ground rent, profits and wages), that is, in the sphere of distribution and not in the sphere of production, their views were an important step forward in the development of social thought.

The discovery by the French historians of the Bourbon restoration — Augustin Thierry, François Mignet and François Guizot (and before them by the great French utopian socialist Saint-Simon) — of the role of the class struggle as the motive force of the revolution in the new age was of great importance in preparing the way for historical materialism.

The pre-Marxist materialists also contributed to this process. Their interpretation of social and historical events was generally founded on idealist positions, and yet some of them made brilliant conjectures. The French 18th-century materialist Helvetius, for instance, pointed out the significance of the environment and circumstances in forming social opinion and human morals; bad morals were the result of bad circumstances, he wrote. From this he drew the conclusion that to change bad morals, circumstances must be changed. But he failed to give a scientific explanation of how this was to be done. In his view, the changing of social conditions was to be brought about by new, improved legislation, which could be introduced only by a ruler of genius. Here he maintained idealist positions.

The successes of natural science also had a certain influence on the birth of historical materialism. The end of the 18th century and the first half of the 19th saw redoubled attempts to produce a science of society that would be a strict social science, on the model of the natural sciences — mechanics, physics, chemistry and biology. These were misguided efforts inasmuch as society was regarded naturalistically, without taking into consideration its specific nature as a social organisation with its own special, intrinsic laws of development.

Marx and Engels were the first to produce a scientific theory of society. They created historical materialism by extending philosophical materialism and materialistically revised dialectics to the interpretation of society, by applying them to the revolutionary practical activity of the working class. Showing the intrinsic, inseparable connection between historical materialism and general philosophical materialism, Lenin wrote:

> Marx deepened and developed philosophical materialism to the full, and extended the cognition of nature to include the cognition of *human society*. His *historical materialism* was a great achievement in scientific thinking. The chaos and arbitrariness that had previously reigned in views on history and politics were replaced by a strikingly integral and harmonious scientific theory, which shows how, in consequence of the growth of productive forces, out of one system of social life another and higher develops.[4]

The universal laws of the development of matter discovered by dialectical materialism operate in society, but here they take a specific form. The dialectical method, applied to society, and the method of historical materialism are, in essence, identical concepts. But if we wish to know the laws of development of human society, it is not enough to know the general principles of philosophical materialism and the laws of dialectics; we must also study the specific forms of their action as they operate within a specific form of the organisation of matter. This means that in addition to general philosophical categories we must have such purely social categories as the socioeconomic formation, the productive forces and the production relations, the mode of production, the basis and the superstructure, social classes, and so on. These categories sum up the major laws of social being and socio-historical knowledge, the laws of the development of human society.

Marx and Engels formulated the basic propositions of historical materialism in the 1840s in *The German Ideology*. The new view of history, of social development, was at first only a hypothesis and method, but it was a hypothesis and method that for the first time made possible a strictly scientific approach to history. In Lenin's words, they made the study of society into a science, because they made it possible to reveal the recurrence and regularity in the development of social relations, to generalise the systems in various countries into the concept of the socioeconomic formation, to reveal the general that unites them and at the same time the inherent differences due to the specific conditions of their development.

In the 1850s Marx undertook his study of the highly complex socioeconomic formation of capitalism. In *Capital* he showed this formation in its inception, movement and development. He established how within it the contradictions develop between the productive forces and the production relations, between social classes, how on the basis of material production relations a corresponding political superstructure grows up, how certain ideas reflecting the outlook and interests of the basic social classes of capitalist society arise. With *Capital* historical materialism became a substantiated scientific social theory.

Marx and Engels did not apply the term "sociology" to their theory because the term was then used by various idealist positivist schools[5], which had nothing in common with a genuine science of society. But the doctrine they created in practice was and is the only scientific "sociological" theory worthy of the name, because it alone provides knowledge of the actual laws and motive forces of social development. Lenin pointed out:

> Just as Darwin put an end to the view of animal and plant species being unconnected, fortuitous, "created by God" and immutable, and was the first to put biology on an absolutely scientific basis by establishing the mutability and the succession of species, so Marx put an end to the view of society being a mechanical aggregation of individuals which allows of all sorts of modification at the will of the authorities (or, if you like, at the will of society and the government) and which emerges and changes casually, and was the first to put the study of society on a scientific basis by establishing the concept of the economic formation of society as the sum-total of given production relations, by establishing the fact that the development of such formations is a process of natural history.[6]

2. The Subject-Matter of Historical Materialism

Human society is in its essence and structure the most complex form of existence of matter. It is a specific, qualitatively unique part of nature, in a certain sense opposed to the rest of nature. This interpretation of the interrelationship between society and nature fundamentally distinguishes historical materialism both from idealism, which in most cases creates an absolute antithesis between society and nature, and from metaphysical materialism, which does not recognise the qualitative difference between them.

Giovanni Vico, the Italian philosopher of the 18th century, wrote that the history of society differs from the history of nature in that it is made by people, and only by people, whereas in nature phenomena and processes take place of themselves, as a result of blind, impersonal, spontaneous forces. The fact that society is the scene of action of people possessed of minds and wills, who set themselves certain goals and fight to achieve them, has in the past and often in our own time been a stumbling-block for sociologists and historians who seek to study the essence, the fundamental causes of social processes and phenomena. Some of them, absolutising the specific nature of social and historical events, metaphysically oppose the natural sciences, which study general, recurrent phenomena and processes, to the historical sciences, which are allegedly concerned only with the individual and unique. Thus, in the 19th century certain German philosophers representing one of the schools of neo-Kantianism (H. Rickert, W. Windelband) believed there must exist two different and even opposite methods of cognition: the so-called nomometric, or generalising method, which is applied by the natural sciences, and the ideographic, or individualising method (concerned only with individual, unique events), which is used by the historical sciences.

But such a metaphysical counterposing of the natural sciences to the social sciences is far-fetched and unjustifiable. We are no more likely to find in nature than in the history of society two phenomena that are absolutely identical (for example, two animals of a species or two leaves on one and the same tree). On the other hand, in society, in history, besides the specific and the individual there is also the general, which manifests itself in economics, in social relationships, in the political and intellectual life of various peoples that are at the same stage of historical development. It is by detecting these general features that we are able to discover the laws of social life.

It might be supposed that since social events and processes are the result of people's own activity, it should not be so difficult to understand them as it is to understand the phenomena of nature. And surely it ought to be easier for people and society to establish their power over social relationships than to subjugate the colossal forces of nature. But this picture is incorrect, as human history and the history of science show.

In the first half of the 19th century the natural sciences had already made considerable progress, but a general science of society was still only in embryo. Step by step humanity was getting to know the laws and forces of nature and bringing them under control. But it turned out to be a far more difficult task to discover the true nature of society and its laws. Even more difficult and prolonged was the task of mastering the social laws and processes and bringing them under the control of society. The possibility of solving these problems came only with the creation of social science, with its application to the practical task of the revolutionary transformation of social life.

Human society, social phenomena and processes are studied by various sciences. Political economy investigates the laws of the rise and development of commodity production. The legal sciences study the laws of the emergence of various political and judicial institutions, the state and law, and their functions. Aesthetics and art criticism study the laws of the rise and development of art, the relationship of art to reality, the methods of artistic creativity. Ethics studies the sphere of moral relationships between people. Thus, although human society is investigated by various sciences, each of them studies only a certain aspect of social life, one or another type of social relationships or phenomena (economic, political, ideological).

Historical materialism does not deal with the separate aspects of social life, but with its general laws and the driving forces of its functioning and development, with social life as an integrated whole, the intrinsic connections and contradictions of all its aspects and relations. Unlike the specialised sciences, historical materialism studies, first and foremost, the *general laws of the development of society, the laws of the rise, existence and motive forces of the development of socioeconomic formations.*

The general social laws, which concern all historical epochs, operate in each socioeconomic formation, in each epoch, in a specific way. Therefore, if we wish to obtain a correct idea of the character and essence of general social laws, we must study their specific functions in the various historical epochs, in the various socioeconomic formations (e.g., under primitive collectivism, "oriental despotism", ancient slavery, feudalism or capitalism). Thus the concept of "general social laws" includes the intrinsic connections and relations that are characteristic of the most general laws of the historically determined socioeconomic formations.

Historical materialism also differs from such an empirical discipline as history. History implies study of the history of different peoples, of events, in their chronological sequence. It treats the course of events not abstractly, in general theoretical terms, but in specific historical form, taking into consideration the concrete conditions of each country, the action of real people and the influence of chance, which sometimes plays a tremendous part in historical events.

Historical materialism, on the other hand, as a *science* of social development, studies not one particular people, or one particular country, but human society as a whole, considered from the standpoint of the most general laws of its development.

Historical materialism, like Marxist philosophy in general, combines both theory and method in one. It furnishes the dialectical-materialist solution to the basic, epistemological[7] question of social science — the question of the relationship between social being and social consciousness. It tells us about the most general laws and driving forces of society and is therefore a scientific general social theory. For this reason historical materialism is both an effective method of studying the phenomena and processes of social life, and a method of revolutionary action. Only with its help can the historian, the economist, the student of law or art find his or her way amid the complexities of social phenomena. Most importantly, it provides the political vanguard of the working class with a scientific guide for revolutionary social practice, for bringing about the proletarian-socialist revolution.

Historical materialism assumes particular methodological significance in a context of vigorous social development, of rapid change, when history takes a sharp turn and when a particularly strict and objective analysis of events, of the behaviour of classes and parties, is needed.

Historical materialism is the mainstay of scientific socialism, which studies the strategy and tactics of the working-class struggle, the laws and driving forces of the proletarian revolution and the construction of socialism.

Historical materialism is also highly relevant to concrete social research. When employing mathematical methods or methods of polling, interviewing, circulating questionnaires and so on, one must have a firm footing in the general social theory of Marxism and its method. In its turn Marxist social science, taken as a general theoretical science of society, relies in its development on specific social research, on the wide use of statistical and other empirical data concerning various aspects of social life. Specific social research reveals the mechanics of the functioning of social laws in diverse, real life conditions.

The classics of Marxism provide splendid examples of the application of the historical materialist method to the concrete study of social processes. "Theory, my friend, is grey, but green is the eternal tree of life." Lenin often cited these lines from Goethe's *Faust* in his polemics against those Marxists who failed to see the new and unexpected things produced by life in its rapid development. Life, what actually happens in the world, in history, is always richer than the most advanced social theory. This is a fact that we need to be particularly aware of in our stormy and dynamic age.

Historical materialism gives us an objective, scientific guide to the course of events, enables us to know and understand them, to predict them scientifically and to see the prospects and trends of social development, thus providing the theoretical basis for revolutionary action.

Bourgeois ideologists maintain that political partisanship is incompatible with science and thus discount the scientific character of historical materialism because it frankly acknowledges that it is a theoretical guide for revolutionary practice. Some of them maintain that scientific knowledge stands above the practical political activity of any particular social class or political party, and thus represents knowledge for the sake of knowledge. They thus divorce theory and practice, at least when it comes to *revolutionary* social practice. But can there be in a class-divided society any social theorists who soar above classes, disregard their interests and do not take a stand on the struggles between them? Such people, of course, do not exist. In fact, we constantly find that the very people who boast of their "uncommittedness" are in practice those who conduct a far from non-partisan struggle against Marxist social theory, who seek to discredit it and replace it with one or another variant of bourgeois social theory.

To the idea of class non-partisanship in social theory, which is essentially hypocritical, Marxists openly affirm that their social theory serves the practical needs of the working class. Lenin stressed that "... there can be no 'impartial' social science in a society based on class struggle", and that to "expect science to be impartial in a wage-slave society is as foolishly naive as to expect impartiality from manufacturers on the question of whether workers' wages ought not to be increased by decreasing the profits of capital".[8]

Class partisanship in social theory certainly does not coincide with a scientific approach when that theory expresses and defends the position and interests of the classes that have become historically outmoded in the course of social development. In doing so, social theory will depart from truth about objective social reality. And, in the opposite case, social theory is objective and scientific if, by truly expressing the dynamics of social reality, it expresses the position, interests and aspirations of the historically progressive classes of society.

3. The Objective Character of the Laws of Social Development

More than a hundred years ago in the preface to his 1859 work *A Contribution to the Critique of Political Economy*, Marx gave the fullest formal statement of the basic propositions and principles of historical materialism:

> In the social production of their life, [people] enter into definite relations that are

indispensable and independent of their will, relations of production which correspond to a definite stage of development of their material productive forces. The sum-total of these relations of production constitutes the economic structure of society, the real foundation, on which rises a legal and political superstructure and to which correspond definite forms of social consciousness. The mode of production of material life conditions the social, political and intellectual life process in general. It is not the consciousness of [people] that determines their being, but, on the contrary, their social being that determines their consciousness. At a certain stage of their development, the material productive forces of society come in conflict with the existing relations of production, or — what is but a legal expression for the same thing — with the property relations within which they have been at work hitherto. From forms of development of the productive forces these relations turn into their fetters. Then begins an epoch of social revolution. With the change of the economic foundation the entire immense superstructure is more or less rapidly transformed. In considering such transformations a distinction should always be made between the material transformation of the economic conditions of production, which can be determined with the precision of natural science, and the legal, political, religious, aesthetic or philosophic — in short, ideological forms in which [people] become conscious of this conflict and fight it out. Just as our opinion of an individual is not based on what he thinks of himself, so can we not judge of such a period of transformation by its own consciousness; on the contrary, this consciousness must be explained rather from the contradictions of material life, from the existing conflict between the social productive forces and the relations of production. No social order ever perishes before all the productive forces for which there is room in it have developed; and new, higher relations of production never appear before the material conditions of their existence have matured in the womb of the old society itself. Therefore [humanity] always sets itself only such tasks as it can solve; since, looking at the matter more closely, it will always be found that the task itself arises only when the material conditions for its solution already exist or are at least in the process of formation.[9]

This formulation of the basic propositions and principles of Marxist social theory highlights its two most important features. First, strict historicism, the consideration of society as something that is in a state of constant development. Second, the consistent application of the materialist view of history as a law-governed process, conditioned in the final analysis by the development of humanity's productive forces, by the level of development of its productive interaction with nature. Commenting on this formulation of Marx's, Lenin wrote:

At best, pre-Marxist "sociology" and historiography brought forth an accumulation of raw facts, collected at random, and a description of individual aspects of the historical process. By examining the *totality* of opposing tendencies, by reducing them to precisely definable conditions of life and production ... and by revealing that, without exception, all ideas and all the various tendencies *stem* from the condition of the material forces of production, Marxism indicated the way to an all-embracing and comprehensive study of the process of the rise, development, and decline of socioeconomic systems. People make their own history but what determines the motives of people, of the mass of people, i.e., what gives rise to the clash of conflicting ideas and strivings? What is the sum-total of all these clashes in the mass of human societies? What are the objective conditions of material life that form the basis of all of man's historical activity? What is the law of development of these conditions? To all these Marx drew attention and indicated the way to a scientific study of history as a single process which, with all its immense variety and contradictoriness, is governed by definite laws.[10]

We noted earlier that even before the appearance of historical materialism, particularly under the influence of the advances in natural science, people sought to understand social life, the history of society, as a law-governed process. But social laws were generally treated in the same way as the laws of the mechanical, physical or biological processes in nature. The specific features that characterise social life, which is created by people who possess minds and willpower, were thus ignored.

The great contribution of Marx and Engels was to reveal in social life, in the history of society, not only that which relates social laws to the laws of nature, but also to show that the socio-historical law differs radically from the law of nature. This is expressed in their description of social development as a *natural historical process*.

The natural historical process is a process that is as necessary and objective, as much governed by law, as natural processes; it is a process that not only does not depend on people's will and consciousness but actually determines that will and consciousness. At the same time, unlike the processes of nature, the natural historical process is a result of the conscious, purposeful activity of people themselves. At first glance this proposition appears to imply a logical contradiction. How can we reconcile the fact that social life, the historical process, is created by people possessing consciousness, will and desire, setting themselves certain tasks and goals, with the fact that history obeys certain necessary, objective laws that do not depend on human will and consciousness?

This contradiction can be resolved if we remember that people (and particularly large groups of people — classes, parties, etc.), in pursuing their aims, in being guided by certain ideas and desires, at the same time always live under certain objective conditions that do not depend on their will and desire and that ultimately determine the direction and character of their activity, their ideas and aspirations.

What is meant by *social laws*?

Any natural law expresses an objective, necessary, relatively stable connection between phenomena, between processes. Similarly, the laws established by historical materialism and other social sciences express a necessary, relatively stable and recurrent connection between social phenomena and processes.

Some social laws operate at all stages of social development. These include the laws of the determining role of social being in relation to social consciousness; the determining role of the dominant relations of production in relation to a particular structure of society; the determining role of the productive forces with regard to economic relations; the determining role of the economic basis in relation to the social superstructure; the dependence of the social nature of the individual on the sum-total of social relations, and so on.

Besides general social laws there are others that hold good only for certain social formations. These are primarily the law of the division of society into classes, which is characteristic only of certain relations of production, and the law of the class struggle as the driving force of history, which holds good only for those socioeconomic formations that are based on antagonism between classes.

Some critics of historical materialism say that a law is a relationship that exists always and everywhere. If the law of the class struggle does not conform to this demand, it is not then a law.

A shorter duration of existence and action is in general one of the features of the laws of social life in comparison with the laws of nature. Other social laws besides the law of the class struggle operate only where and when the requisite conditions and relations exist. Nevertheless they are objective, real laws expressing intrinsic, relatively constant connections between social phenomena and processes. After all, even the laws of the biology of the Earth do not operate on the Sun. But this does not lead anyone to doubt their reality, their objectivity.

Some bourgeois economists and sociologists elevate social laws (for example, the laws of the existence and development of capitalism) to the rank of eternal, natural, intransient laws; they see capitalism with its property inequality and relations of domination and subjection at all stages of development of society. Criticising such views of social and economic laws, Engels wrote:

> To us so-called "economic laws" are not eternal laws of nature but historical laws which arise and disappear; and the code of modern political economy, in so far as it has

been drawn up with proper objectivity by the economists, is to us simply a summary of the laws and conditions under which alone modern bourgeois society can exist — in short, the conditions of its production and exchange expressed in an abstract way and summarised. To us, therefore, none of these laws, in so far as it expresses *purely bourgeois relations*, is older than modern bourgeois society; those which have been hitherto more or less valid through out all history really express only those relations which are common to the conditions of all society based on class rule and class exploitation.[11]

Every law operates under definite conditions and the results of its action depend on those conditions, which vary from one formation to another and within each formation, and assume specific forms in different countries. Thus, capitalism in every country has acquired certain features connected with the historical past of that country, with a greater or smaller share of pre-capitalist economic structures. But these peculiar features do not affect the main thing; they do not abolish and cannot abolish the general laws inherent in capitalist society. There are no national laws of the development of capitalism, laws that are characteristic of each separate country; the laws of each separate socioeconomic formation, though specific in relation to the general social laws, are themselves general laws for all countries that are part of a given formation. Here, as in other fields, there is dialectical unity of the general and the particular, the international and the national. Ignoring or violating this unity, overstressing the national to the detriment of the general, the international, may lead to nationalist tendencies. Here there is a dividing line which the Marxist, the internationalist in politics and dialectician in theory, should see and understand.

4. People's Conscious Activity and Its Role in History

In regarding social development as a natural historical process do we not prevent ourselves from obtaining a correct understanding of the role of people's creative, revolutionary transforming activity? Does this not lead to belittlement of the historical activity, the historical initiative of the progressive social forces, to belittlement of the role of the subjective factor?

Those who take the subjective idealist view of history have often accused the Marxists of fatalism. Bourgeois sociologists maintain that the Marxist conception of the objective character of the laws of social development underestimates people's free, purposeful activity, that it is anti-humanist. They claim that it regards the economic factor as all, while ideas and various forms of social consciousness — philosophy, morality, religion — are nothing, and from the standpoint of historical materialism have no significance whatever. This is how the critics of Marxism present the case. But they confuse historical materialism with economic, vulgar materialism. The two trends are, however, radically opposed to each other.

Historical materialism in no way ignores the significance of politics, of social consciousness; on the contrary, it recognises their tremendous role in social life. Reactionary ideas and reactionary policy (for example, racist ideas, the policies of fascism) play an extremely negative role. They may and do bring great disasters upon the working people.

By contrast, progressive, revolutionary ideas — philosophical, economic, political and moral — and the policies based on them play a great part, particularly when these ideas become widespread among the masses, when they act as a mobilising, organising and transforming historical force.

Historical materialism, like Marxism as a whole, took shape and developed in the struggle against two opposite trends: First, against the subjectivism of the Young Hegelians; second, against providentialism and fatalism that belittle the significance of people's conscious, creative activity (against bourgeois objectivism, against "socialist" opportunism with its theories of the peaceful growing of capitalism into socialism, and so on).

The bourgeois critics of historical materialism try to discover a contradiction between the revolutionary activity of the Marxist parties and their teaching on historical necessity, particularly on the inevitable collapse of capitalism. These critics say, if we know that a lunar eclipse is inevitable and bound to occur according to certain laws, no one would think of creating a party for promotion of such an eclipse, but the Marxists teach that capitalism is bound to collapse and yet they create political parties to fight capitalism and establish socialism.

It would be foolish and absurd, of course, to create parties for the "organisation" of a lunar eclipse or the coming of spring and summer. Human activity does not participate in the motion of the Earth round the Sun, or in the motion of the Moon. The Earth rotated round the Sun, and the Moon around the Earth long before humans appeared on Earth. But history was made and is being made by people, and only by people. The laws of social development, unlike the laws of nature, are laws of *human activity*. Outside this activity they do not exist. Therefore, social revolutions, including socialist revolutions, occur only as a result of the struggle of the progressive classes on the basis of using the objective laws of social development, particularly the laws of class struggle. The more profound and comprehensive our knowledge of the laws of social development, the laws of social revolution, the higher is the consciousness, the solidarity, unity and organisation of the working people, the more successful the struggle for socialism, the swifter the progress of history.

Just as knowledge of the laws and processes of nature offers us the best chance of taming its spontaneous forces, so does knowledge of the social laws controlling the forces of social development allow the progressive classes to consciously create history, to fight for social progress. By getting to know the objective laws of social development the progressive social forces are able to act not blindly, not spontaneously, but with knowledge of what they are doing, and, in this sense, freely.

The laws of social development usually function as *tendencies*. They break their way through many obstacles, through a mass of chance events, through conflict with opposite tendencies supported by hostile forces, which have to be paralysed and overcome in order to ensure the victory of the progressive forces and tendencies.

Conflict between these various trends or tendencies means that in every historical period there exists more than one possibility. Thus, the productive forces created by capitalism provide — for the first time in human history — the possibility for the building of a socialist society, once they are freed from the constraints of capitalist production relations and subordinated to the collective management of the working people. The alternative possibility, however, is not the continued existence of capitalism, but the greater and greater aggravation of the contradiction between capitalist relations of production and the immensely powerful forces of production created by capitalism. If this tendency is allowed to run its course then humanity's productive forces will be driven toward stagnation and destruction due to ecological degradation, with the collapse of capitalism into a new form of barbarism, or even — as a result of a global nuclear conflagration — the destruction of the human race itself. The formation of revolutionary Marxist organisations in all countries, their conversion from groups of propagandists for socialism into popular parties capable of mobilising masses of people in the struggle for workers' power and socialism, is therefore a task of the highest order and utmost urgency. It calls for the highest levels of conscious activity, commitment and dedication. Without such parties, the struggle for socialism will not be victorious and humanity as a whole will suffer never-before-experienced levels of misery and degradation, and run the risk even of physical extermination.

Historical necessity is, therefore, not the same thing as predetermination. In real life, thanks to the effect of objective laws and various trends of social development, there arise certain possibilities, the realisation of which depends on the activity of the masses, on the course of the *class struggle*.

Knowledge of the laws of historical necessity, of the objective laws of social development, far from freeing people from the need to act, demands their active, conscious participation in order to utilise these laws to meet their social needs. The teaching of historical materialism on the natural historical process does not belittle the role of human beings, of their conscious activity, but rather shows the significance of this activity, of the struggle of the progressive social forces. Ignorance of these laws, failure to take into consideration actual conditions and means of struggle, condemns the masses of the working people, the working class and its parties, either to hopelessness and passivity or to adventurism and defeat.

In this way historical materialism resolves the old philosophical problem of the relationship between freedom and necessity, the problem of free will and determinism.

> Freedom [Engels observed] does not consist in the dream of independence from natural laws, but in the knowledge of these laws, and in the possibility this gives of systematically making them work towards definite ends. This holds good in relation both to the laws of external nature and to those which govern the bodily and mental existence of men themselves — two classes of laws which we can separate from each other at most only in thought but not in reality. Freedom of the will therefore means nothing but the capacity to make decisions with knowledge of the subject. Therefore the *freer* a man's judgment is in relation to a definite question, the greater is *the necessity* with which the content of this judgment will be determined; while the uncertainty, founded on ignorance, which seems to make an arbitrary choice among many different and conflicting possible decisions, shows precisely by this that it is not free, that it is controlled by the very object it should itself control. Freedom therefore consists in the control over ourselves and over external nature, a control founded on knowledge of natural necessity; it is therefore necessarily a product of historical development.[12]

What Engels has to say about the laws of nature fully applies to social laws, to the relation between freedom and necessity in social life. Social laws, while they are not known and while people act against them, operate as spontaneous forces that are hostile to people. But when we know these laws and their nature, the conditions and direction in which they operate, we are able to master them and make use of them.

The history of humanity has certainly not always proceeded in a straight, ascending line. There would be something very mystical about it if it consisted only in forward movement. However, despite its reverses, its zigzags, despite such historical disasters as wars, barbarian invasions, and the decline and fall of powerful states, human history, taken as a whole, has logically proceeded in an ascending line, from one socioeconomic formation to another, from the lower to the higher, as measured by the level of development of the social productivity of human labour.

Historical movement is multifarious, not uniform, and includes much that is specific and connected with the peculiar features and conditions of development of various peoples. But in this lies the great significance of historical materialism, which has revealed from the seeming chaos and infinite diversity the law, the regularity and recurrence in the main and most essential things that characterise the development of humanity.

Is there any *meaning* in the history of humanity, in the development of society, or is this movement as meaningless and elemental as the flow of rivers that sweep away everything in their path? There are no grounds, of course, for acknowledging any meaning imported to history from without, such as divine predestination, a prearranged program or supernatural destiny for humanity. At the same time the history of society in every epoch has its own definite content. The masses, the progressive social forces that make history, blaze the trail for new, more advanced economic, political and other social relations, and fight to accomplish certain historical tasks. People may be more or less fully aware of these tasks, or they may misapprehend them, sometimes in a mystified religious, fantastic form. In the great transitional periods of history the conscious, creative activity of the masses, of the progressive classes, attains new heights. Thus the history of humanity is not entirely spontaneous and social consciousness also plays its part.

The content of the present epoch is the struggle between the forces of capitalism and socialism, the revolutionary transition from capitalism to socialism. The conscious struggle of the working class and its allies for socialism accelerates historical movement. And this movement takes place through the overcoming of various difficulties, profound contradictions and antagonisms; it therefore proceeds not in a straight line. Here, too, there are zigzags and setbacks. But taken as a whole, the contemporary historical process is heading towards socialism, and in this lies its most profound meaning. ❦

CHAPTER 2
SOCIAL BEING AND SOCIAL CONSCIOUSNESS

In complete accord with the materialist world outlook, historical materialism proceeds from the proposition that social being is primary in relation to social consciousness, to "public opinion"

1. SOCIAL CONSCIOUSNESS AS THE REFLECTION OF SOCIAL BEING

Social consciousness is a reflection of social being. It may be a more or less correct reflection or it may be false. It does not determine the system of social life and the direction of social development, as the idealists assume. On the contrary, it is social being that ultimately determines social consciousness, the ideas, aspirations and aims of individuals and social classes.

What, then, is implied by the concept of "social being", which holds such an important place in historical materialism?

In philosophical materialism the category of being is regarded as identical with the concept of existence. Accordingly, social being is understood by Marxists as the material life of society, the material interactions and relations between people. For example, let us take exchange value, understood as the relationship between producers of commodities. Exchange value, according to Marx, is just as objective and material as the thing produced, the use-value. At the same time exchange-value is not something substantial that can be perceived by the senses. Exchange-value is the objective material relationship between commodity producers. This means that materiality in the social sense must not be fully identified with materiality in the sense of something substantial, tangible. Of course, society cannot exist without the material, substantial embodiment of the achievements of human labour. The instruments of labour, buildings, ploughed fields, canals are all the creation of human hands, the materialisation of human activity and ideas. But they are not the elements that constitute "social matter". This is composed of *the totality of associations humans enter into to maintain their existence*, including the reproduction of people themselves, the system of social relations that forms between people in the process of the production of material necessities of life, i.e., the production, or economic, relations, and the other relations that people form in the course of their social life (legal and political, religious, moral, artistic, etc).

Social being is primary because it exists outside and independently of social consciousness; social consciousness is secondary because it is a reflection of people's social being, of their social relations.

The question is sometimes asked: how are we to understand the independence of social being from social consciousness? Do not people themselves create their means of production? Is not the distinguishing feature of human labour people's own purposeful activity? Do not people themselves establish their relations with one another in the process of production? Reasoning on these lines, the Russian Machist Bogdanov[1] concluded that people could not combine together except with the help of consciousness and, consequently, social life in all its manifestations was conscious, mentally active life. Hence he inferred that social being and social consciousness were identical.

People themselves build their social life. But by no means always and by no means everywhere do they build it *consciously*. Of course, they perform every separate act of production consciously. But it does not follow from this that they are always conscious of the character of the social relations into which they enter in the process of production, of how these relations are changing, or what the social consequences of these changes are. Driven on by vital necessity, people work, produce goods and exchange them, and the economic relations thus formed do not depend on their conscious choice or desire, but on the level of social production they have achieved. From the fact that people enter into intercourse as conscious beings, Lenin explains, it certainly does not follow that social being is identical to social consciousness. Social consciousness may be a more or less correct reflection of social being, but it can never become identical to it because, first, social consciousness does not determine social being and, second, does not even entirely embrace it.

What is more, the will, aims, desires and aspirations of people, conditioned by their social or personal interests, embodied in their actions and making their appearance on the stage of social life, clash, interweave and come into contradiction with one another, and the outcome of it all is often that the desired is only rarely achieved. The clash of countless actions and aspirations of millions of people has often led to results that no one could foresee and no one sought to achieve. "Liberty, equality, fraternity" were the slogans that inspired the French people in the revolution of 1789 to 1793. But the liberty turned out in practice to be the liberty to sell labour-power, the equality turned out to be the formal, legal "equality" of the worker and the capitalist as buyers and sellers of commodities, and the fraternity, the "national unity" of exploiters and exploited in defence of the interests of the capitalist ruling class.

When they unleashed aggressive war against the USSR in June 1941, the Nazi imperialists sought to destroy the Soviet workers' state. But what happened in practice? The defeat of fascism, the overthrow of capitalist rule in a whole series of countries in Eastern Europe, including in the eastern part of Germany.

Characterising social development as a natural historical process, Engels wrote:

> . . . history is made in such a way that the final result always arises from conflicts between many individual wills, of which each in turn has been made what it is by a host of particular conditions of life. Thus there are innumerable intersecting forces, an infinite series of parallelograms of forces which give rise to one resultant — the historical event. This may again itself be viewed as the product of a power which works as a whole *unconsciously* and without volition. For what each individual wills is obstructed by everyone else, and what emerges is something that no one willed. Thus history has proceeded hitherto in the manner of a natural process and is essentially subject to the same laws of motion. But from the fact that the wills of individuals — each of whom desires what he is impelled to by his physical constitution and external, in the last resort economic, circumstances (either his own personal circumstances or those of society in general) — do not attain what they want, but are merged into an aggregate mean, a common resultant, it must not be concluded that they are equal to zero. On the contrary, each contributes to the resultant and is to this extent included in it.[2]

Only after the socialist revolution, when society acquires control over social relations, do people begin to achieve their aims on an ever increasing scale. Yet even in this period social development continues to remain a natural historical process, conditioned by objective causes and laws that exist outside the consciousness of people and determine their will, consciousness, aims and tasks. Thus, only as society advances toward socialism does it gradually overcome the spontaneity of social development, subordinating it to the conscious, collective will of society. But even here social processes are determined by objective conditions, by actual possibilities that people must take into consideration and proceed from in their actions.

2. The Concept of Intellectual Culture

When we speak of social consciousness we deliberately ignore everything individual and personal and consider the views and ideas that are characteristic of a given society as a whole or of some definite social group. Although social consciousness is directly or indirectly created by individuals, it is not the sum-total of the "consciousness" of individuals within a given society. Just as society is more than the sum of its individual members, social consciousness is something more than the sum of the "consciousness" of its individual members. It is a qualitatively specific intellectual system, which, although engendered and conditioned ultimately by social being, has a relatively independent existence and exerts a powerful influence on every individual, compelling him or her to reckon with the historically shaped forms of social consciousness as something that is real, although non-material.

The social consciousness in its historically shaped forms is a component part of the intellectual culture of society. So we must first deal with the meaning of this concept.

In its generic sense the term "culture" (derived from the Latin *cultura*) means cultivation and is normally used in contrast to nature, regarded as things in their natural state, independent of people and their labour. By culture we mean above all the modes and results of people's activity. Culture is usually divided into *material* and *intellectual* culture. This is a conventional division, because the making of tools and the objects generally required to satisfy people's material needs would be impossible without the participation of their thinking. On the other hand, the products of intellectual effort — ideas, artistic images, social norms and rules — exist in a certain material form — in books, paintings, music, documents, and so on.

Intellectual culture comprises the results of people's intellectual activity — science, philosophy, art, morals, politics, law and their corresponding institutions (research centres, schools, theatres, libraries, museums, etc.) — and also the level of their intellectual, aesthetic and moral development. The concept of culture is connected with people's accumulation of knowledge and experience in one or another field of activity, their assimilation and acceptance of a particular system of values and evolution of a certain pattern of behaviour. Every individual from early youth comes under the influence of a certain culture — its objects, ideas, values and standards of behaviour. The individual's very upbringing and education consist, in fact, in his or her adaptation to the existing culture, in assimilating the knowledge, skills and abilities amassed by society, and also its intellectual values and standards of behaviour. Upbringing and education, the development of the public system of education, are in themselves important indices of the level of culture of a given society.

Intellectual culture bears the imprint of the characteristic features of the given socioeconomic formation, the classes that created it, and in this sense it corresponds to the superstructure erected on the given economic basis.

The intellectual culture of a society divided into antagonistic classes does not form an integrated whole. As Lenin observed:

> The *elements* of democratic and socialist culture are present, if only in rudimentary form, in every national culture, since in *every* nation there are toiling and exploited masses, whose conditions of life inevitably give rise to the ideology of democracy and socialism. But every nation also possesses a bourgeois culture (and most nations a reactionary and clerical culture as well) in the form, not merely of "elements", but of the *dominant* culture.[3]

This does not imply that the working class throws aside the whole content of a bourgeois culture. It faces up to the task of mastering all the wealth of culture that humanity has produced in conditions of oppression by exploiters. "We must take the entire culture that capitalism left behind and build socialism with it", Lenin argued. "We must take all science, technology, all knowledge and art."[4]

The relations between classes leave a significant imprint on the content of the intellectual culture in a class-divided society. This means that ideology is an extremely important element in any culture. Culture also manifests the specific features of social psychology that are characteristic of the age or a class.

3. Social Psychology and Ideology

What is ideology? What is social psychology? The material economic relations, the social conditions in which people live, their everyday activity and accumulated experience are reflected in their mental activity in the form of feelings, moods, thoughts, motives and habits. These are usually described as social psychology.

The growth of social psychology is directly influenced by the conditions of people's social being, by their activities. Social psychology does not take the form of a generalised system of views and beliefs, but manifests itself in judgments, emotions, feelings, moods, voluntary acts, etc. At the level of social psychology people's ideas and views have no theoretical expression; they tend to be empirical, and the intellectual elements in them are mingled with the emotional elements.

Social psychology is a part of people's ordinary consciousness. The term "ordinary consciousness" is used in Marxist literature in a wider sense than the term "social psychology". "Ordinary consciousness" implies not only the reflection of the social conditions but also the results of the empirical observation of nature that people perform in the course of their everyday life, the knowledge and skills they acquire in the process of labour, and so on.

People's psychology in a class-divided society inevitably bears the stamp of the features of a particular class and expresses the conditions of its life. Even before the consciousness of a class becomes imbued with ideology, its psychology exhibits certain features that sharply distinguish it from the consciousness of the class that opposes it.

There are psychological differences between classes whose relations are not antagonistic. For instance, in capitalist society there are differences between the psychology of the proletariat and that of the working farmers. These differences are based on the latter's possession of private property, of which the proletariat has none, and also on the specific features of their labour and the resultant different conditions of life in town and country. The psychology of the intellectuals also has its specific features, depending on the intellectual's social status and the character of his or her work.

The classics of Marxism teach proletarian revolutionists to pay close attention to the social psychology of the masses, particularly in the periods of revolutionary upswing. They point out the tremendous part played by the masses' awareness of the injustice of the social system based on exploitation. Although such awareness cannot serve as a scientific proof of the necessity for a new system, it is an expression of the fact that the masses do not want to go on living in the old way, that the existing conditions have become intolerable and should be changed. A revolutionary workers' party studies the state of the mass consciousness and strives to raise it to the level of revolutionary political consciousness, that is, to give the masses a clear scientific explanation and evaluation of social processes and to organise the masses for a struggle for political power.

Whereas social psychology is the ordinary consciousness that is shaped directly in the process of people's everyday activity and intercourse, *ideology* is a more or less coherent system of views, propositions and ideas (political, philosophical, moral, aesthetic and religious).

Of course, at the level of ordinary consciousness a person uses concepts and molds them into judgments in accordance with the laws and forms of logic, but at this level he or she thinks in more elementary concepts, which do not take a person beyond the bounds of personal experience and his or her immediate environment. Ideology, on the other hand, is concerned with more complex concepts, based on a wider (generalised) experience, which is both historical and contemporary. Ordinary consciousness takes shape of its own accord, spontaneously, in the process of people's life activity and interaction, and is the product of their immediate perception of the surrounding world, whereas ideology is the product of conscious activity, demanding special efforts on the part of ideologists. Characterising the ideology of the bourgeoisie, Marx and Engels noted "... inside this class one part appears as the thinkers of the class (its active, conceptive ideologists)".[5]

As regards their social status, the ideologists of a certain class need not necessarily belong to that class. But by expressing in the language of ideology the interests of a class, they serve it and represent its intellectual agents. In the words of Lenin, "... the intelligentsia are so-called just because they most consciously, most resolutely and most accurately reflect and express the development of class interests and political groupings in society as a whole".[6]

Many liberal intellectuals scorn ideology in general, this being expressed in the demand for the "deideologisation" of social life, or in the claim that ideological battles have become outdated and irrelevant. One of the early proponents of this view, Daniel Bell, even called his 1960 book *The End of Ideology*. But this very theory is itself an ideology. As C. Wright Mills, the US Weberian sociologist, put it, the "end of ideology" is in fact the ideology of the end, that is, of the decline of bourgeois society.

The advocates of the theory of "deideologisation" also try to present matters as if there were a divergence between the views of Marx and Engels concerning ideology, on the one hand, and those of Lenin, on the other, as if only Lenin recognised the possibility of a scientific ideology and its significance for a revolutionary movement, while Marx and Engels regarded any ideology as the sum-total of the illusions, mystifications and false notions that people have about themselves.

Marx and Engels actually did use the term "ideology" to denote false, illusory consciousness. But they used it in regard to those ideological theories that considered thoughts and ideas as independent essences which supposedly develop independently and obey only their own intrinsic laws. They were referring to those ideologists who did not acknowledge or were not aware of the fact that the material conditions of the life of the people in whose heads the thinking process takes place ultimately determine the course of this process. Such an ideology, which implies an idealist interpretation of history, is in itself false consciousness and gives rise to mystifications and illusions. As for the ideology that provides the working class with a guide to revolutionary action, it is characterised in the *Communist Manifesto* in the following words:

> The theoretical conclusions of the Communists are in no way based on ideas or principles that have been invented, or discovered, by this or that would-be universal

reformer.

> They merely express, in general terms, actual relations springing from an existing class struggle, from a historical movement going on under our very eyes.[7]

We must therefore draw a distinction between scientific ideology, which is an accurate reflection of material social relations, and ideology that reflects these relations in an illusory, distorted and even fantastic form.

In class-divided society the decisive factor in determining how much truth there is in the ideology of a certain class is the historical role played by that class in satisfying the vital needs of society at a given stage of its development. The ideology of a progressive class becomes capable of more or less correctly reflecting these needs and acquiring scientific views, although with varying degrees of depth and consistency, which depends ultimately on the character of these needs and the specific features of the given stage of social development.

In the period of the rise of the bourgeoisie the objective course of economic development was adequately reflected in its ideology — in philosophy, political economy, law, and so on. At the same time this ideology contained quite a few illusions, namely, the notion that the historically transient bourgeois system was eternal and in accord with "the natural rights" of people, their nature and reason.

Only the proletarian socialist ideology could shake off all illusions and establish itself as entirely scientific. This happened because all former classes that had historically achieved leadership of society sought to perpetuate their rule. The historic mission of the proletariat, on the other hand, is to abolish all division of society into classes, and for this reason the creators of the proletarian ideology were able to produce a truly scientific theory of social life.

As a part of social consciousness ideology, also influences the development of natural science. The data of the natural sciences cannot be theoretically generalised without a definite world outlook. It is absurd to talk of "bourgeois" and "proletarian" mathematics, physics, chemistry and so on, just as it is absurd to take a class position or class approach to questions that are neutral in regard to the interests of classes. But the development of the natural sciences shows that they are not neutral towards philosophy, that they are the scene of a struggle between world outlooks, that the achievements of natural science quite often serve as the point of departure for diametrically opposed philosophical conclusions by the ideologists of hostile classes.

To sum up, we may give the following definition of ideology: *ideology is a system of views and ideas directly or indirectly reflecting the economic and social peculiarities of society, expressing the position, interests and aims of a definite*

social class and designed to preserve or change the existing social structure in its class interests.

4. THE RELATIVE INDEPENDENCE OF SOCIAL CONSCIOUSNESS. CONNECTION AND MUTUAL INFLUENCE OF ITS FORMS

Social consciousness is determined by social being and yet it possesses a certain relative independence. When radical changes occur in the economic structure of society, the material basis of social life, this does not mean that corresponding changes in social consciousness will automatically follow. There is a *continuity of development* and also interaction between the various forms of consciousness, both in social psychology and ideology.

First we must note the tremendous part played by tradition and habit in people's consciousness, particularly in ordinary, everyday consciousness. A distinction must be made, however, between the habits and traditions that hinder the development of the new forms of life and new consciousness, and those that should be preserved and further encouraged. The assimilation of progressive traditions and habits (revolutionary and labour traditions, habits of observing certain rules of community life, etc.) is of great importance for social progress.

The relative independence of the development of ideology plays a special role. Its history is marked by the fact that ideology is a systematised assembly of ideas. Although its development is ultimately determined by economic development, every form of ideology and every form of social consciousness has its own continuity. For example, political ideology depends on the economic basis to a greater degree than philosophy. The latter reflects the basis less directly and therefore has relatively greater independence of development.

Facts of non-correspondence of economic and ideological development may be illustrated by examples from every sphere of ideology. From the history of philosophy, for example, we know that French materialism attained a higher level of development than English materialism, although France lagged behind England in its economic development. The materialism of the 19th century Russian revolutionary democrats was more radical and more fully developed than that of the French, although economically Russia was less developed than either England or France. The fact that the French bourgeoisie was politically more radical than the English and the revolutionary democrats of Russia saw the profound contradictions of tsarist Russia and expressed the aspirations of the exploited peasantry was highly significant in this respect. Important, too, was the fact that materialism in Russia, while it had its own traditions, relied on the achievements of European philosophical thought and developed it further. Thus, although the materialism of modern times was on the whole called forth by the development of capitalism, it depended in its development on such non-economic factors as the internal continuity of the development of philosophical thought and its own internal needs, which involved the posing and solution of certain philosophical problems.

Advanced ideology poses the vital questions of social development and in this sense anticipates its objective course, but this should not be interpreted as meaning that consciousness ceases to be determined by being. The point is that consciousness reveals certain tendencies of development of social being and more or less accurately reflects them. Being able to foresee the processes and tendencies of development makes it possible to use the transforming power of progressive social ideas and testifies to their active role in social development.

The relative independence of social consciousness is also expressed in *the interconnection and reciprocal influence of its forms*. This means that in the history of one or another ideological form, which is ultimately determined by economic development, certain problems arise and are solved in connection with the development of other ideological forms as well.

Certain forms of consciousness that provide the fullest concentration of the consciousness of a given society (primarily its leading class) come to the fore in every historical epoch. We know that in the Greece of the 5th century BC philosophy and art (theatre, sculpture, architecture) played a particularly important part in social consciousness. In the Europe of the Middle Ages religion exerted the predominant influence on philosophy, morals, art and the political and legal outlook. Medieval philosophy was the servant of religion. Even materialist and atheistic thought could in those days appear only in religious guise. In the conditions of capitalist society religion has relatively less influence on people's hearts and minds, and there is a considerable growth in the role of secular ideology — philosophical, political and legal beliefs and theories — to which religion has to adapt itself.

At certain periods the various forms of social consciousness (religion, philosophy, art) have served as most important instruments for the propaganda of political ideas, as a means of political struggle. Thus in classical tragedy, according to André Bonnard, "the struggle of the tragic hero against Destiny is nothing else, expressed in the language of myth, but the struggle of the people of ancient Athens, between 700 and 500 BC, to liberate themselves from the oppressive social restraints ..."[8]

In France in the second half of the 18th century, in Germany at the turn of the 19th, and in Russia from 1840 to 1870, philosophy and literature became the main arena of political struggle for the progressive social forces that wished to solve the vital problems of social development, in particular, people's liberation from the fetters of medieval, feudal relationships. This role of philosophy and literature in the political struggle sprang not only from the specific conditions of the economic and political development of these countries, but also from the profound, organic link between progressive philosophy, progressive art and the life of the people, their longing for freedom from oppression.

The connection between philosophy and art is not confined to their interaction, direct or indirect. Great works of art always contain profound philosophical meditations on social life (Greek tragedy, Shakespeare, Goethe, Pushkin, Tolstoy, Dostoyevsky). History furnishes many examples of works in which philosophical thought and artistic creativity are combined, in which the philosopher emerges as a writer or poet. Such are the philosophical tales of Voltaire, some of the works of Diderot (*Le Neveu de Rameau*), and Chernyshevsky's *What Is to Be Done?*

While philosophy, as a rational world outlook, is opposed to religion with its appeal to blind faith in supernatural forces, idealist philosophy quite often not only aligned itself with religion (in the fight against materialism) but also evolved directly into a religious philosophy and merged with religion (Kierkegaard, some of the existentialists and personalists). In certain cases, substantial elements of a philosophical system have contributed to the foundation of a new religious doctrine. Thus, for example, much of the ethical doctrine of Roman Stoic philosophy, as developed in the 1st century AD, became the foundation of the ethics of the new religion of Christianity.

The interaction between religion and art, and between religion and morality, has compelled attention since time immemorial. To this day we hear assertions (mainly from theologists) that religion was the source of both art and morality. Studies of the history of primitive culture, however, show that the origin and development of art and morality (and religion itself) are connected with certain social conditions and needs which we will examine later. For many centuries religion played the part of humanity's official moral mentor, but this does not imply that morality arose "on the basis of religion", or that it cannot exist without religion. The aesthetic value of many paintings and sculptures on religious themes is not a derivative of these themes. They were created by outstanding artists and, like the Parthenon and the Gothic cathedrals, remain works of art that give us aesthetic pleasure independently of religious feelings.

All forms of ideology and also the various spheres of natural science, contribute to the formation of people's world outlook. The fundamental questions of world outlook throughout the history of class society have been answered in various ways by religion and philosophy from definite social positions. Political and legal ideologies exert a considerable influence on people's world outlook (under certain conditions this influence is even more considerable than that of religion and philosophy).

Enough has been said to indicate the complexity of the interaction between the various forms of social consciousness. We must therefore be careful to avoid the mistakes of vulgar, economic materialism, which tries to infer all ideological phenomena directly from the economic basis. The connection between the basis and social consciousness is not so simple. It is effected through the medium of the political system of society and political relations, the class struggle, the interaction between the forms of social consciousness themselves and, finally, the interconnection between social and individual consciousness.

5. The Correlation Between Social and Individual Consciousness

Although society is a social organism and the individual in a society can be regarded as analogous to the cell in a biological organism, society would, of course, be unthinkable without the people of whom it is composed, and therefore social consciousness is unthinkable without the consciousness of individuals.

The general conditions of the social environment in which people live determine the unity of their views and aspirations, which is based on the unity of their interests. And even a consensus will always find individual expression among individuals. Sharing a certain social origin and status with others offers the individual only the possibility but by no means an absolute guarantee of a corresponding social orientation.

The point is that individual consciousness has a biography that differs from the biography of the social consciousness.

The *social consciousness* is controlled by social laws. Its history necessarily follows the history of social being and any changes (evolutionary or revolutionary) that occur in the social consciousness are ultimately determined by corresponding changes in social being. The *individual consciousness* is born and dies with the individual person. It expresses the unique features of the individual's path in life, the peculiarities of his or her upbringing, and various political and ideological influences.

For the individual consciousness, the objective environment which influences its formation is the result of the interaction of the macro-environment — social being (in class society, the conditions of life of a class) — and the micro-environment — the conditions of life of a certain section within a class, a social group and also the immediate environment (family, friends, acquaintances) and, finally, the conditions of personal life. All other conditions being equal, the specific paths of the individual's development determine the difference between his or her consciousness and the conscious world of other individuals and create a wealth of human personalities.

The social consciousness and the individual consciousness are constantly interacting and enriching each other. Every individual throughout his or her life, through relationships with other people, through education and training, experiences the influence of the social consciousness, although his or her attitude towards this influence is not passive but active and selective.

The norms of consciousness evolved historically by society nourish the individual's mentality, influence his or her beliefs and become the source of the individual's moral precepts, aesthetic notions and feelings.

Social consciousness does not merely enter individual minds; it is a collective mind, a unique and complex synthesis of individual minds. According to Engels, human thought "exists only as the individual thought of many milliards of past, present and future men ... The total thought of all these human beings."[9]

Certain beliefs or ideas emanating from an individual may become, and do become, the possession of society, acquire the significance of a social force, when they reach beyond the bounds of personal existence and become part of the general consciousness, forming the beliefs and standards of behaviour of other people.

The character of the social system has a decisive influence on the individual's assimilation of the achievements of social thought and on his or her own social "response". Where the ruling class has a monopoly of education, the broad masses are, in effect, deprived of the ability to broaden their mental horizons and to develop their inherent talents to the full.

In contemporary capitalist society the ruling class uses all available media for conditioning the mass consciousness and public opinion, but the development of the democratic and socialist forces of society increases their role in forming public opinion, designed to combat the omnipotence of the stock market and the banks, militarism and war, racial and sexual discrimination etc. Public opinion in class society thus inevitably reflects the struggle of class interests and ideologies.

Thus we see that not every conflict of opinions is ideological conflict. The ideological struggle, however, does occupy a highly important place in the life of society, particularly in the present age.

* * *

We have stressed that social consciousness is dependent upon social being and that different products of social consciousness are, to one extent or another, reflections of social being. However, it would be wrong to conclude from this that social consciousness reflects social being like a mirror reflects objects placed in front of it. Precisely such a position on the passive nature of social consciousness, of the intellectual life of society, has been ascribed to Marxism by bourgeois ideologists. By establishing the fact that social consciousness depends on social being, that social consciousness reflects social being, Marxist social theory in no way belittles the significance of social consciousness.

Having given a correct, scientific, definition of social consciousness and its relation to social being, historical materialism also indicates its place in the life of society. One cannot transform society by transforming ideas alone. To make society better, to make life truly worthy of human beings, it is necessary to reorganise social being. And social consciousness plays a highly important part in this. Marxist theory, which itself is part of social consciousness, gives people knowledge of the methods to transform their social life. When assimilated by the majority of the working class, Marxist theory stimulates them to work for the revolutionary transformation of social being. That is why Marx himself stated that "theory ... becomes a material force as soon as it has gripped the masses" [10] ❦

CHAPTER 3

FORMS OF SOCIAL CONSCIOUSNESS AND THEIR SOCIAL FUNCTION

In class society social consciousness assumes various forms: socio-political and legal theories and beliefs, philosophy, morals, aesthetics, religion and science. Each of these forms, in reflecting social being and actively influencing it, has its own particular object and mode of reflection, influences social being and people's consciousness in its own particular way and is characterised by its specific role in the ideological and political struggle between classes.

At the early stages of development of society, social consciousness was not broken down into separate forms. The harsh existence of hunter-gatherer societies with their extremely low level of material production had its correspondingly primitive and undifferentiated consciousness. Mental work had not yet been separated from manual labour, and people's consciousness was "directly interwoven with the material activity and the material intercourse of men, the language of real life".[1] But the rudiments of such forms of social consciousness as aesthetics, morality and religion are to be found at certain stages of development of labour activity even in pre-class society.

With further division of labour, the appearance of private property, classes and the state, social life became much more complex, and so did social consciousness. The division of labour into physical and mental, and the monopolisation of the latter by the ruling class, signified an increasing separation of consciousness from people's material practice. Consciousness became relatively independent of social being. It could now be regarded as completely independent of being and even primary in relation to being, it could "proceed to the formation of 'pure' theory, theology, philosophy, ethics, etc".[2] In reality all these "pure" forms of consciousness in some way or other expressed the real conditions or relationships of class society and acted as the ideological reflection of the interests of certain classes.

We shall now briefly examine the separate forms of social consciousness, their specific features and functions, in connection with the historical conditions and social needs that brought them into existence.

1. Political and Legal Consciousness

Political consciousness is the system of ideas and attitudes, sentiments and objectives of classes concerning the political organisation of society, the forms and uses of state power. It can be considered on the plane of ideology and/or social psychology.

Political psychology is: the feeling of class solidarity or hatred, pessimism or optimism, patriotism or internationalism, political illusions etc. *Political ideology* is the most concentrated expression of the interests and objectives of a social class. It *is the systematised theoretical expression of the interests of a definite class in relation to other classes and in relation to the state, the class struggle and social revolution.* It is a vital weapon in the struggle for political power, in the establishment, defence, substantiation and reinforcement of a definite political order and its economic foundation.

Closely connected with political consciousness is *legal consciousness*, since it originates together with the state and law. Law is created and enforced by the state and is therefore binding upon the entire community under the given state's control. In the *Communist Manifesto* Marx and Engels characterise bourgeois law as follows: "...Your jurisprudence is but the will of your class made into a law for all, a will whose essential character and direction are determined by the economical conditions of existence of your class".[3]

Legal ideology is the systematic, theoretical expression of the interests of a class in relation to the nature and purpose of legal relationships, norms and institutions, questions of legislation, the courts and so on.

The legal principles and theories of the ruling class seek to legitimise its social system. Law imparts a legal character — "lawfulness" — to the dominant relations of production that exist within a given socioeconomic formation. Second, legal principles and theories propose and justify legal institutions, standards and forms best corresponding to the given socioeconomic system and the dominant form of ownership of the means of production.

Like any form of theoretical consciousness, political and legal ideologies express their propositions in logical form and rely on the previous development of the given branch of knowledge. They are expressed in specialised works on the theory of state and law. But in dealing with the political consciousness, we are concerned not only with political doctrines and theories, but also with political programs and platforms, with political strategy and tactics. Their essence is most clearly demonstrated by the example of the activity of the Marxist party. Its program, based on the theory of scientific socialism, shows the ultimate aim of the working-class movement and maps out the line of march and basic tasks to be followed to achieve it. Its strategy sets out the basic means to implement its program, while its tactical orientation provides a definite line of conduct for the specific situation it faces.

2. Moral Consciousness and Ethics

Like politics and the law, morality is also a regulator of human behaviour.

Historical materialism rejects the theological theories of morality being generated by "the will of God" and developed by the influence of religion. Elementary moral consciousness long preceded religion. It was only later, in class-divided society, that the first ruling-class ideologists (the priests) invested morality with a religious sanction.

Nor does moral consciousness derive from humans' biological or "animal" nature. This view identifies morality with instinct (female animal's protecting its offspring, herd instinct). In actual fact, animal instinctive behaviour has nothing in common with moral relations among human beings, since, unlike moral relations, instinctive behaviour does not involve conscious actions.

Morality was the first form of social consciousness. In primitive-communal society numerous rules of conduct, reflecting the elementary demands of the clan and the tribe, regulated the individual's behaviour. Behaviour complying with these elementary rules was approved of and encouraged, while any violation of the rules was disapproved of and could result in an individual being banished from the clan and the tribe (and consequently being cut off from the collective labour activities essential to his or her survival). The moral consciousness originated as a direct reflection of the individual's relations with other members of his or her clan and tribe and with the clan or tribe as a whole. In its embryonic form it represented collective concepts of desirable and undesirable, and of permissible and impermissible, conduct.

With the disintegration of clan and tribal society into individual families and social classes, the individual was brought into a more complex set of social relationships. Class society stimulated the development of individual self-consciousness and confronted the individual with a multitude of new problems of individual and social behaviour. These problems concerned the attitude to be taken towards the new social community, towards the people of a certain class, towards the state etc They had a significance that went far beyond the previous customs and traditions of the clan or tribe. In other words, new norms of behaviour were required and various beliefs came into being concerning these new norms as well as the old customs and traditions.

As the social life of society became more complex, specific moral codes (collections of fundamental norms, rules and commandments) and doctrines came into being; for a long period they were mainly of a religious nature. With the development of philosophy, morality became a branch of philosophical knowledge, forming the subject of *ethics* (the theory of morality).

The developed moral consciousness — the individual's awareness of his or her connection with other people in his or her everyday life — is part of the individual's general world outlook and, in some way or another is connected with the solution to the questions of the essence of humanity, its position and role in the surrounding world, the individual's ideas concerning the meaning of his or her life, of good and evil, the moral ideal and moral values. The choice of a course of action and its evaluation often involve complicated meditations and psychological experiences concerning the moral character of these actions. A person educated in the spirit of a certain morality is conscious of his or her moral duty (i.e., his or her personal obligations in relation to other people and a certain community), can evaluate his or her own actions and morally condemns himself or herself for choosing the wrong course, for shirking his or her obligations toward others. People's moral self-consciousness, their awareness of personal responsibility for their own behaviour, for their individual course of action, their evaluation of their own behaviour, is expressed in conscience.

The specific feature of morality as a way of regulating human conduct is that it does not rely directly on any special institutions designed to enforce moral standards through coercion (as distinct from the law, which is backed by the coercive power of the state, by the police, the courts, the prison system). Morality is supported by the force of persuasion, example, public opinion, education, traditions, by the force of the moral authority of individuals, organisations or institutions. Moral standards are therefore not as detailed and strictly regulated as legal norms. At the same time they extend to relationships between people that are not regulated by any state agencies or social organisations (relationships of friendship, comradeship, love etc.).

Moral judgment of behaviour is bound to consider the social consequences of an action (i.e., the consequences for a certain community, class or society), because there are no other objective ways of testing the individual's motives. But the individual's motives play a tremendous role in the moral evaluation of his or her personality, particularly as outwardly similar actions may result from different motives and thus reveal different moral qualities among individuals.

Unlike the administrative, legal and other norms that are designed directly to create and consolidate a certain socioeconomic system, morality is concerned mainly with people's thoughts and individual behaviour. The paramount feature of morality is its educational function. By influencing the individual, his or her psychology and consciousness, it performs its function as a regulator of behaviour and helps to create corresponding moral relations between people at work, in everyday life and social intercourse. This does not contradict either the fact that morality has a social (class) nature, or that moral standards and judgments extend to the behaviour of whole collectives (classes, governments, nations etc.).

The moral consciousness is for millions of people a powerful stimulus to action. For this reason a revolutionary party is bound to be concerned about its formation. The revolutionary criticism of the declining system includes its moral as well as political exposure. Its purpose is to awaken the anger of the masses against the system, to inspire them with faith in their strength and in the victory of the new system.

The ethical systems elaborated by the ideologists of certain classes, like their morality, bear the stamp of their time, of the specific features of those classes. Ethics in the past was primarily concerned with the grounds for moral (virtuous) behaviour. In inferring the demands of moral behaviour from allegedly eternal "human nature", pre-Marxist ethics regarded it as either altruistic or egotistical. Accordingly, precedence was given either to the individual's interest (happiness, pleasure, delight), usually idealised, or the general interest, which also took the idealised form of a universal moral law to which everyone must subordinate their personal aspirations and desires. Pre-Marxist ethics sought, but could not find, ways of combining personal and social interest, happiness and duty, selfishness and self-sacrifice. The problem itself was posed without regard for the fact that the basic contradiction of class society was not the contradiction between the personal and general interest, but the contradiction between the classes, each of which evolves its own particular morality, its own notions of good and evil.

In developed class society, we find at least two and sometimes several moral systems, each of which has a different social significance. Thus in the capitalist countries of Europe at the end of the 19th century Engels observed three types of morality: feudal-Christian, bourgeois and proletarian. The first had been inherited by bourgeois society from the Middle Ages (and was upheld by the Roman Catholic church), the second was the predominant morality of the existing capitalist society, and the third expressed the interests of the working class. What is the connection between the first two systems of morality? The main connection is that they are both founded on private property as the pillar of society. Hence the inevitability of the first becoming adapted to the second. As the US sociologist Jerome Davis put it, "... the result of the interlocking control of religion by capitalistic interests has been that ethical standards of the Christian community have largely conformed to the ethical standards of capitalism".[4]

Proletarian-socialist morality teaches the workers to suit their conduct to the interests of *their* class, to dedicate their lives to the cause of the proletarian revolution and the building of socialism. The proletarian revolutionist upholds a morality that has an openly class character, but it has the aim of liberating all humanity from all forms of oppression. When this problem is solved, morality will lose its class character. "A really human morality which stands above class antagonisms and above any recollection of them", Engels explained, "becomes possible only at a stage of society which has not only overcome class antagonisms but has even forgotten them in practical life".[5]

3. Aesthetic Consciousness and Art

The artistic attitudes of a society are aesthetic consciousness. It embraces aesthetic feelings, tastes, concerns, notions, ideals and the concept of beauty.

Art is one of the most ancient forms of social consciousness; it dates back to pre-class society. The study of primitive cultures shows that beginning from the Paleolithic period, people gradually learned not only how to make the tools they needed but also how to create works of art. Labour perfected people's creative abilities, developed their thinking, exercised their hands, differentiated their feelings and developed the desire for fine work, for rhythm and symmetry; it fashioned the ability to generalise and to reproduce objects and phenomena in the form of imagery.

The result of thousands of years of labour activity was that art became possible as a form of aesthetic perception of the world, as activity creating objects designed not for hunting animals or tilling the soil but for embodying the people's creative imagination, their ideas and feelings. The need that art satisfied was the need for beauty, for creating things that would delight people. This need itself developed with the development of artistic activity as one of the forms of people's creative activity. The latter demanded specific aesthetic abilities, cultivated aesthetic feelings, tastes, evaluations, experiences and ideas, which are a specific form of people's reflection of the world.

In class society art became an independent field of activity, isolated from material production. Art became largely the occupation of an elite — poets, painters, sculptors, musicians, etc. It was subjected to specialised theoretical analyses. A new philosophical science appeared — *aesthetics* — the study of people's perception of beauty, its essence and laws. Art began to be studied in its various branches.

Outside the professional sphere art developed in the form of folk art (mythology, folklore etc.), which had deep roots in pre-class society and in the course of the centuries has produced unfading artistic values.

One of the fundamental questions of aesthetics and the study of art is the question of the relationship of the aesthetic consciousness (notions of the beautiful, the ugly etc.) and art to reality. This question has received various answers from philosophers, art theoreticians and artists themselves. The materialist theories in aesthetics maintain that social life is the determining factor in the formation of the aesthetic consciousness. The idealists, on the contrary, assume that the aesthetic consciousness and art are independent of social relations.

However, the historical development of aesthetic notions testifies to the fact that they differ considerably among people of different classes and different epochs. Thus things that were considered beautiful in one stage of social development would be considered ugly in another.

Scholars studying art in primitive-communal societies almost unanimously note that animals' skins, claws and teeth are greatly valued by people in these societies as ornaments. It was not that they found their colour and patterns particularly attractive. As he decorated himself with an animal's skin, claws, teeth or horns, a primitive warrior was showing others that he was as quick and strong as the beast he had defeated. This example illustrates that the aesthetic notions of beauty in the remote past were directly linked with people's production activities — in this case, hunting.

Let us consider another example drawn from social anthropology. We know, for instance, that women of many African tribes wore iron rings on their arms and legs. From our point of view, this is certainly very uncomfortable, yet the discomfort did not prevent many African tribal women from wearing such "chains" of beauty. Why did these women like to wear such heavy iron rings? The reason is that they made them appear beautiful to themselves and others. This resulted from a rather complex association of ideas. The passion for such ornaments was observed among tribes which used iron for weapons and tools but in which its supply was limited. Among these peoples iron was thus regarded as a precious metal. And everything precious seems beautiful because it is associated with the idea of *wealth*.

We find further proof of the inherent connection of aesthetic notions and social production in other kinds of art. Thus many African tribespeople have the keenest sense of rhythm. Basuto women, who wear metal bangles on their arms, which tinkle at every movement, often gather together to grind corn, accompanying the rhythmical movement of their arms by singing. The beat is the main thing in Basuto music, and the more rhythmical a song, the more beautiful it is considered. The beat is important because in primitive agrarian societies, to coordinate their collective labour activities, people chanted in rhythm with their work, and every kind of work had a chant adapted to its rhythm. As the productive forces developed and private labour replaced collective labour, the significance of rhythm in work decreased.

Generalising these facts, we can conclude that in primitive-communal society, people's aesthetic notions and art forms were directly influenced by their production activities. But in a class-divided society the immediate impact of economic activities on the aesthetic notions and art is much less obvious. Thus, while the Australian Aboriginal clans had a dance representing herb-gathering by women, no dance popular among French aristocratic women in the 18th century can be linked with production activities because they engaged in none.

To be able to understand what the Aboriginal dance was about, it is enough to know what role herb-gathering played in the life of an Aboriginal clan. But to see what the minuet is about, it is not enough to be familiar with the 18th century French economy. The minuet is one of the art forms expressive of the social psychology of the idle rich. This psychology underlies most of the customs and "polite manners" of aristocratic "high society". At first sight economic life, social relations of production, seem to be ousted in this case by purely psychological factors. That, however, would be a superficial judgment, for it must not be forgotten that the very existence of a strata of idle rich within the ruling class of a society is the result of its economic development.

The dependence of art and aesthetic views on social conditions is thus highly complex. There are many intermediate links between the situation and the interests of a given class and their artistic reflection.* The social and political struggle and its reflection in various forms of consciousness and also the psychology of certain sections of society play a tremendous role in this respect. The artistic reproduction of

* To this must be added that the connection of various forms of art with social life is not always the same. Music is connected with society and classes by far more complex relations than, for example, literary fiction or painting. But in all its forms art cannot be profoundly understood without a scientific analysis of the whole structure of social relations in their interaction.

reality is also greatly influenced by the personality of the artist, his or her talent and skill, his or her world outlook and the school of art to which he or she belongs, his or her links with certain traditions etc.

It may be taken as a general law of the development of art that the most significant works of art, which form part of the golden treasury of human culture, have been artistic embodiments of living truth, of the progressive ideals and aspirations of the people of a certain epoch.

Art that is bound up with the life of the common people is a powerful factor in social progress. It performs its function through artistic perception of the world, through the satisfaction of people's aesthetic needs. It reflects reality in artistic images and through them influences the thoughts and feelings of people, their aspirations, actions and behaviour. Since they are expressed by certain material means, works of art are passed on from one generation to another and serve both as a means of knowing social life and as a means of the ideological, aesthetic and moral education of young generations.

In aesthetic thought there have existed and continue to exist theories that reject the social role of art and regard it as an end in itself. Such theories usually express a maladjustment of the artist to his or her social environment and lead the artist, under certain conditions, to depart from any social commitment and become involved in a one-sided enthusiasm for formalistic experimentation and the like.

The subject of artistic expression is for the most part the life of society, particularly the sphere of personal relations. Art also portrays nature. But even such portrayal always implies certain human feelings, emotions, moods and so on. This demand is all the more true of the portrayal of people, their inner world and social interaction.

The portrayal of the ugly and beautiful, the tragic and the comic, the heroic and the trivial in the life of society and the individual presupposes a profound knowledge of social reality, its development and meaning. The aesthetic "yardstick" that the artist uses to measure reality is not simply a manifestation of his or her subjective will. It is molded in the process of the whole socio-historical practice of humanity.

Thus the cognitive (and also the political, moral, educational, etc.) significance of art must be considered in connection with its ideological and aesthetic function. When the artist reproduces reality in the form of images, he or she makes an ideological and aesthetic evaluation of reality, that is, the artist expresses his or her attitude to it in accordance with his or her aesthetic ideal, his or her notions of the beautiful. This shows how important it is that these notions should correspond to the objective qualities of reality and be based on a correct understanding of the paths of its development and transformation. The artist is "tendentious" even in his or her selection of material for a work of art, not to mention the fact that he or she pronounces judgment upon phenomena of social life, advocates one thing and condemns another, awakens certain feelings and aspirations.

The artist seeks to give a generalised reflection of life, to show the essential, important aspects of reality (people, their relationships). The difference between the artistic image and the scientific concept is that the generalisation of reality in the image is given as a living and concrete whole that can be perceived by the senses. In a scientific work on political economy, for instance, the capitalist is but the personification of capital, his or her personal features are of no importance. In the artistic work the capitalist is a generalised but also individualised, sensually perceptible image, a definite personality with his or her inner world and concretely manifested deeds and actions.

From what has been said we may define art as *a specific form of social consciousness reflecting reality in aesthetic terms*. Art has the special property of giving aesthetic pleasure, of "infecting" people with lofty ideas, feelings and emotions.

Art that is linked with the interests of the working people and socialism seeks to fulfil such a mission. Though it is far from imposing on the artist any strict demands that would limit the range of his or her thought or imagination, it sees its task in serving the millions of people who are fighting for a better future. Herein lies the *partisanship of art* and its true freedom. Such art cannot be adapted either to the tastes of a handful of snobs or to primitive tastes. The working people, said Lenin, have gained the right to a real and great art.

Although works of literature, music, painting, etc., have no direct utilitarian significance, certain forms of art (for example, architecture, the decorative arts, modern industrial design, etc.) combine a utilitarian purpose with aesthetic notions.

4. Religion

Marx and Engels regarded religion and philosophy — the forms of social consciousness that express people's world outlook — as the most remote from the economic basis.

Religion is of more ancient origin than philosophy. Its emergence in pre-class society was conditioned by the lack of development of production and production relations. As Marx wrote, primitive social relations "are conditioned by a low stage of development of the productive powers and corresponding limited relations between men in the process of creating and reproducing their material life, hence also limited relations between man and nature. These real limitations are reflected in the ancient worship of nature, and in other elements of tribal religions".[6]

The early forms of religion are connected with the deification of natural forces, plants and animals. Vestiges of these forms (animism, totemism) survive even in later religions. Thus the Egyptian god Horus (whose earthly representative was the pharaoh) had a human body and the head of a falcon. The ancient Greek god Zeus, although endowed with human features, could turn into a bull, an eagle or a swan.

The spontaneously formed social relations, which were the product of people's own material and mental activity, acquired a special power over people as the division of labour, private property and classes appeared. Consequently, the deification and worship of the phenomena of nature were replaced by the deification of social forces, and this accordingly produced a change in religious notions. The supernatural forces that were conceived to dominate people's lives were given human form, i.e., became gods, ruling over both nature and social life. In the ancient Greek religion, for example, Mars was at first the god of vegetation, and afterwards became the god of war, while Hephaestos was at first the god of fire and later became the god of the blacksmith's trade.

The history of religion also shows that among no people did religion ever begin with monotheism, with the doctrine of one universal god, as is maintained by certain theologists; on the contrary, monotheism was preceded by polytheism, involving the worship of several gods.

In wars between peoples, the gods of the conquered yielded place to the gods of the conquerors, who often assumed some of the features of the gods of the vanquished people; the uniting of tribes and communities brought about combinations or even the merging of gods and other objects of worship. When large monarchical states were formed, the multiplicity of religious faiths that had been characteristic of tribal unions and the early type of state (where one supreme deity usually emerged from a number of deities) was replaced by the worship of one, almighty god which assumed the attributes of all the other gods.

While all other forms of social consciousness reflect reality more or less adequately, *religion alone is the form of social consciousness which gives a distorted, fantastic picture of the external world.* Marx said that religion "is the *fantastic realisation* of the human essence", of social reality.[7] Concerning the peculiar quality of religion as a distorted view of the world, Engels wrote: "All religion ... is nothing but a fantastic reflection in men's minds of those external forces which control their daily life, a reflection in which the terrestrial forces assume the form of supernatural forces".[8]

Religion should not be conceived of merely as some kind of belief in the world being built upon a certain pattern and being ruled by gods and other supernatural forces. Religion is not just a definite interpretation of reality, however much distorted. If that were so, it would have been shattered long ago, for it would be easy to prove that this conception of the world has no foundation in experience and to replace these fantastic notions by a scientific conception of the world.

In addition to its highly distorted interpretation of reality, religion comprises an *emotional element*, an emotional attitude to the world. A person who has a religious view of the world conceives of himself or herself as part of this fantastic world with which he or she associates certain hopes and expectations. This complex of feelings bred by religion makes the latter extremely tenacious.

Religious sentiments refer to *religious psychology,* which is of a dual nature, being an expression of helplessness, weakness and fear on the one hand, and of hope on the other, which sometimes grows over into religious protest, ecstasy and fanaticism. Writing of this level of religious consciousness, Marx underlined that "*religious* distress is at the same time the *expression* of real distress and also the *protest* against real distress".[9]

Thus in Marxist theory two levels of religious consciousness are differentiated, i.e., the world-view level and the emotional level. Religions notions and ideas constitute the "mythological" (world-view) element of religion — a body of myths dealing with gods and other supernatural forces and with their relation to the world and to humanity. The emotional level of religion — just as its world-view level — represents a twisted, distorted level of human consciousness. Religion distorts not only people's world outlook, but their feelings, their emotional responses to reality as well.

It would, however, not be enough to dwell on these two levels of religious consciousness alone. After all, we have stated that forms of social consciousness influence and shape human conduct. The distorted conception of the world inherent in religion as a form of social consciousness compels believers to behave in a similarly distorted manner, manifested in *religious worship*. This consists of the performance of certain rites, offering sacrifices and prayers to their deity. These rites have their origin in primitive magic. Just as primitive communities tried to make natural forces fulfil their desires and intentions by the performance of magical ceremonies (invocations, sacrifices etc.), so do religious people today seek help from a god by means of certain rites and by obeying certain prohibitions laid down by the modern religions.

Religious activity is not, however, confined to worship. Groups, associations and organisations of believers adopt a definite attitude towards society and social issues, participating in the life of society, social conflicts, the class struggle etc. These activities are marked by the religious conception and attitude toward the world.

Sorcerers, witch-doctors etc. were the intermediaries between people and the spirits which people in primitive societies believed animated the natural forces around them. Class society brings into being a special professional group of servants of religion — priests. The priesthood acquires great power over people's minds. Its ideological influence is reinforced by its connection with the state and by the establishment of a given faith as a state religion. Religious worship is further developed, and the ceremonial of religious services involving music and song plays an important part in fostering religious feelings and strengthening the faith.

The three elements of religion — (1) religious notions, (2) religious feelings and (3) worship and ritual — vary in importance depending on the social conditions.

Religion is the most conservative ideological form in that it perpetuates its precepts in the name of a supernatural, all-powerful being. At the same time history shows us that under the influence of great social upheavals some religions are supplanted by others. The ancient religions in the Roman empire were conquered by Christianity in the period of the decline of slave society. Moreover, Christianity inherited certain definite features from the old religions, for example, recognition of the Old Testament of Judaism, and the myths of the peoples of Mesopotamia, concerning the suffering, death and resurrection of the gods, all this being rolled into one with vulgarised versions of Greek philosophy, particularly that of the Stoics.

Having emerged in the Roman empire as the religion of the poor and oppressed masses, Christianity subsequently became the official ideology of the ruling classes and lost many of the essential features of early Christianity: its democratic spirit, its disapproval of rites and ceremony. With the development of feudalism "Christianity grew into the religious counterpart to it, with a corresponding feudal hierarchy".[10]

In the 16th century, on the basis of the growth and consolidation of the bourgeoisie, Protestantism with its idea of immediate communion between God and the individual (thus eliminating the need for an expensive, parasitic priesthood), its appeal to individual conscience and action, its preaching of such virtues as thrift and diligence, broke away from the feudal-Christian Catholic Church. The development of capitalism compelled Catholicism, while preserving its dogma, to adapt itself to the new conditions and evolve its own social doctrine designed to reconcile labour and capital, justify colonialism and so on.

What has been said does not by any means contradict the fact that at certain periods, for example in the Middle Ages, the revolutionary masses gave their demands a religious form: " ... the sentiments of the masses were fed with religion to the exclusion of all else; it was therefore necessary to put forward their own interests in the religious guise in order to produce an impetuous movement".[11]

But the positive social content that in certain historical periods took the form of religious consciousness does not negate the basic proposition that religious consciousness is a retrograde consciousness, and for this reason religion can never be an adequate form of expression of the essential interests of the masses and the meaning of human life. It always was and always will be "the opium of the people", a means of reconciling working people to oppressive social relations by offering them an illusory happiness in an "afterlife".

Marxism took up the banner of militant atheism from the old materialists and developed their criticism of religion on the basis of the latest discoveries of natural and social science. It revealed the social roots of religion in class society and showed that the struggle against religion is not merely a matter of educating the masses, as was assumed by the early materialists. It must be, above all, a struggle against the oppressive social conditions that engender or maintain religion. Only on this basis can there be really fruitful atheistic enlightenment, which is an inseparable part of the work of building a scientific world outlook.

5. Science

Science comes into being only when society achieves a certain stage of maturity, and the state of science is one of the basic indicators of social progress.

Primitive society possessed only the rudiments of scientific knowledge. Scientific knowledge involves the separation of intellectual labour from physical labour, and the appearance of a written language, which makes it possible to record knowledge, preserve it and pass it on to succeeding generations.

The rudiments of science arose as a direct response to practical needs confronting the ruling classes of the earliest civilisations. Empirical inquiry into such fields as astronomy, mathematics and mechanics were called into being by the needs of large-scale irrigation, and the building of great public works such as canals, temples and aqueducts.

The second stage in the history of science begins at the end of the 15th century with the emergence in Europe of modern experimental natural sciences and the simultaneous vigorous growth of the social and political sciences and philosophy. The basic cause of this breakthrough was the emergence of the new, bourgeois social structure within the womb of feudal society. "If, after the dark night of the Middle

Ages was over, the sciences suddenly arose anew with undreamt-of force, developing at a miraculous rate, once again we owe this miracle to production", wrote Engels.[12]

The growth of scientific knowledge, particularly in mechanics and mathematics in the 16th, 17th and 18th centuries, was directly connected with the needs of developing production, navigation and trade, and paved the way for the Industrial Revolution in England at the end of the 18th century. In its turn, the transition to machine production gave science a new technical base and powerful stimulus for development.

Summing up the history of science, Marx observed that "along with capitalist production the *scientific factor* is for the first time consciously developed, applied and created on a scale of which previous epochs had not the slightest conception".[13] We see this most fully in late monopoly capitalism, where the development of scientific knowledge becomes the point of departure for the revolutionising of production, for creating whole new branches of industry.

But what is science? There is no one answer to this question, because science is a many-sided social phenomenon combining both intellectual and material factors. Nevertheless, the usual definition of science as a system of knowledge of the world gives us a starting point.

All knowledge, including scientific knowledge, must be regarded as reflection of nature and social being. All processes of nature and social life, without exception, can form the subject-matter of scientific inquiry. This is one of the things that distinguishes science from such forms of social consciousness as political or legal ideology or morality, which reflect only social relations.

The interrelationship between science and religion has a different structure. These are essentially opposed phenomena. Religion gives a false and distorted reflection of reality, whereas science, taken as a whole, provides a true reflection of nature and society. The mistaken hypotheses and theories that arise in the process of development of science do not alter the substance of the point, because error in science is either the result of the pressure of reactionary ideology or a by-product of the quest for truth. Religion is hostile to reason, whereas science is the highest achievement of human reason, the embodiment of its strength and effectiveness.

Religion appeared before science, at an extremely low level of practical achievement, when people were totally dominated by natural and social forces and were quite unable to understand and bend them to their will. The birth of science, on the other hand, is a direct result of humanity's increased practical power. The development of science and the increasing dominion of humanity over the spontaneous forces of nature and society are interconnected. As Engels observed, "... it is in the measure that man has learnt to change nature that his intelligence has increased".[14] Thus, taking into consideration the opposition between science and religion, we can begin to define science as a system of objectively true knowledge generalising practice, from which it is acquired and by which it is tested. But to go any further than this we must bear in mind also the distinction between science and ordinary everyday knowledge, and the distinction between science and art.

Everyday, empirical knowledge acquired directly from practice can exist without science and apart from it. The people of ancient times, for instance, were aware that day regularly follows night, that iron is heavier than wood, and so on. Even in our days, the peasant or the craftsworker in small-scale production in the economically backward countries makes do with the empirical knowledge that has been handed down from generation to generation. Such knowledge also plays a considerable part in everyday life. For example, a mother knows that her child is ill if the child starts shivering.

The thing that distinguishes science from such prescientific empirical knowledge is that science not only provides knowledge of the individual aspects of objects and the external connections between them, but above all tells us the *laws* that govern nature and society. The knowledge that iron is heavier than wood may indeed be acquired without science, but the concept of specific gravity, not to mention the reason for the greater specific gravity of iron, compared with wood, is a matter for physics and chemistry. Awareness of the fact that day follows night is instilled in our consciousness by empirical observation, but we could never explain the causes of the succession of day and night and the periodic lengthening and shortening of the days in the course of the year without astronomy. Fever as a sign of illness can be detected without the help of science, but a correct diagnosis and prescription of the necessary medicines can be made only by medical science based on biology and chemistry.

Scientific laws express the necessary connections between natural or social phenomena. As such they also reveal the essence of these phenomena. Thus, for example, chemistry has established that water is a specific unity of the chemical elements hydrogen and oxygen, H_2O. This statement is true of necessity, not by virtue of any "logical" or "conceptual" connections, but by virtue of the real nature or essence of water. Any chemical substance that is not H_2O in its essential composition is not and *cannot* be water, however much it may resemble water in its appearance. Human beings did not always know this; it was a *discovery* people made about the essence of water. Real natures or essences do not lie around on the surface for our immediate appropriation. They have to be uncovered by investigation, observation and theory.

To acquire such knowledge is the essential task of science. As Aristotle observed: "There is scientific knowledge of a thing only when we know its essence".[15]

Art, like science, also plays a cognitive role in respect of the phenomena of social life. Realistic art, like science, can tell us about deep-going social processes and the psychology of a particular class. But unlike art, which always expresses the general through the individual, the concrete, science presents it in the form of abstract logic, by means of concepts and categories.

To sum up, the specific nature of *science* lies in the fact that it *is the highest generalisation of practice capable of embracing all phenomena of reality, and provides true knowledge of the essence of phenomena and processes, the laws of nature and society in an abstract, logical form.*

The structure of science is extremely complex, but it can be reduced to three basic interacting components.

First, science includes *empirical knowledge*, and not only the knowledge which is borrowed from ordinary consciousness for the purpose of analysis and generalisation, but also the knowledge obtained through experiments and observation. New theoretical fields in natural science are usually opened by the experimental discovery of new facts that refuse to "fit" into the framework of the existing theories and for some time may defy a satisfactory theoretical explanation. This was the case with the discovery of radioactivity at the end of the 19th century; not until 20 years later was it explained as the conversion of chemical elements. Thus, new facts provide a stimulus to the development of theory.

Second, science is a sphere of *theoretical knowledge*. It is the business of theory to explain facts in their totality, to discover the operation of laws in empirical material and to bring these laws together in a unified system. In every field of science the process of accumulation of facts sooner or later leads to the creation of a theory as a system of knowledge, and this is a sure sign that the given field of knowledge is becoming a science in the true sense of the term. The study of mechanics became a science thanks to Isaac Newton, who at the end of the 17th century discovered the basic laws of the mechanical motion of bodies and built them into a system. The study of biological organisms became a genuine science only with Darwin's theory of evolution of species according to natural selection. In the second half of the last century the study of electricity became a genuine science only when James Maxwell produced a consistent theory of the electromagnetic field. The same period saw the great work performed by Marx and Engels transforming the study of society into a science with the development of the materialist theory of history, and of political economy into a science with the development of a consistent labour theory of value.

The essence of science as a theoretical system is its laws, which reflect the objectively necessary, essential connections of phenomena in one or another sphere. The laws of science may be truly understood only if we take into consideration their interconnection as an essential part of the system of scientific knowledge. Another part of theoretical science consists of hypotheses, without which science cannot develop and which in the course of practical testing are either rejected or else corrected, cleansed of error and become theories.

Third and last, an inseparable part of science is its *philosophical foundations and conclusions*, in which theory finds its direct continuation and culmination. Scientific theory may have varying degrees of universality, and the greater the degree of universality, the nearer the given theory comes to philosophy. It is not surprising therefore that the most important synthetic theories of natural science are distinctly philosophical in character. For example, the interpretation of the law of the conservation and conversion of energy and the law of entropy that forms the basis of thermodynamics would be impossible without an elucidation of the philosophical questions of the eternity and infinity of matter and motion, their quantitative and qualitative indestructibility. The theory of relativity establishes the connection between space, time and matter; the quantum theory reveals the interrelation between continuity and discontinuity at the level of interactions of sub-atomic objects. These are not only physical but also philosophical problems.

What has been said above refers also to the generalising theories in biology and astronomy, and even more so to the social sciences.

In the social sciences ideological factors play a part in the interpretation of facts, that is, at the level of theory, whereas in the natural sciences they usually function at the level of philosophical interpretation of theories. For this reason the absolute opposition of science to ideology, which is so characteristic of contemporary bourgeois philosophy and sociology, does not stand up to criticism. Nevertheless bourgeois ideologists make a great fuss about the necessity of "cleansing" science of ideology, their principal intention being to "cleanse" the social sciences of Marxism and completely subordinate them to bourgeois ideology.

As for natural science, both positivism and religious philosophy insist on its complete "deideologisation", although from different standpoints. In their speeches at the 14th International Philosophical Congress in Vienna (September 1968), during the debate on the problem of "Philosophy and Natural Science" the neopositivist A.J. Ayer and the neo-Thomist[16] Joseph Meurers agreed that natural science can "only measure quantities". For Ayer this is the end of cognition in general, but for Meurers the essence of the phenomena of nature can be known only by religion, so natural science can and should be "liberated" from materialist philosophy. In this way both philosophers impoverish natural science and limit its scope. In actual fact, science is penetrating ever deeper into the essence of phenomena and processes and embracing an ever wider picture of the world, and for this reason its philosophical content is steadily increasing.

While it remains a phenomenon of the intellectual life of society, science is at the same time embodied in the sphere of its material life. It is a special field of human activity, *both theoretical and practical.* At the earliest stages of scientific development, scientists not only contemplated nature, they also acted; they invented instruments, carried out observations, made experiments and thus gathered new facts for science. Take for example, the ancient astronomical instrument known as the gnomon, invented by the ancient Greeks. This was a vertical pole on a horizontal plane which they used to determine not only the altitude of the sun above the horizon but also geographical latitude.

In modern times such forms of scientific practice as instrumental observation, and particularly experiment, have been rapidly developed, and today there is not a single science that can do without a solid experimental base. In many branches of science this base demands tremendous expenditure and is technologically far more complex than any form of production.

The division between theory and practice in many branches of science has demanded a division of labour between scientists. For example, experimental physicists conduct experiments, control instruments and provide the first generalisation of the data received, while theoretical physicists devote themselves entirely to generalising experimental data and developing theory.

The main distinguishing feature of practical activity in science is that it is subordinated to the work of acquiring knowledge, of developing theory. The material and mental factors are interwoven not only in science but in any field of human endeavour, and the dialectics of the interaction of these factors must be taken into account when considering either of them. Whereas material production and work cannot exist without the intellectual element, no form of social consciousness can exist without the material element. This is particularly true of science, which presupposes a number of special forms of practical activity (experiment, observation), which are often known as "practical science". The existence of "practical science" should not, however, be taken as an argument against regarding science as primarily a phenomenon of the intellectual life of society, a special form of social consciousness.

6. PHILOSOPHY

There exist a wide range of vitally important questions that are not dealt with by the specialised sciences, e.g., what is the essential nature of the world around us? Or, to put it differently, what is the relationship between matter and consciousness? Do our perceptions and thoughts about the world around us correspond to the reality of the external world? What is the nature of humanity and what is its place in the world? These and similar questions make up the content of a special form of social consciousness, philosophy.

Philosophy is a world outlook with its own specific content and form, a world outlook which offers theoretical grounds for its principles and conclusions. This is what distinguishes philosophy from the unscientific, religious world outlook, which is based on faith in the supernatural and reflects reality in forms conjured up by the imagination and emotions.

A philosophical world outlook is a system of highly generalised theoretical views of nature and society. Philosophy seeks to substantiate a definite orientation in political, scientific, moral, aesthetic and other spheres of social life.

Everybody forms his or her own particular view of the surrounding world, but this view often consists of no more than fragments of various contradictory ideas without any theoretical basis. The philosophical world outlook, on the other hand, is not merely the sum total but a system of ideas, opinions and conceptions of nature, society, the individual human being and his or her place in the world. It does not merely proclaim its principles and try to make people believe in them; it gives logical arguments for these principles.

By no means every theoretically substantiated world outlook is scientific in character. The actual content of a philosophical world outlook may be scientific or unscientific or even anti-scientific. Only the world outlook that bases its conclusions on the findings of contemporary science, that uses scientific method in its thinking and allows no place for various kinds of anti-scientific, mystical and religious views and superstitions may be considered scientific. Of course, the very idea of scientificality must be considered historically. For example, the world outlook of the French materialists of the 18th century was scientific because in addition to the historically transient element in their teaching there was something that proved to be historically intransient, and this has been inherited by modern materialism. There were also scientific ideas and propositions in the great idealist philosophical systems (for example, in Descartes,

Leibnitz, Kant, Fichte and Hegel) to the extent that they had a true grasp of ideal relationships and connections.

The subject matter of philosophy has changed historically in close connection with the development of all aspects of humanity's intellectual life, with the development of science and philosophical thought itself.

Philosophy first arose in the commercially oriented city-states of ancient Greece. The most ancient form of world view, which immediately preceded philosophy in history, was religion. In religious mythology with its belief in imaginary spirits and gods as the creators and rulers of the world, great importance was attached to questions of the origin and essence of the world. Philosophy grew out of the myth-steeped religious consciousness, while simultaneously fighting it, and thus took shape in its struggle to furnish a naturalistic, as opposed to a supernatural, explanation of the world. The emergence of philosophy coincides historically with the beginnings of scientific knowledge, with the need for theoretical inquiry. In fact, philosophy was the first historical form of theoretical knowledge, of science.

Initially, philosophy tried to answer the questions that had already been posed by the religious-mythological view of the world. But philosophy had a different way of tackling these questions. It based itself on a theoretical analysis that was in accord with logic and practical experience.

The early Greek philosophers (Thales, Anaximenes, Anaximander, Parmenides, Heraclitus and others) were mainly interested in understanding the origin of the diverse phenomena of nature. Natural philosophy (philosophical doctrine concerning nature) was the first historical form of philosophical thought.

As specialised scientific knowledge was accumulated and thinkers began to develop specific methods of research and notions about the laws prevailing in various realms of nature, a process of differentiation of the hitherto undivided body of theoretical knowledge occurred, and mathematics, medicine, astronomy and other disciplines broke away and formed separate sciences. But this process was not one-sided. As the range of problems studied by philosophy diminished, there was a corresponding development, deepening and enrichment of the purely philosophical notions, and various philosophical theories and schools emerged. Such philosophical disciplines were formed as ontology — the study of being, or the essence of all that exists; epistemology — the theory of knowledge; logic — the science of the forms of correct, that is to say, consistent, argued thinking; the philosophy of history, ethics, aesthetics, and later, philosophy itself.

The age of the Renaissance, and particularly the 17th and 18th centuries, accelerated the process of differentiation. Mechanics, physics, chemistry, biology, jurisprudence, and political economy became independent branches of scientific knowledge. This progressive division of labour in the sphere of scientific knowledge brought about a qualitative change in the goal of philosophy, its place in the system of knowledge and its relationship to the specialised sciences. Philosophy was no longer able to devote itself to solving the special problems of mechanics, physics, astronomy, chemistry, biology, law, history and so on, though it was still better equipped to deal with general scientific questions, with questions of world outlook, which are often implied in the work of the specialised sciences, but which cannot be solved within their terms of reference and by their specialised methods.

We know from history that the interrelationships between philosophy and the specialised sciences have been extremely complex and contradictory in character, since the specialised sciences (with the exception of mathematics and mechanics) were for a long time restricted mainly to empirical research, while the general theoretical questions concerning these sciences were dealt with by philosophy. But philosophical inquiry into the theoretical problems of the specialised sciences was not based on sufficient factual material (as a rule such material had not been accumulated); such inquiry was therefore abstract and speculative, and its results often conflicted with the latest facts discovered by science. This was where the opposition arose between philosophy and the specialised sciences, which assumed a particularly acute form in those philosophical doctrines that were connected with religion and sought to provide a justification for the religious world outlook, which is incompatible with science.

Some philosophers created encyclopaedic philosophical systems designed to counterpose the philosophy of nature to natural science, the philosophy of history to history as a science, or the philosophy of law to the science of law. These philosophers usually assumed that philosophy was able to go beyond the bounds of experience, to provide "superscientific" knowledge. Such illusions were exploded by the development of the specialised sciences, which proved that physical problems can be solved only by physics, chemical problems by chemistry and so on.

At the same time, the opposite tendency, the reduction of philosophy to the status of a specialised science, was to be observed in a number of philosophical doctrines. The successes of the specialised sciences, particularly mathematics and mechanics, prompted philosophers to study the methods by which these successes had been obtained, so that they could find out whether these methods could be used in philosophy. Philosophers often attempted to apply, for example, the axiomatic method of mathematics for building up philosophical systems; attempts were also made to universalise the principles of classical mechanics, so that, basing itself on these principles, philosophy could explain not only the phenomena of inanimate nature, but also biological and even social processes.

The development of the specialised sciences demonstrated, however, that there are problems that can be dealt with by philosophy as well as by the sciences. In fact, such problems can be solved only by their joint efforts. There are also some specific philosophical problems that philosophy alone can solve, but even here a solution can be obtained only if philosophy relies on the sum-total of the scientific data and advanced social practice.

But philosophy that relies upon scientific data begins to loose its character as "philosophy", as explanations about the world relying simply upon pure thought. It was in this sense that Engels declared that with the development of the dialectical materialist conception of nature and of human history, philosophy is reduced to study of the "realm of pure thought", to the "theory of the laws of the thought process itself, logic and dialectics". In the realm of the study of nature and human history, philosophy as such "becomes unnecessary and impossible" since in these spheres of knowledge, it "is no longer a question anywhere of inventing interconnections from out of our brains, but of discovering them in the facts" of material reality.[17] ❦

CHAPTER 4

MATERIAL PRODUCTION: THE BASIS OF SOCIAL LIFE

The subject matter of historical materialism is human society and the most general laws of its development. The first step towards discovering these laws was to establish the role of material production in the life of society. It will easily be understood that society cannot exist without producing the material goods needed for human life. This proposition is obvious and had been recognised even before the time of Marx and Engels. But Marx and Engels did not stop there; they established the law-governed dependence of all social relations on the relations people enter into to produce material goods.

In the process of production people do not only create material products; production does not only provide people with means of existence. *In producing material goods people produce and reproduce their own social relations*. The study of social production, its structure, its constituent elements and their interconnections, therefore, makes it possible to penetrate into the essence of the historical process, to reveal the deep-going social mechanisms that operate in the life of society.

1. SOCIETY AND NATURE, THEIR INTERACTION

Material production furnishes the key to the interpretation of both the internal structure of society and its interrelationship with the external environment — surrounding nature. Production is, above all, the process of interaction between society and nature. In this process of interaction, people obtain from surrounding nature the necessary means of existence. Labour, production, is at the same time the basis of the formation of humans as social beings, their emergence from nature.

In his work *The Part Played by Labour in the Transition from Ape to Man,* Engels showed that labour is the driving force, the basis of humanity's evolution.

To begin with, our pre-human ancestors used any simple object that came to hand to protect themselves from beasts of prey or to capture prey themselves, and to regularly gain access to fruits, nuts, and other vegetable foods. This activity as yet belonged to the category of "those first instinctive forms of labour which remain on the animal level".[1] But it was this primitive activity of humanity's ancestors that marked the beginning of the development of human labour itself into a form in which it constitutes humanity's unique possession.

From the simple use of objects provided by nature, which is sometimes observed among modern-day apes, our ancestors gradually passed on to making tools, and this was the essential factor in the emergence of human labour itself. Labour activity had two decisive consequences. First, the organism of humanity's ancestors began to accommodate itself not only to the conditions of the environment but to labour activity. The specific features of humans' physical organisation — upright walk, differentiation of the functions of the front and rear limbs, development of the hand and the brain — evolved in the long process of adaptation of the organism to the performance of labour operations. Second, because it meant concerted action, labour stimulated the emergence and development of articulate speech, of language as a means of communication, the accumulation and transmission of labour and social experience.

Two important stages may be noted in the process of the formation of humanity. The first of them is marked by the beginning of regular tool-use, and of tool-making. This is the stage of humans-in-formation (*Australopithecus africanus*, *Homo habilis* and *Homo erectus*). The oldest evidence of the use of stone tools, found at Hadar in Ethiopia, dates from 2.5 million years ago. The remains of humanity's oldest ancestors, the Australopithecines and *Homo habilis*, also belong to this period. This confirms the intrinsic connection between the development of labour and human evolution.

The second major qualitative stage was the appearance in Africa about 100,000 years ago, in the middle Paleolithic age, of modern humans (*Homo sapiens* — "rational man"). Since the emergence of *Homo sapiens,* no radical changes in humanity's physical type have occurred. In this period, corresponding major changes took place in production, involving the making of various instruments of labour (from wood, stone, bone and horns).

The stages in the evolution of humanity and the instruments of labour were at the same time the stages in the formation of human society itself in its primary form, namely, tribal society. Humans are social beings; they have never lived and could not appear outside society or before society. Nor, however, could society appear before humanity; the new forms of relations between individuals developed only because humanity's ancestors were becoming people.

All kinds of features distinguish humans from other animals. The most important of them, however, are production of the instruments of labour,[2] articulate speech and abstract thought. The first of these is primary. According to Marx and Engels, people "... begin to distinguish themselves from animals as soon as they begin to *produce* their means of subsistence".[3] Modern paleontologists follow the same approach, classifying fossil skeletons of primates as belonging to the human rather than the simian evolutionary line if they show evidence of having engaged in labour (using and making tools for that purpose). Whatever apelike physical features these early transitional forms retain, the passing over from the use of biological organs for food foraging to the use of tools to procure their subsistence sets them apart from their simian relatives.

Taken in its most general forms, the process of production is what humans do to the objects and forces of nature in order to obtain and produce their means of subsistence: food, clothing, a place to live and so on. This process presupposes human activity, or labour itself, affecting the objects of labour. Unlike the instinctive forms of human activity, human labour, in the true sense of the word, is purposeful activity, which results in the creation of an object which, as Marx put it, already existed in a person's imagination, that is, ideally. Comparing the behaviour of the bees, which so skilfully build their honeycomb of wax, with the activity of the architect, Marx observed that even the worst architect is superior to the best bee in that, before he or she builds a house, the human has already created it in his or her own mind.

Labour activity takes place with the help of the corresponding means of influencing the object of labour — tools.[4] These are the essential means of human labour.

Tools bring about the transition from the immediate, direct actions, characteristic of the animals, which use their natural organs — claws, teeth etc. — to essentially human actions mediated by the instruments of labour. The latter continue, as it were, humans' natural organs, performing at first the same functions as the natural organs, but intensifying their effect.

Society may be described as a special type of organism.[5] Whereas the biological organism has a system of natural organs performing certain functions that are needed for its existence, the development of human society, involves the improvement of artificial organs — tools, instruments of labour.

Because human development is expressed primarily in change of its social organs — the instruments of labour — it has no natural boundaries. In the process of labour humans, unlike the animals, actively influence the natural environment, changing it and adapting it to their needs.

To sum up: *Human labour differs from the activity of even the most developed animals in that, first, it exerts an active influence on nature, instead of merely adapting to it as is characteristic of the animals; second, it presupposes systematic use and, above all, production of the instruments of production; third, labour implies purposeful, conscious activity; fourth, it is from the very beginning social in character and inconceivable outside society.*

For these reasons, social development differs from biological development. Humans develop as social beings without any radical changes in their biological nature. Hence the difference in the character and rate of both processes. Radical changes in social life take place within periods that would be quite insufficient for any significant changes to occur in the development of the biological species (not counting, of course, the changes that occur in nature thanks to humanity's activity). Thus, for example, when humans developed the ability to fly, they accomplished in a mere fifty years of technological evolution what it took biological evolution fifty million years to achieve by genetic variation.

The rapid change in human social development compared to the rate of change in our biological features has been largely due to the appearance of new mechanisms of continuity in social development compared with biological evolution. In the organic world the accumulation and transmission of information from one generation to another is effected mainly through the mechanism of heredity, which forms the basis of the inborn instincts, and in the higher animals also through parents' transmission to their progeny of certain skills. In social life a tremendous part is played by each generation's inheritance of the means of production created by the previous generation, and also by the continuity of social experience embodied in language, culture and traditions. Whereas biological transmission of properties is limited by the information that can be stored in the apparatus of heredity (in the genes), the inheritance of social experience occurs constantly and has no limits. Viewed in the most general sense, culture is the embodiment of this experience, the sum-total of the material and intellectual values created in the course of human history.

Each generation enriches culture with new achievements. In contrast to the biological world, where all changes take place spontaneously, unconsciously, human society is afforded ever greater possibilities of consciously and purposefully changing the conditions of its material life and regulating its interrelations with nature.

Any material system presupposes a definite type of connection between its constituent elements. The specific nature of social life is determined by the production, or economic, connection. All forms of social relationships are made up in the final analysis on the basis of the relations between people arising in the process of production — the production relations, which cement the social organism and give it its unity.

The qualitatively new forms of connection that make up the social organism have corresponding specific laws of development that differ from biological laws. Marx and Engels, already in their day, showed the misguidedness of attempts to apply biological laws to the explanation of social phenomena. Like other laws of nature, biological laws do not regulate or determine the development of social phenomena. Society is governed by its own specific laws, which are revealed by historical materialism and other social sciences.

This does not imply, however, that society develops in isolation from nature. The development of society is inconceivable without certain natural preconditions. Chief among these are the natural conditions surrounding society, usually called the *geographical environment*, and the physical organisation of the people themselves.

The concept of the geographical environment embraces, of course, not nature as a whole, which is infinite, but that part of it which affects society directly or indirectly, which constitutes the natural conditions of human life and activity. Some writers define the geographical environment as the sphere of nature that is changed or transformed by society. As we shall see later, the part of nature that surrounds humanity actually does bear the imprint of our activity, but humans' life is also influenced by forces of nature that are beyond their control (for example, solar radiation, the internal energetics of the Earth, which are revealed in movements of the Earth's crust, and so on).

Various naturalistic theories have attempted to ascribe the determining role in history to these natural preconditions. Thus, the exponents of geographical determinism (the French philosopher Charles Montesquieu, the English historian Henry Thomas Buckle, the French geographer Elisee Reclus, and others) tried to attribute the differences between the social system and histories of various peoples to the influence of the natural conditions in which they live. In fact, however, we find extremely different social systems in similar geographical conditions, and one and the same kind of social system in different geographical conditions (for example, the tribal system was to be found at various times in Europe, Asia, Africa, America and Australia). Nor can the historical succession of socioeconomic formations be attributed to the influence of the geographical environment, if only because it occurs far more quickly than changes in this environment, which do not depend on the influence of society.

The basic methodological fault of the naturalistic theories in sociology is that they see the source of social development as something outside society. The influence of external conditions on any developing system, including society, cannot be denied or underestimated, of course. But change in such a system is not simply the imprint of changing environment, the passive result of its influence. A system has its own internal logic of development and in its turn exerts an influence on the environment.

If we adopt the modern classification of systems, society may be regarded as one of the so-called open systems, which exchange not only energy but also matter with their environment. Between society and nature there occurs a constant metabolism, a constant exchange of substances, which takes place, as Marx showed, in the process of labour, of production. From the vegetable and animal world people obtain their means of nutrition and raw material for making objects of use. Mineral resources provide them with the material for producing the means of production. Production involves the use of various sources of energy: first of all, people's own muscular strength, then the strength of the animals they tame, of wind and water, and finally the power of steam, electricity and the energy of chemical and nuclear processes.

The geographical environment influences the development of society in various ways at various stages of its development, but the direct influence of geographical conditions on people's nature and their social organisation is never of prime importance (as Montesquieu and other geographical determinists maintained). The main thing is their mediated influence — through the conditions of production. At the lower cultural stages, when humans are mainly concerned with obtaining ready-made products, more importance attaches to the natural means of subsistence: fertile soil, an abundance of fish and so on. At the higher stages, when mechanised industry develops, the existence of the natural means of production, such as waterfalls, navigable rivers, forests, metals, coal and oil, is of far greater importance.

The development of economic activity is not, of course, always the same among different peoples. It depends largely on the geographical conditions under which they live. Among the tribes inhabiting the fertile areas of the northern subtropics — the Tigris and Euphrates river valleys (Mesopotamia), the valley of the Nile, and so on — the productive forces developed more quickly than among the tribes that lived in conditions of the Far North and the Far South.

At the same time, the uneven rates of development of production are also connected with different social conditions, with how relations took shape between different peoples — with their interconnection or isolation, their mutual intercourse or conflict, and so on.

The influence of geographical conditions is always mediated by social conditions, primarily by the level of development of production. People make various use of the properties of their environment: more and more new materials are brought into production, humanity penetrates new regions of nature (the depths of the earth and sea, outer space etc.) and masters them in order to satisfy its needs. This means that society's links with nature become increasingly widespread and many-sided.

With the development of production, society's dependence on natural conditions is relatively diminished. The production of synthetic materials reduces industry's dependence on natural raw material; the transmission of electricity over long distances reduces the need to deploy factories near the sources of power.

The reduction of dependence on natural conditions in any particular geographical environment is predicated on the increase of humanity's influence over nature. Whereas natural conditions change comparatively slowly if left to themselves, their rate of change may be accelerated by humanity. Humans' natural environment bears the stamp of their production activity.

Geographical conditions on Earth are to a significant extent the result of the activity of living organisms, which are responsible, for example, for the formation of limestone, dolomite, marble, coal, peat, fertile soil, an oxygenated atmosphere and so on. The active role of life on Earth is expressed in the concept of the *biosphere* of the planetary envelope, which includes the organisms and also inanimate matter that is taken over and transformed by life. If there were no life on Earth, it would look as barren as the Moon. With the appearance of humanity, the "pressure of life" on the planetary envelope became immeasurably more powerful.

Humanity influences the vegetable and animal world, exterminates certain species of plants and animals and introduces and changes others. A considerable area of the vegetable world has been shaped by humanity. In ancient Greece there were only a few varieties of apple; now there are more than ten thousand. The area of cultivation of many plants has expanded under human influence. Potatoes, which first appeared on the plateau between the mountains of the Andes in South America; maize, which first grew in America; the water-melon, which came from Africa, and other useful plants have all spread to other countries thanks to human activity.

The scale of humanity's influence on our planet's crust is comparable with that of the most powerful geological forces. According to one estimate, people have extracted from the earth in the last five centuries not less than 50,000 million tons of carbon, 2000 million tons of iron, 20,000 million tons of copper and 20,000 tons of gold and so on. Humanity's production activity brings to the surface not less than five cubic kilometres of rock per year. People drive canals through continents, and win back land from the sea. By watering deserts, drying marshland and altering the course of rivers, they change even the climatic conditions of their life. The climate is also indirectly influenced by humanity's production activity because the burning of oil, coal and peat annually returns to the atmosphere about 1500 million tons of carbon. The amount of carbon in the air is one of the factors controlling the temperature on Earth.

The effect of nature on society is totally spontaneous, but the effect of society on nature is always the result of humanity's conscious struggle for existence. Besides the intended transformation of nature, human activity also has unforeseen results, which in many cases subsequently cause tremendous losses. Karl Marx observed that cultivation, when it progresses spontaneously and is not consciously controlled, leaves deserts behind it.[6] The parasitic felling of timber, for instance, upsets the flow of rivers, widens ravines and causes drought. Huge areas of land are eroded and become unsuitable for cultivation. The use of chemical pesticides and weed killers often not only destroys the insects and the weeds but also poisons many other plants and animals. As the scale of humanity's activity increases, the danger of its uncontrolled influence on the natural environment also increases. One of the side effects of humanity's activity, for example, is the upsetting of the balance between various processes in nature and pollution of air and water with so much industrial waste, radioactive matter etc., that this is beginning to constitute a threat to humanity's own existence.

Yet it is not humanity *per se* that is to blame for this danger, but the subordination of its activity to considerations of private profit or narrow utilitarianism. The overcoming of this problem will require the planned use of natural resources on the scale of whole countries and continents. This is beyond the scope of capitalist society; to achieve this there must be social ownership of the decisive means of production. It also demands, of course, wise and effective planning of production, and good management, which is not achieved automatically even in conditions of social ownership of the decisive means of production. It presupposes democratic control and accountability informed by the best available scientific knowledge.

To sum up: *Humanity's influence on nature depends on the level of the productive forces, on the character of the social system and on the level of development of society and people themselves.*

In principle the same is true of another natural precondition of human history — humans' bodily organisation, their biological properties.[7] It is these biological properties that give them their need for food, clothing, and so on. But the means by which people satisfy these needs are determined not by biological but by social conditions. Procreation also proceeds according to human biological properties and yet the growth of population is primarily a social phenomenon, regulated by the laws of the development of society.

From the naturalistic standpoint, population growth is regarded as a factor independent of the laws of social development and even determining that development. Moreover, some sociologists treat it as a positive factor and regard the increase of the population as one of the causes that impel people to seek new sources of food and thus promote the development of production (such, for example, was the view of the Russian sociologist Kovalevsky); others (the British economist Thomas Malthus at the close of the 18th century, and his followers today, the neo-Malthusians) see the rapid growth of population as a source of social problems such as environmental degradation and poverty.

According to Malthusian "law", the means of (agricultural) subsistence grow in arithmetical progression as opposed to the geometrical progression of population growth. The population increases faster than its food supply, and hence, so Malthus maintains, come the starvation, unemployment and poverty of the working people. His conclusion is that to improve their position, the working people should control the number of births in their families.

In reality the relation between the growth rate of the population and production of the means of subsistence is not something given once and for all. With a relatively conservative technical base and slow development in the pre-capitalist socioeconomic formations, there was pressure of excess population on the productive forces, which often led to large-scale migrations of population. On the other hand, in conditions of rapid technical progress, the growth of production of the means of subsistence considerably outstrips the population growth rate, as is seen, for example, in the increase of per capita production. But such average figures fail to reveal the extremely uneven distribution of food resources. Hundreds of millions in Asia, Africa and Latin America are systematically underfed. The reason is economic backwardness resulting from the heritage of colonialism, the neo-colonial economic structure and the exploitation of underdeveloped countries by the corporations and banks of the developed capitalist countries.

In the countries of developed capitalism, it is not overpopulation that exerts pressure on the productive forces, but rather the productive forces that exert pressure on the population, and create a relative surplus of population (a permanent pool of unemployed workers). This was what Marx saw as the law of population inherent in the capitalist mode of production.

The conclusion reached by Marx from his analysis of the problem of population under capitalism is of great importance in social theory. His conclusion is that every historically determined mode of production has its own specific laws of population, which are historical in character. Marx considered that an "abstract law of population exists only for plants and animals, and even then only in the absence of any historical intervention by man".[8]

Size of population, its growth, density and territorial distribution undoubtedly exert an influence on the development of society. For example, when we determine the initial possibilities of development of production in a particular country we must take into consideration both its natural resources and its population. Without sufficient numbers and density of population, it will be impossible or difficult (as, for example, in many parts of the far north and in deserts) to exploit natural resources.

At the same time, the actual number of people that go to make up a society depends on the degree of development of production. At the beginning of the Neolithic age (about 15,000 years ago) the primitive tribes that had spread over all continents counted only a few million people. By the beginning of the present era (AD) the world's population was between 150 and 200 million people, while by 1000 AD, it had risen to about 300 million. The total population since then has increased almost twenty times.

Acceleration in the rate of population growth is not a cause of change in the mode of production and people's conditions of life; rather it is one of the results. Population increase depends on the ratio of deaths to births. Both these processes are influenced by a large number of social factors: economic relations, standard of life, housing conditions, medical development, health services and so on. The rates of growth of the population also depend on social and economic conditions.

The characteristic situation at present in the developed countries is as follows: a low or average birth rate (15 to 20 people per 1000 of population), low death-rate (about 10 deaths per 1000 of population), a small or average natural increment, a high expectancy of life (65 to 80 years) and consequently a relatively slow replacement of generations. In most of the semi-colonial countries of Asia, Africa and Latin America, we find another type of reproduction of population: a high birth rate (20 to 50 per 1000 of population), considerable mortality (about 20 or more deaths per 1000 of population), a rather high natural increment, rather low expectancy of life (average 45 years in the African countries) and a rapid replacement of generations. Clearly the decisive factor producing these different patterns is the disparity in average living standards (incomes, health care, education, social security).

The neo-Malthusians maintain that the present "demographic explosion" is no less dangerous than the atom bomb. The US biologist Paul Ehrlich compares the increasing numbers of the Earth's population to a wild-fire cancer growth and has predicted, since the early 1970s, that within the next ten years new extensive famine areas will make their appearance. Like other Malthusians, however, he refuses to see the social causes of famine.

Scientific calculations show that fuller use of agricultural land and increasing its yields would make it possible to feed ten times more people than there are at present in the world. There is no doubt that the use of the tremendous food resources of the seas and oceans and further advances in synthesising food products by chemical means will reveal possibilities of feeding an even greater number of people. The realisation of these possibilities, however, depends not only on finding more rational means of using the biosphere, but on solving social problems, overcoming economic and cultural backwardness in many countries and eliminating the imperialist (super)exploitation of the working people of the underdeveloped countries.

It would be a mistake to imagine that Marxism always and everywhere, regardless of the specific conditions of place and time, demands increase of the birth rate. This vulgarised notion distorts the true nature of the opposition between Malthusianism and Marxism, which lies not in acknowledging or denying the admissibility of measures to regulate population growth but in the completely different ways of solving social problems that they propose. For the Malthusians, starvation and poverty are caused by excessive growth of population; for the Marxists, they are caused by the obsolete social system. The former see reduction of the birth rate as a panacea for social ills; the latter maintain that the chief means of solving the urgent social problems of modern times — including excessive population growth — is to replace capitalism by socialism.

The development of society must be explained in its own terms; the key to the transformation of society lies in society itself. To understand the true inner causes of development of society, we must trace the role of material production as the basis of social life and progress.

2. The Productive Forces of Society

Material production is the sphere of social life in which the material product is created that is afterwards consumed by society as a whole, by further production or by individuals.

No matter how high the level of its development, a society cannot exist and develop without material production. One has only to imagine the effect of even a brief stoppage in production. The bakeries, the footwear and cloth factories would cease to operate, the trains would stop running, there would be no electricity, no water supply and so on. A complete cessation of production would entail the destruction of society. There can be no society without material production.

Although production is a permanent condition of the life of society, the mode of production varies in the various stages of its development.

In the process of production, people interact with nature and with one another. These two types of relationship constitute the inseparably connected aspects of any concrete mode of production — the *productive forces and the production relations*. Consequently, analysis of the mode of production in its general form entails discovering what the productive forces and production relations are and how they are interconnected.

The productive forces are the forces by which society influences nature and changes it. These forces express the relation of society to nature, but nature itself, of course, cannot be included among the productive forces of society.

Nature is the universal *object of labour*. Not all of nature, of course, is the immediate object of labour, but only that part of it which is drawn into production, inasmuch as it is used by humans.

From nature humans extract the raw material from which things are made in the process of labour. But with the exception of the extracting industries, the ploughing up of virgin land and so on, production is usually concerned with objects that have previously had some labour put into them. Thus the steel that goes into making a machine-tool has previously been forged. Raw material (for example, cotton, grain, ore) and semi-manufactures are human-made objects of labour. People not only acquire in nature ready-made objects of labour but also create them. Industrial progress involves the use of more and more new materials. Modern industry uses various rare metals, new alloys and new kinds of synthetic materials — plastics, synthetic fibres. New materials widen the field of people's production.

The *means of labour* are the thing or complex of things that people place between themselves and the objects of labour, and that people use to act on the objects of labour. The means of labour include: first, instruments of labour (tools, machinery, engines etc); second, buildings in which to conduct labour activities; third, transport and communications facilities; and fourth, reservoirs and tanks for storing objects of labour.

The objects and means of labour, that is, the material elements of the process of labour, constitute in their totality the *means of production*.

The composition of the means of production is extremely varied and changes from one epoch to another. Industrial and agricultural production today makes use of machines and engines and various subsidiary means of production that are needed for transporting and storing products and for other purposes. Out of all the means of production that have been applied in any particular epoch and are typical of it, Marx concentrates on those that directly serve as the conductor of people's influence on nature — *the instruments of labour*. In Marx's phrase these constitute the bone and muscle system of production and are the most important indicator of the relationship of society to nature, of the labour productivity achieved by society. At the same time, the instruments of labour are only a part of the whole technological complex, and in defining technological trends we must take into consideration all the complex interdependencies and interactions that occur within that complex.

The instruments of labour are the determinant of the development of production. "It is not what is made but how, and by what instruments of labour, that distinguishes different economic epochs."[9] For every new generation, the instruments of labour that it inherits from previous generations become the point of departure for further development and thus form the basis of the continuity of history.

The instruments of labour become an active force that transforms the object of labour only in contact with living labour, with human beings. People, the working masses, are a productive force thanks to their knowledge, experience and the skills needed to put production into practice.

To sum up: *The social productive forces are the means of production created by society and, above all, the instruments of labour, and also the people who put them into operation and produce goods.*

While the instruments of labour are the *determining* element in the productive forces, inasmuch as they determine the character of society's relation to nature, the working people, with their knowledge and experience, *are the most important* productive force of society. It is people who use machinery, who operate the instruments of labour and carry on production. The functioning of the instruments of labour depends on the skill, knowledge and experience of people, on how fully they are able to utilise the available machines and to what extent they have mastered these machines. At the same time, these very qualities of people depend on the available instruments of labour, on what tools, implements and machines they are using.

This dependence of people's experience and skills on the technology of production is one of the expressions of the general dependence of the subject on the object, of the personal factor in production on its material factor. At the artisan stage, people's experience and skills take shape empirically and acquire the character of traditions passed on from one generation to the next. In the Middle Ages craftsmen made a secret of their discoveries and experience, which were closely guarded from the eyes of strangers. Under these conditions, changes in the traditional instruments of labour were punished rather than encouraged, thus intensifying stagnation in the process of production.

With the transition to machine production, education, culture and the scientific knowledge needed for working with machines assume ever increasing significance. Navvies cannot simply throw down their spades and start driving excavators. They must master the new machine, even though the excavator performs the same work as they did. At the same time, machine production, particularly in some of its forms (for example, line production), creates a need for unskilled and semi-skilled labour.

People not only make use of the available instruments of labour, but also create the new ones; the instruments of labour are the materialised force of human knowledge. Human experience, technical knowledge and skills are essential for improving the instruments of production, for the work of inventing things and for rationalisation of production. The development of technology itself and the use of its possibilities depend on people's experience, skills, technical knowledge and culture.

The development of the productive forces is the development of the instruments of labour and correspondingly of people themselves, of their cultural and technical standards. The level of development of the productive forces is indicated by the *productivity of social labour*. A major factor in the growth of the productivity of labour is the creation of more productive instruments of labour, that is, *technical progress*. The improvement of the existing instruments of labour and the creation of new ones that are more productive, of new technology, the development of the power base and the corresponding re-equipment of all branches of the economy are the mainspring of the development of social production.

In the course of the history of society, the productive forces have achieved tremendous development. Historically, production begins with the making and using of the most primitive stone, bone and wooden implements — the stone chisel and point, the club and spear, needles and other utensils made of bone. The discovery of how to make and use fire was one of the greatest achievements of humanity's early stage of development. This discovery, as Engels said, finally divided humans from the animal kingdom. Another great step forward was the emergence of pottery. Humanity's possibilities were considerably expanded by the invention of the bow and arrow. People thus accumulated a collection of primitive implements that enabled them to engage in hunting, fishing and vegetable collecting. As tools improved, they tended to become more and more specialised for certain operations. At the earliest stage of primitive society, people produced only the instruments of labour, while taking their means of existence ready-made from nature (appropriative economy), which made them heavily dependent on natural conditions.

The great revolution in the development of primitive production was the transition from appropriation to production of the means of existence, which was connected with the emergence of *agriculture and livestock-breeding*. This transition occurred in the Middle East early in the Neolithic period (around 12,000 years ago). The collecting of the seeds of wild wheat and barley for grinding into flour prepared the way for the planting and harvesting of cereal crops , while the hunting of herds of grazing animals (gazelles, wild goats, sheep and cattle) helped to introduce livestock-breeding.

The tilling of the soil with digging sticks and then primitive hoes demanded an enormous amount of labour. But this was a fundamentally new step in human development because it allowed people to use a new and powerful means of production — the soil. A radical change in the productivity and organisation of agricultural production occurred with the invention of the simple scratch plough drawn by oxen. Further progress involved the use of metal tools, at first of copper and bronze, then of iron. Plough agriculture, cattle-breeding and metal tools raised production to a new level. There was now a basis for the division of social labour into craft and agricultural production and, later, into mental and physical labour. People began to produce more, and it became possible to accumulate wealth. All this had its social consequences and prepared the transition from the primitive-communal system to class society. We should also mention the tremendous importance that the invention of a written language had for the development of production and for human culture as a whole.

In class society, production developed at first on the basis of artisan's tools. Marx describes this base as conservative in the sense that the instrument of the artisan is specialised and may achieve certain forms that set a limit to its development. For example, knives, axes, spades and hoes may change somewhat in being adapted to various forms of activity, but only within certain limits. Of course, these instruments improved and production developed on their basis, giving rise to various branches.

Besides the muscular force of animals, the power of water and wind (wind mills, the water-wheel) were used, and more complex instruments were introduced. Humanity was enriched with important inventions that were to play a great part in the development of technology: the mechanical clock, gunpowder, printing and the production of paper, the compass. All this shaped the conditions for a new qualitative leap in the development of the productive forces — the emergence of *machine production*.

Manufacture provided the immediate technical preconditions for the appearance of machines. Cooperation in labour, that is, the joining together of people for the performance of various tasks, had always taken place on a certain limited scale — in quarries and mines, in workshops, in building and so on. Manufacturing differs from simple cooperation in that it is based on a detailed division of labour for the production of a certain kind of goods. This division of labour in manufacturing leads to specialisation of tools and of the workers themselves, in the course of which they become the performers of particular functions.

Whereas a craftsman created the whole product, in manufacturing the production of this item is broken down in specialised operations, which are performed by different workers. This increases the productivity of labour and creates preconditions for the replacement of the individual worker's operations by the machine.

Machine industrial production began in the 18th century, when England became the scene of the Industrial Revolution. Marx linked this revolution with the appearance of working machines — the loom and the spinning-machine. Such machines replaced a large number of workers by performing operations that had been previously performed by hand. But the working machine demands a motor, and such a motor was invented in the form of the steam-engine. This motor, the transmission mechanism and the working machine constituted the first production mechanism of machine industry.

The Industrial Revolution, which had begun in England in the 18th century, spread during the 19th century to other European countries, to North America and by the end of the century to Russia and Japan. Machine production formed the material and technical base of capitalism.

In contrast to the artisan basis, the technical basis of machine production, according to Marx, is revolutionary, because the possibilities of its development are practically unlimited, while the conscious application of science to production makes technical innovation inevitable. The development of machine production has revealed what tremendous forces human labour can bring into operation.

The history of machine production has developed through four main stages:

1. Machinist-operated machines driven by steam engines that were produced by handicraft labour. This was the genesis of the Industrial Revolution and of industrial capitalism.

2. Machinist-operated machines driven by steam engines that were also produced by machinist-operated machines (the first technological revolution in machine

production, which began at the end of the 1840s).

3. Assembly-line combined machines tended by semi-skilled machine operators and driven by electricity (the second technological revolution, which began in the late 1890s).

4. Continuous-flow production machines semi-automatically operated by electronic apparatus (the third technological revolution, which began in the late 1940s).

In the 19th century, when analysing the prospects of the further development of the productive forces, Marx showed that the development of machine production was shifting from the application of separate machines to the system of machines and, in future, would move on to the creation of automatic production in which people would be excluded from the direct process of material production and retain only the task of controlling, adjusting and repairing machines and designing new ones. The emergence of micro-electronics, which since the late 1960s has made possible the generalisation of the semi-automatic production system that characterises the third technological revolution, has also begun to create the technical basis for full automation ("robotisation"). However, the large-scale introduction of automatic production of automatic machines — a fourth technological revolution in machine production — has been extremely limited since — as Marx also stressed — it is incompatible with the capitalist mode of production (robots do not buy goods and services or produce values!).[10]

With the development of machine production, in general production becomes increasingly the field for the technological application of science, while science emerges as a direct force of production, with scientific labour being transformed into a specific form of proletarianised labour (i.e., labour subordinated to the needs of capitalism and controlled by capital). As Marx observed:

> In machinery, the appropriation of living labour by capital achieves a direct reality in this respect as well. It is, firstly, the analysis and application of mechanical and chemical laws, arising directly out of science, which enables the machine to perform the same labour as that previously performed by the worker. However, the development of machinery along this path occurs only when large industry has already reached a higher stage, and all sciences have been pressed into the service of capital; and when, secondly, the available machinery itself already provides great capabilities. *Invention then becomes a business, and the application of science to direct production becomes a prospect which determines and solicits it.*[11]

It would be wrong to understand this thesis of Marx's in the sense that science in general merges with production and loses its relative independence, ceases to be a sphere of intellectual production.

The transformation of science into a direct productive force implies, first, that the instruments of labour, the technological processes, are becoming a result of the materialisation of scientific knowledge; new technology cannot be created without science, and even the existing technology cannot function without it. Second, scientific knowledge becomes an essential component of the experience and knowledge of all working people taking part in the process of production. Third, the actual control of production, of the technological process, particularly in automated systems, becomes a result of the application of science. Fourth, the very concept of production is widened and comes to include not only the production process but also research and development, so that the spheres of science and production tend to penetrate one another.

The overall effect is to expand the human component of the productive forces, which already include not only manual workers but technicians, engineers and even scientists who are directly concerned with the scientific and technical servicing of the production process.

Mechanisation and "scientification" of production create the basis for bringing together physical and mental work, lead to the intellectualisation of the labour of the workers, make it more meaningful and creative, evoke important changes in the professional structure of labour and rapidly increase the proportion of skilled workers, technical and engineering personnel.

Continuous-flow production lines make special demands on the individual, on his or her ability to take independent decisions, to assume responsibility and to combine his or her own personal interest with that of the collective. Thus, whereas in manufacturing (craftworker-operated machine production) the worker was a "partial" worker, whereas the development of assembly-line (conveyor-belt) production turned the worker into an "appendage of the machine", the development of semi-automated, continuous-flow production processes necessarily implies the improvement of the workers' creative abilities and their liberation from unskilled and monotonous labour. The all-round development of the individual — the goal of socialism — becomes, when considered from the standpoint of modern semi-automated production, a need of the productive forces themselves. Here we cannot fail to see evidence of the fact that the trend of scientific and technological development objectively demands the replacement of capitalism with socialism.

Bourgeois writers spend a lot of time accusing Marxism of regarding humans merely as a "productive force" and attaching no value to them as individual personalities. In reality, however, humans as a productive force are people of work and a people at work, and this means creative individuals. Recognising people as a productive force certainly does not imply that they are belittled or reduced to the status of a thing. On the contrary, it means recognising people as creators, recognising their ability to do things that have raised them above the animal world and have given them the ability to control nature. It is not recognition of people as a productive force that belittles them, but the oppression of workers, the conversion of their labour into a curse, and the workers themselves into slaves. Such social conditions reduce people to the status of a thing, but Marxism is opposed to all forms of oppression. The challenge of Marxism is that humans as a productive force should be free workers, with a highly developed, creative personality. This is real and not illusory humanism.

In the conditions of capitalism, where modern technical progress gives rise to increasingly acute social antagonisms, we find various kinds of "technical mythology", which absolutise the role of technology and regard it as a force hostile to people. It is claimed, for example, that the development of science and technology bodes ill for humanity. Already technology is supposed to be creating various dangers for humanity, making its life more and more standardised and impersonal.

The authors of such concepts divorce technology from people, underestimate the role of the working class, the working masses as a whole, and ignore the significance of social conditions, on which the ultimate outcome of technical development primarily depends. If under capitalism life actually is becoming more standardised and people are losing their individuality, the cause is not technological progress in itself but the domination of private ownership of the means of production, implying a relationship based on exploitation.

The development of technology and the productive forces must, therefore, not be regarded apart from its connections with social *production relations*.

3. Production Relations

Production has always been and remains social. In creating material, goods people enter into various relations with one another, and only within the bounds of these relations does their relation to nature exist.

People have never produced anything purely as individuals in complete isolation from one another. The idea of anybody being able to produce in absolute isolation, outside society, is a pure figment of the imagination. As we have said already, humans emerged from the animal world and developed only in society, in intercourse with others of their own kind. In the first stages of the development of society, production was collective in the direct sense of the term. When it lost its collective character and was carried on by separate families, the production relations between people did not disappear. They were retained and afterwards extended along with the development of the social division of labour and the growth of commodity production and exchange. As the division of labour developed, every producer became increasingly dependent on the others, inasmuch as he or she obtained from them his or her raw materials and implements and sold them his or her products. Finally, with the appearance of large-scale machine production, these interconnections between producers became even more organic, as expressed in the extensive socialisation of the process of labour.

Various relations are formed between people in the production process. There are, for example, relations conditioned by the technical division of labour between various specialised trades. These are relations between workshops of a factory, between the workers performing certain interrelated production operations, and so on. They may be described as the work (production-technical) relations, or more accurately, the division of labour within a production unit. They are conditioned by the instruments of labour available to the producers and their technical knowledge and skills. The division of labour, the technical cooperation necessary for production, involved with a specific technology is *both* a force and a relation of production.

Social production (economic) relations are a different matter. Their character depends on how the means of production are distributed in a society or, in other words, how the problem of the *ownership of the basic means of production* has been solved in that society.

In principle, in the most general form, this problem may be resolved in two ways: Either the means of production belong to the whole of society, or they belong to individuals or a part of society, while the other part of society is barred from any participation in ownership. In other words, ownership of the means of production may be social or private. But ownership is not simply the right to something in law, i.e., property. Ownership is a real economic relationship between people, mediated by their indirect relationship to things — to the means of production. The social relations that people enter into in undertaking production are not the result of any deliberate act; they come about by an unconscious and spontaneous adaptation to the material productive forces at their disposal. But in entering into these relations in the process of production, people become conscious of the need to make them socially recognised and obligatory. In undertaking production, then, it is necessary for people to socially regulate their mutual relations to the means of production. This is how *property* relations arise.

In social production, the means of production become the property of various people or groups of people. For in carrying on production and the distribution of the results of production, it is necessary that some arrangement should be made, binding on all members of a given society, by which it is known who is entitled to dispose of the various means of production and of the product which is produced by working with them. Property relations, therefore, are ways of socially regulating people's mutual relationships in the process of utilising the means of production and disposing of the product, of making the relations of production obligatory relations, binding on society and all its members.

We can therefore define the social relations of production as *the mutual relations into which people enter in the process of production and disposal of the product*, and of which they become conscious as *property relations*.

If the means of production are owned by the whole of society, the members of society stand in an equal relationship to the means of production, and collectivist relations of cooperation and mutual help are established between them. The forms of this cooperation, like the forms of social ownership, may differ. For example, in history social ownership is found in the forms of the property of a clan, tribe or primitive commune, and the property of the working class as a whole in a post-capitalist society, held and administered by the workers' state.

If, on the other hand, the owners of the means of production are individuals, if the means of production are in the hands of only a part and not the whole of society, property acquires a private character, people are placed in an unequal relationship to the means of production, and relations of domination and subjection, relations of exploitation, appear.

What is meant by *exploitation*? When the instruments of labour are primitive and, consequently, the productivity of labour is low, only a rudimentary technical-productive division of labour is possible. All members of the society are compelled to work in common to survive. This leads to common ownership of the means of production and the fruits of production, such as they are, are accordingly shared by the whole community, by the whole clan or tribe. But when the instruments of labour become more powerful and consequently labour productivity increases, labour produces a surplus over and above what the producers require to satisfy their own essential needs. There thus arises the possibility for a minority in society, if they can appropriate this surplus, to live off the labour of others. This possibility becomes a reality when this minority appropriates the means of production that the labourers utilise to produce the surplus, i.e., when the mass of producers are forced to accept these means of production as the private property of this minority. For the producers, exploitation therefore means that only a part of their total labour is used to meet their own requirements, the rest being appropriated and used by another, by virtue of the latter's private ownership of some form of means of production. By taking other people's surplus labour, the exploiters can live well without having to work.

Exploitation means that some people, the minority of society, by virtue of their ownership of large-scale property, live without labour off the fruits of the labour of others, the majority.

In his 1859 preface to *A Contribution to a Critique of Political Economy*, Marx defined different basic types of socioeconomic formation based on the exploitation of labour — Asiatic, slave, feudal and capitalist. At each of these stages of social development there also existed or exists the small private property of the peasants and craftsmen, based on personal labour.

The form of property in each of these types of society determines the mode of exploitation of the producers. The Asiatic mode of production* first appeared in ancient Iraq and Egypt in the 4th millennium BC, in the Indus river valley in the 3rd millennium BC, in northern China in the 2nd millennium BC. This mode of production arose on the basis of and was dependent upon an agriculture that required large-scale public works carried out by the community as a whole. The basic means of production — the land and the water — were the private property of a despotic ruler. The labouring population — the village communities of craftsmen-peasants — owned their instruments of labour (tools, oxen) but were dependent upon the ruler and the vast apparatus of officials he commanded (headed by a priestly and military nobility) for the organisation of the construction and maintenance of the large-scale irrigation systems (canals, dykes, reservoirs). The king and the priestly and military nobility exploited the rural population through the forcible extraction of tribute (in both goods and labour services).

It is typical of slave production relations, which arose in ancient Greece and Rome, that not only the means of labour, but also the labourers themselves became the

* The fact that this mode of production also arose outside Asia — in ancient Egypt and in ancient Mexico and Peru — makes the designation "Asiatic" misleading. Marx used this adjective to designate this mode of production because he first became aware of it during his studies of the impact of British capitalism on India and China during the 18th and 19th centuries. Since this mode of production was based upon large-scale irrigation works organised by a despotic state which extracted suplus labour from village communes as tribute, later Marxists have used a number of different terms to designate it, e.g., "hydraulic", "communal" and "tributary"

property of other people, the slave-owners. The latter appropriated to themselves the whole product of the slave's labour, allowing the slaves only as much as was necessary to keep them alive.

The system of feudal relations, which arose in medieval western Europe, was based on large-scale property in land. The craftsmen-peasants (serfs) were personally dependent upon the feudal landowner for the provision of a small plot of land on which to live and make a living. This enabled the feudal lord to exploit the serfs by requiring them to provide labour services to him free of charge.

The economic structure of capitalism is based on the capitalists' private ownership of the basic means of production — the factories, mines etc. — and on free labour, i.e., labour that is free of personal dependence, and free of possession of means of subsistence. Economic necessity compels the worker to sell his or her labour-power as a commodity to the owner of capital, and only in this form can the worker become united with the means of labour and begin the process of production. The capitalist extracts surplus labour from the worker by purchasing his or her labour-power at a price on the market (the wage rate) that is lower than the value (amount of socially necessary labour) of the commodities which the worker produces while working for the capitalist.

Thus property relations have fundamental significance in the history of humanity. Whole epochs of human history differ from one another depending on the dominant forms of property. Indeed property relations are always an expression of a *definite system of production relations*. The bounds of these relations are determined by the movement of the material product, which begins in the sphere of material production, passes through a definite cycle there, and then through exchange and distribution reaches the consumer and ends in the sphere of individual consumption. Consumption itself depends on production, but at the same time is opposed to it in the sense that it takes a material product out of the sphere of production relations.

Consequently, production relations imply not only the forms in which the producer is united with the means of labour in the process of material production, but also the relations of exchange of activity and the products of activity, and the distribution of the material goods produced. The need for the exchange of activity and its products stems from the existence of a social division of labour — the division into craft/industrial and agricultural, mental and physical labour etc.

The character of distribution — the forms and size of the incomes of various classes and social groups — also depend on the form of property.

Like the productive forces, relations of production also belong to the *material* side of social life. The material character of production relations is expressed in the fact that they exist objectively, independently of human will and consciousness. Their existence and character are determined not by people's wishes, but by the level of production that has been achieved. Moreover, the production (or economic) relations established between people are not only not determined by people's social consciousness; they are not even completely grasped by it.

The productive forces and relations of production are the two inseparable aspects of social production. Only in abstraction can the forces of production be considered without production relations, or vice versa. In reality they are as inseparable from each other as content and form, if in this case we regard the productive forces as content and the relations of production as the social form. Just as, in general, content determines form, so do the productive forces determine production relations. In their turn, the production relations endow the functioning of the forces of production with a certain social quality. Although the production relations depend on the state and character of the productive forces, it is the production relations that determine the social nature of every mode of production.

4. Dialectics of the Development of the Forces and Relations of Production

Having considered the features of the productive forces and production relations as the two sides of the mode of production, we can now pass on to an analysis of their interconnection and interaction.

The interaction of the productive forces and production relations obeys a general social law that has operated throughout history, *the law of the correspondence of the production relations to the character and level of development of the productive forces*. This law characterises an objectively existing dependence of the production relations on the development of the productive forces, and establishes the fact that the production relations take shape and change under the determining influence of these forces.

Marx pointed out that what "distinguishes the various economic formations of society — the distinction between for example a society based on slave-labour and a society based on wage-labour — is the form in which this surplus labour is in each case extracted from the immediate producer, the labourer".[12] The form of extraction of surplus labour, of exploitation, i.e., the relations of production in a class-divided society, are determined by the society's productive forces. "It is always the the direct relationship of the owners of the conditions of production to the direct producers — a relation always naturally corresponding to a definite stage in the development of the methods of labour and thereby its social productivity — which reveals the innermost secret, the hidden basis of the entire social structure ..."[13]

When humans had only just emerged from the animal state, the stone tools and other implements that people used, although they were instruments of individual use, were so primitive and unproductive that the individual armed with these tools would have been unable alone to produce the material goods they needed for subsistence. People were compelled to work together, to support one another because of the weakness of the individual in the face of the mighty forces of nature. Thus the main productive force here was the strength of the collective itself, and it was on this basis that primitive collectivist relations arose.

Further development of the productive forces, the transition from stone to bronze, then iron, tools and the replacement of primitive wooden hoes with ploughs drawn by domesticated cattle raised the productivity of labour, with the result that it became possible for people to perform productive activity on an individual or a family basis. This laid the basis for the dissolution of the primitive commune, based as it was on collective labour activities and the common sharing of its products. These developments in the productive forces also allowed the appearance of a regular social surplus product (i.e., the product remaining after the satisfaction of essential needs of the producers) and along with it a division between mental and physical labour. With the appropriation of the means of production and the social surplus product by those who no longer engaged directly in material production, society became divided into classes, into exploiters and exploited.

The law of the correspondence of production relations to the character and the level of development of the productive forces manifests itself at this stage of production in the fact that private-property production relations correspond to the private character of the productive forces. It would seem that only small private property based on personal labour of the producers corresponds to the instruments of individual use. But this form of property never created a specific mode of production because it was incapable by itself of ensuring progress in the economic and cultural spheres. For this reason, we find developing alongside it various forms of private property based on the appropriation of other people's labour, that is, on exploitation, made possible by the appearance of surplus labour and the surplus product.

In the preface to his *Contribution to the Critique of Political Economy*, Marx wrote:

> In broad outlines, Asiastic, ancient, feudal, and modern bourgeois modes of

production can be designated as progressive epochs in the economic formation of society. The bourgeois relations of production are the last antagonistic form of the social process of production ... the productive forces developing in the womb of bourgeois society create the material conditions for the solution of that antagonism.[14]

The progress that is referred to here is the increase in the productivity of labour due to the higher level of development of the productive forces made possible by the dominant relations of production of each of these modes of production.

While each of these modes of production is based on the exploitation of labour, it is only the capitalist mode of production which gives the productive forces a level of development and a social character that make it objectively possible to put an end to exploitation.

In the process of the rise of capitalism the immediate producer was turned into the "partial worker" of a manufactory on the basis of use of instruments of labour that were private in character. But gradually capitalism develops machine production, endowing the process of production itself with a social character. The use of machines makes it objectively necessary to combine people together in large collectives and to introduce the division of labour on a wide scale throughout society. There comes into being the modern proletariat, a class that is totally separated from the means of production and economically fettered to capital.

All this brings a qualitative change in the character of the productive forces. The product is now the result not of the labour of the separate producer but of a group, of the collective labour of many people. It is appropriated not by those who produced it, but by the owner of the means of production — the capitalist. Under capitalism a contradiction develops between the social character of the process of production and the private capitalist form of appropriation, which is the basic contradiction of capitalist society. This contradiction shows itself in the cataclysms of the spontaneous capitalist economy, in anarchy of production and crises of overproduction, and in the class struggle of the proletariat.

The creation of capitalist monopolies reflects within the framework of capitalism the social nature of the contemporary productive forces, as do the attempts of monopoly capitalism to introduce certain principles of planning and regulation into the spontaneous development of capitalist production. But all this does not change, and cannot change, the nature of capitalism, because the basic means of production remain private property.

The mechanism of competition, of the concentration and centralisation of capital, leads to the actual concentration of ever more wealth in the hands of a small group of capitalists. At the same time, the separation of the producer from the means of production, hired labour, exploitation and other features of capitalist relations remain and tend to grow. This fundamental contradiction cannot be resolved in the framework of capitalism because only social ownership of the means of production can correspond to the social character of the process of production. The development of large-scale industry not only creates the material preconditions for socialist ownership of the means of production but also makes it imperative to move on from capitalism to socialism.

To sum up, *each form of production relations exists for as long as it provides sufficient scope for the development of the productive forces.*

But as development of the productive forces proceeds, the existing relations of production gradually come into contradiction with the developing productive forces and become a brake on them. Marx observes that people never voluntarily give up the productive forces they have brought into being, but this does not mean that they do not give up the production relations that have till then served as the form of development of these forces. "On the contrary, in order that they may not be deprived of the result attained and forfeit the fruits of civilisation, they are obliged from the moment when their mode of carrying on commerce no longer corresponds to the productive forces acquired, to change all their traditional social forms."[15]

If the production relations change under the influence of the progress of the productive forces, then what, it may be asked, causes the development of the productive forces themselves?

Here we must consider the action of a whole set of various causes. In our examination of the interaction of geographical conditions, the growth of population and production, we found that geographical conditions and population growth exercise a significant influence on production and may stimulate or retard it. But they are not the basic source of development of the productive forces.

The development of the productive forces has an inner logic of its own. The more complex instruments of labour arise on the basis of their simpler predecessors. In any relatively developed economy, an important change in one industry inevitably affects the others. For example, the development of industrial production leads to the technical reequipment of agriculture, to the mechanisation of construction; the intensification of agriculture demands production of artificial fertilisers, which stimulates the development of the chemical industry and so on. As technology develops and new and more efficient tools and machines appear, the existing machines become obsolete and demand replacement. Society is compelled to reckon with this logic of the development of production.

There are both interaction and contradiction between the material and personal elements of the productive forces. By changing nature, people change themselves, develop their abilities and raise their cúltural level. The experience and knowledge gained are objectified in new means of labour, but people in their turn are obliged to adapt themselves to these new means of labour once they have appeared and come into use. This is the internal driving force of the development of production. But the internal needs of the productive forces still do not explain why production develops faster in some cases and slower in others, more or less evenly in some cases and through booms and crises in yet others. Nor can this be ascribed to the development of science. All technology is materialised knowledge, and without the development of human knowledge there could be no technical progress. Today research and development are a powerful source of technical progress. But the development of science itself, its actual growth rate, depends in greater measure on the development of production.

The *needs of society, of people, are the most important factor in the development of production*. Directly or indirectly, production always serves the purpose of satisfying certain human needs, and a complex dialectical interconnection between these needs and production establishes itself in a society. The needs themselves are evoked by the development of production, the satisfaction of some needs gives rise to new ones, and this is bound to influence production in some way or another. But the relation of people's needs to production is mediated by production relations: the needs do not influence the productive forces directly, but do so through production relations.

Every form of production relations subordinates production to a particular aim, and this aim has certainly not always been the needs of the majority of people. The mass of the population in class society, the classes, are motivated by various stimuli, which are specific in every specific case; slave-owning society was stimulated in one way, capitalist society in another. The active nature of the production relations shows itself in the fact that they evolve in people certain definite *stimuli to action*.

The ruling classes in class-divided societies subordinate the development of production to their interests and needs. As long as the exploiting classes appropriate the social surplus product in natural form, satisfaction of their own consumption is the stimulus to production. This, however, sets a limit to their interest in increasing production and labour productivity. By contrast, in the capitalist mode of production, the social surplus product is appropriated not in natural form, but as money, as surplus value. Moreover, the share of the social surplus product that each capitalist can appropriate is dependent upon the amount of capital they possess. Capitalists are therefore driven to continuously accumulate capital, to maximise their profits. Thus, it is the objective laws of expanded production and reproduction, the laws of production of maximum profit, the laws of capitalist competition, that have constituted and still constitute the driving forces of development of capitalist production, of its productive forces.

But what stimulates the actions of the working masses, the direct producers? This depends on the position of the direct producer in the system of the given production relations. A certain form of production relations is progressive inasmuch as it creates for the masses advantages as compared to their previous situation. The peasant farmers under the "Asiatic" or tributary mode of production had little incentive to increase their labour productivity, since all of their surplus product was taken as tribute by the ruling class. Similarly, the slaves in ancient Greece and the Roman empire had no interest whatever in increasing the productivity of their labour, because it was impossible for the slave to benefit from this — all of the slave's surplus labour was appropriated by his or her owner. Under feudalism the immediate producers — the serfs — were provided by the feudal landowner with a small plot of land on which to live and produce their means of subsistence. The serfs owned tools, draught animals and productive livestock, seed, fodder and other means of production and had a certain interest in raising productivity in working on their own plots. The wage-worker confronts the owner of all the means of production — the capitalist — as a formally equal owner of commodities. In selling his or her labour-power, the higher the worker's skill, the higher the wage the worker receives, and therefore the wage-worker is compelled to some extent to develop the productive capacity of his or her labour-power. But working for a capitalist forces the worker to regard his or her work only as a source of livelihood. The whole complex mechanism of capitalist production and reproduction is so constructed that it compels the worker to strain every effort and ability. The wages system also serves this aim. The worker's fear of being thrown out of production and becoming unemployed has no less force than the slave overseer's whip.

So, the causes of the development of the productive forces must not be considered in isolation from the social conditions in which this development occurs, that is, from the system of the given production relations. The development of the crude technology of primitive society and that of modern machine technology cannot be ascribed to the same causes. Each historically definite mode of production has its own *specific causes (sources) and economic laws* of development of the productive forces that are valid for that mode of production, and the character of these laws depends on the character of the production relations.

The effect of the production relations is positive when the production relations correspond to the productive forces and thus promote their development, and negative when this correspondence is upset and the production relations act as a brake on the development of the productive forces.

The active role of the production relations does not mean that the forms of property by themselves drive forward or hold back the development of the society's productive forces. Only people develop production or, on the contrary, are not interested in its development. They develop and change their mode of production, which constitutes the basis of their history. The interaction of people and instruments of labour — the key elements of the productive forces — manifests itself always in the form of certain definite production relations, and it is these that determine the concrete motives stimulating people to actions.

The law of the correspondence of the production relations to the character and level of development of the productive forces *determines not only the development of the given mode of production, but also the necessity for the replacement of one mode of production by another*. As the productive forces develop in the womb of the old society, new production relations are conceived that form a certain economic structure, the embryo of the new mode of production. "Asiatic" depotism and slavery are conceived already in the womb of the primitive-communal system, elements of serfdom are formed in the womb of slave-owning society and the capitalist system in that of feudal society.

In the old mode of production there occurs a quantitative accumulation of new elements, the development of the new economic structure. The developing productive forces come into conflict with the old production relations prevailing in society. This conflict cannot be resolved, that is, the new production relations cannot establish themselves without getting rid of the old relations, whose existence is supported by the ruling class and the political superstructure (the state institutions) that it has created.

The transition from the old production relations to the new ones is impossible by means of a simple quantitative change. Here there must be a qualitative transition, the revolutionary destruction of the old obsolete and hidebound economic, social and political forms, which opens the road for the establishment of a new mode of production.

The emergence of the socialist mode of production has its own special features. In the womb of the old society, under capitalism, there arise only the material preconditions of the socialist mode of production in the form of the enormous socialisation of production, the creation of modern productive forces that are social by their nature. But the new production relations of socialism corresponding to the newly emerging productive forces do not take shape and cannot take shape in the conditions of capitalism.

The opportunists and revisionists always denied and still deny this Marxist proposition. They maintain that "bits" of socialism, including even its production relations, arise already in the conditions of capitalism, that the transition to socialism lies in their gradual expansion within capitalism, that this transition takes place by purely evolutionary means, without the revolutionary overthrow of capitalist rule.

In contrast to the opportunists, Marxists proceed from the fact that socialist production relations, based on social ownership of the means of production, cannot arise under capitalism in the framework of separate enterprises and economic units, as capitalist relations, for example, were formed in the womb of feudalism. For socialist production relations to arise, there must be socialisation of the means of production on the scale of the whole society, and only the revolutionary seizure of political power by the working class can bring this about. So the socialist system cannot arise in any other way than by means of revolution and the conscious, planned building of the new society.

The Marxist proposition on the braking effect of the old production relations should not be interpreted in an oversimplified, mechanistic way, as, say, the effect of the brakes that stop a train. Since the beginning of the 20th century, for example, capitalist production relations have become a brake upon the development of the productive forces, but this is not to say that the development of production has come to a halt. Rather, it means that capitalist relations of production have become a restriction, a constraint, upon the fullest possible development of the productive forces.

Marx observed that once the productive forces have developed to their highest point upon the economic basis of a particular social order, unless this basis (i.e., the dominant relations of production) is changed, "further development [of the productive forces] appears as decay" of the existing mode of production.[16] How and when does this become expressed in the capitalist mode of production? Engels gave a preliminary answer to this question in the "theoretical" part of his 1878 book *Anti-Dühring*. In it he explained that capitalism begins to decay when the contradiction between objectively socialised productive forces and capitalist property relations forces the capitalists themselves to introduce forms of social ownership of the means of production — giant trusts that seek to regulate production in whole industries, joint-stock companies in which the capital in the form of means of production is no longer owned by a single capitalist, and state-capitalist businesses:

> If the crises [of overproduction] demonstrate the incapacity of the bourgeoisie for managing any longer modern productive forces, the transformation of the great establishments for production and distribution into joint-stock companies, trusts and state property shows how unnecessary the bourgeoisie are for that purpose. All the social functions of the capitalist are now performed by salaried employees. The capitalist has no further social function than that of pocketing dividends, tearing off coupons, and gambling on the Stock Exchange, where the different capitalists despoil one another of their capital.[17]

In his 1916 work *Imperialism, the Highest Stage of Capitalism,* Lenin showed that these features of a moribund, parasitic and decaying capitalism had matured within the developed capitalist countries at the beginning of the 20th century with the merger of banking and industrial capital, through monopolistic joint-stock companies, into finance capital, which brings the national economy under the parasitic domination of a financial oligarchy and subordinates the majority of states in the world to the parasitic financial overlordship of a small number of "usurer-states".

It may be objected that, while Lenin showed that with monopolist-imperialist capitalism bourgeois society enters upon a new and higher stage of its development, he did not and could not show that this stage was the "highest" possible to capitalism; that it might conceivably advance to a still higher stage. The answer to that objection is that it proceeds from the assumption that the possibilities of development open to a given historically conditioned mode of production are unlimited. The whole of the facts and processes analysed by Marx, and Lenin, show that, on the contrary, only a specifically limited and conditioned development is possible to each historically determined social order. As Marx explained:

> In so far as the labour process is a simple process between man and nature, its simple elements remain common to all social forms of its development. But each particular historical form of this process further develops the material foundations and social forms. Once a certain level of maturity is attained, the particular historical form is shed and makes way for a higher form. The sign that the moment of such a crisis has arrived is that the contradiction and antithesis between, on the one hand, the relations of distribution, hence also the specific historical form of relations of production corresponding to them, and, on the other hand, the productive forces, productivity, and the development of its agents, gains in breath and depth. A conflict then sets in between the material development of production and its social form.[18]

Two outstanding phenomena indicated by Engels as characteristic of the culminating stage of capitalism are shown by Lenin to have become generalised in the imperialist stage of capitalism. These are, firstly, parasitism, and, secondly, the partial recognition of the social character of production. Each separately, and still more, both together, evidenced the fact that in the imperialist stage the conflict between objectively socialised productive forces and capitalist relations of production had matured.

Parasitism first becomes apparent when (by the formation of joint-stock companies, trusts, cartels etc.) all the social productive functions of capitalist firms are devolved by the bourgeoisie upon salaried employees, and the bourgeoisie becomes a purely parasitic class, playing no necessary role in the social organisation of the labour process. The process of bringing the entire economy under the direction of a tiny financial oligarchy includes objectively the launching and flotation on the stock exchange of a host of speculative companies, development syndicates, investment trusts etc. The immense mass of capital required by each gigantic finance-capitalist monopoly is accumulated by every sort of device for collecting the spare cash of all, even the poorest, into a huge heap of money capital, which the financial oligarchs can turn into actual capital loaned or invested in enterprises all over the world. It is not only that in the imperialist stage the place once occupied by the industrial and commercial bourgeoisie is now occupied by a bourgeois financial oligarchy — an aristocracy of *rentiers*, whose sole occupation is collecting income from stocks, bonds and other commercial paper. The other side is the subordination of the development of the world's productive forces, particularly in the colonial and semi-colonial areas, to the exploiting dominance of this financial oligarchy. While using its monopoly control of home production to reduce the volume of production to the level of ascertained market requirements, finance capital is impelled by its need and greed for ever-expanding profits to continually revolutionise the economy of the more backward areas of the world, while keeping them firmly in the grip of its monopolistic control.

Not incidental to the development of parasitism into a universally dominant system is the rise to general importance of reckless speculation and the swindling which invariably accompanies it. Gambling in commercial paper grows into an accepted and usual way of getting rich. Whereas, on the plane of the exchange of commodities between (relatively) small producers, swindling was a phenomenon only incidental to the process of production as a whole — since each swindle was cancelled by a counter-swindle in the final outcome — in the monopolist stage of capitalism swindling (dignified by the name "financial manipulation") is developed into a system and becomes a regular and usual mode of capital accumulation. This fact, that in its stage of domination by finance capital, the first concern of capitalism is not so much the immediate extraction of surplus value (which, of course, is extracted in greater masses than ever) as the *diversion* of the already extracted surplus value into the grip of the dominant parasites is clear evidence that monopoly capitalism, despite the immense impetus it gives both to capital accumulution and to the growth of the material means of production, is nonetheless *decadent.* Lenin cited the fact that as long ago as 1893 the income British rentiers derived from overseas investments was *five times as great* as Britain's income from foreign trade — from the export of commodities — as an example of decadent and parasitic development.

Thus finance capital sums up within itself and develops with accelerating rapidity all the general contradictions of captalism — particularly that between the increased socialisation of the material process of production (which it develops on a *world* scale) and the private appropriation of the product, from which arises as a consequence the increasing anarchy in social production as a whole. Finance capital from its nature is forced deliberately to strive for the attainment of both the *anarchy* and *socialisation* of production on a world scale.

Lenin's description of the monopolist stage of capitalism as its *highest stage* was an application of the conception of Marx and Engels that the complete *socialisation* of the labour-process involved the *separation* of the *productive function* of capital from the *ownership* of capital — a separation which becomes obvious when, in its parasitic rentier form, capitalist profit becomes mere appropriation of the surplus labour of others, with the owners of capital being completely separate from the actual labour process. Once this becomes generalised, it is obvious that (a) no further development is possible *within* this relationship; (b) that the driving force of the antagonism between capital and wage labour, making development of some kind inescapable, will precipitate a transition to a qualitatively new social form corresponding to the socialisation of production; and (c) that this potential new social form has its material basis in the positive and negative poles of the social antagonism itself, i.e., in associated production by associated owners for their common satisfaction. This conclusion was already anticipated by Marx when joint-stock companies were only just beginning to be formed:

> In joint-stock companies, the function [of management of the labour process] is separated from capital ownership, so labour is completely separated from ownership of the means of production and of surplus labour. This result of capitalist production *in its highest development* is a necessary point of transition towards the transformation of capital [as means of production] back into the property of the producers, though no longer as the private property of individual producers, but rather as their property as

***associated producers*, as *directly social property*. It is furthermore a point of transition towards the transformation of all functions formerly bound up with capital ownership of the reproduction process into simple functions of the associated producers, into *social functions*.[19] ❦**

CHAPTER 5

THE SOCIOECONOMIC FORMATION

An intrinsic feature of historical materialism is its concrete historical approach to society. The majority of bourgeois sociologists proceed from an abstract metaphysical interpretation of society in general, as a category outside history. By contrast, Marxism approaches society dialectically, considering it not as something immutable, but as something developing, and therefore seeks out the qualitatively specific stages of its development — the specific socioeconomic formations.

The Marxist concept of the socioeconomic formation allows us to place the study of history on a concrete basis. Since the history of society is formed out of the history of specific socioeconomic formations, we must study the laws of their development and transition from one formation to another. This is how Marx proceeded. In *Capital* he analysed the laws of the establishment and development of the capitalist socioeconomic formation and showed its historically transient character and the necessity for its replacement by a new and higher one — the socialist (or communist) socioeconomic formation. The concept of socioeconomic formations is a cornerstone of Marxist social theory.

1. THE CONCEPT OF THE SOCIOECONOMIC FORMATION

The basis of social life and historical development is the way in which people organise the production of the goods required for the satisfaction of their physical and socially recognised needs — the social relations of production.

The relations of production are connected with all other social phenomena and processes. This connection may be direct or more or less remote, but it does exist, and the discovery of this connection is a most important feature of the materialist conception of history. No matter what social phenomena we take — the state, science or morality, language or art and so on — they cannot be understood in their own terms, but only as phenomena engendered by society and corresponding to certain social needs. Just as people's way of life in a particular society is basically characterised by their relations of production, so all other social phenomena depend ultimately on the prevailing relations of production and proceed from them.

Thus the inner unity and interconnection of all social phenomena inherent in each society arise according to certain laws. All aspects of social life are organically interconnected and ultimately subordinated to the relations of production. The relations of production are the material and economic basis of society, of the socioeconomic formation; they determine its entire internal structure. For this reason Lenin characterised the socioeconomic formation as a single, integrated "social organism", that is, *as a system of social phenomena and relations internally connected with one another and depending on one another*. The socioeconomic formation is not an aggregate of individuals, not a mechanically assembled block of miscellaneous social phenomena, but an integrated social system, each of whose components (that is, the various social phenomena) must be regarded not by itself, not isolated, but only in its connection with other social phenomena, because each of them plays a definite and unique role in the functioning and development of society. This integrity is expressed by the concept of the socioeconomic formation. This concept embraces all the aspects of the life of society at a particular historical stage — from the material and technical base that characterises it to its inherent way of thinking.

The history of society is made up of the histories of particular peoples living in various geographical and historical conditions and possessing their own particular cultural features. History is extremely diverse, and this has led some philosophers and sociologists to maintain that it never repeats itself, that all events and phenomena are wholly individual and the task of historical science can be only to describe these individual events, and evaluate them from the standpoint of some ideal. Such an approach to history is bound to lead to subjectivism because the very choice of ideals and values for judging history becomes arbitrary and loses the objective criteria that are needed to distinguish what is essential, paramount, determining in history, and what is derivative and secondary.

The Marxist theory of society overcame this subjectivism by singling out from the totality of social relations *production relations as the most important and definitive*. It was production relations that provided the objective criterion for distinguishing the essential and inessential in social life. This also revealed the repetition and regularity of the general features in the history of individual peoples at one and the same stage of historical development. For example, despite the diversity of history and forms of political organisation and culture of Australia, Brazil, France, Japan, Indonesia and the United States, all these countries share the common features of having a working class and a bourgeoisie, relations of exploitation and an economy based on commodity-capitalist production, and consequently these countries are at the stage of bourgeois society and belong to the capitalist socioeconomic formation. Science is thus presented with a wide field for comparison, for singling out the general in the history of countries and peoples and for defining more closely on this basis the specific features of their development.

The concept of the socioeconomic formation makes it possible not only to single out the general features to be found in the system of various countries that are at the same stage of historical development, but also to distinguish one historical period from another. Every socioeconomic formation is a definite stage in the development of human society.

While every society is always characterised by a set of social relations of production, not every set of relations of production constitutes a *mode of production*. A mode of production is a set of relations of production in which there is a dominant property form that tends to reproduce itself automatically by the normal functioning of the economy. A mode of production is therefore an economic structure which cannot be fundamentally changed by evolution, adaptation or self-reform. It has an internal logic which can be transcended only if it is overthrown.

In periods of historical upheaval, of transition from one mode of production to another, socioeconomic formations come into being in which the predominant relations of production have a hybrid character, i.e., with characteristics drawn from the previous mode of production combined with those anticipating the new mode of production. Such hybrid relations of production are not structures that tend to automatically reproduce themselves. They can either lead to the restoration of the old socioeconomic order or to the emergence of a new mode of production, the outcome depending on a number of factors — mainly the sufficient or insufficient growth of the productive forces and the relative strength of contending class forces acting within the society and upon it from outside. Thus, for example, in the 15th and 16th centuries socioeconomic formations arose in the Netherlands, northern Italy and in England in which the predominant relations of production were neither feudal (between lords and serfs) nor capitalist (between capitalist employers and wage-workers) but between commodity producers who owned their means of production, i.e., the relations of petty commodity production.

Moreover, the totality of relations of production in a socioeconomic formation based on a distinct mode of production is almost never homogeneous — there exist alongside the dominant property form (dominant and self-reproducing relations of production) other relations of production — vestiges of previous relations of production which were historically transcended long ago, or relations of production that are anticipatory of a new mode of production. Thus in France on the eve of the bourgeois revolution of 1789-93, the totality of relations of production included the dominant relations of production of the feudal mode of production (the relations between lords and serfs) as well as the relations of production characteristic of the emerging capitalist mode of production (the relations between capitalist employers and wage-earning workers). In most of the developed capitalist countries today there continue to exist vestiges of petty commodity production in agriculture (petty-bourgeois farmers, working without wage labour), i.e., of the relations of production characteristic of the period of transition from feudalism to capitalism.

The history of society is the history of the development and replacement of socioeconomic formations. Marx defined five basic socioeconomic formations in the history of humanity that may be distinguished from one another according to their mode of production: primitive-communal, "Asiatic" (tributary), slave, feudal and capitalist. The primitive-communal system coincided with the emergence of humanity and provided the preconditions for the further development of human society. It was superseded by the antagonistic class formations of the tributary, slave, feudal and capitalist societies, characterised by social inequality, exploitation of labour and class struggle. The sequence of these formations is not a fixed pattern that the history of every people must obey, because some peoples are held up in their development while others bypass whole formations. History also produces various transitional forms.

The above-mentioned pattern of socioeconomic formations, showing the basic stages in historical progress, reveals the main line of human development, which is of great importance for the methodical study of concrete history and for tracing the dialectics of the historical process.

Thus the concept of the socioeconomic formation is based on recognition of the unity and integrity of the historical process. Varied though the paths of historical development of individual peoples may have been, there is in history a certain repetition, regularity, a certain law. Moreover, the separate stages of historical development are qualitatively specific systems of social relationships.

Every society is a manifestation of a specific type of socioeconomic formation, an integrated social system functioning and developing according to its own specific laws on the basis of the given relations of production. The economic skeleton of the socioeconomic formation is formed by the historically determined production relations, but the whole body, its flesh and blood, as it were, comprises other social phenomena and relations, forming the complex structure that we must now investigate.

2. STRUCTURE OF THE SOCIOECONOMIC FORMATION: BASIS AND SUPERSTRUCTURE

Every socioeconomic formation is a specific social organism; it differs qualitatively from other formations. But socioeconomic formations do have certain general structural features that are inherent in all or, at least, the majority of such formations. Knowledge of these general structural elements allows us to work out the principles of approach to the study of each individual formation, each concrete society.

Every society is characterised by a *definite totality of social relations*. Social relations are a special form of connections and interactions existing only in society and arising in the process of people's social activity, i.e., activity in the sphere of production, in the regulation of social life, in their intellectual life and so on. These relations are called social relations not only because they exist only in society, but also because they emerge from the interaction of large numbers of people, of social groups and classes.

Social relations are extremely varied. Their different types include: economic, political, legal, socio-psychological and moral relationships. To find any regular interconnection in this diversity we must make up our minds which relations are essential, or primary, and which are derivative, or secondary.

Lenin wrote that by introducing materialism into the analysis of history, Marx had divided all social relations into "material" and "ideological" social relations, the latter forming a superstructure built upon the former.[1]

In carrying on the economic activities of production and distribution people enter, as Marx said, "into definite relations that are indispensable and independent of their will, relations of production which correspond to a definite stage of development of their material productive forces".[2] These relations of production arise as objective, material facts of social life, independently of what people may think about them. Because they exist independently of people's will, Lenin defined the social relations of production as the "material social relations".

But people act consciously, have ideas about themselves and their aims in life, and in their conscious activity are organised within all kinds of social institutions and organisations to serve all kinds of consciously conceived aims — political, legal, religious, moral, artistic, philosophic. Lenin defined these forms of social organisation as "ideological social relations" because they arise only after preliminary passage through people's consciousness. For example, the relations between members of a proletarian party are built consciously; a political party is organised by people who consciously accept its aims and the means it seeks to realise them (its program); here the idea precedes the organisation. The reverse is true of a social group such as the proletarian class, which is formed spontaneously in the sphere of economic relations from people who have been deprived of the means of production and compelled under pressure of economic necessity to sell their labour-power to the owners of capital.

While "ideological" social relations do not exist independently of people's consciousness, of their ideas and aims, they are nevertheless still material, objective relations, i.e., the associations people form to realise their ideas and aims exist outside their consciousness; they are the material embodiment of those ideas and aims.

This distinction between "material" and "ideological" social relations enables us to define the concepts that characterise the structure and specific quality of each socioeconomic formation — the *basis* and the *superstructure*.

At whatever stage of social development, people are engaged together in a system of material production; on the basis of their production relations they work out ideas and associate in social organisations, through which they represent to themselves their various consciously conceived interests and organise themselves in pursuit of those interests. Thus people conceive and adopt religious, political, legal, philosophical, moral, aesthetic ideas and associate in organisations intended to embody, propagate and achieve them. But they do not do this in a vacuum. They are members of a society kept going by economic activities, linked together by definite production relations which arise independently of people's ideas and conscious aims. Such relations of production constitute the necessary basis for any social life; without relations of production there can be no social life at all, and therefore no ideas and aims in people's minds and no forms of social organisation developed in accordance with their ideas and aims. The relations of production, therefore, always constitute *the basis upon which people come together for any conscious social purpose* — the basis of all their "ideological" social relations.

It follows that the ideas and institutions people adopt are always conditioned by their basic social relations, the relations of production. And the ideas which gain currency (i.e., become part of *social consciousness*) and the institutions through which people carry on their conscious social life, change with changes in the relations of production. Aims, outlooks and beliefs, and likewise organisations created to embody, propagate and realise them, arise in response to the opportunities, needs and interests — including, of course, conflicting interests — which are inherent in the relations of production. It is only through the "ideological" social relations, the social superstructure, that people, social classes, become conscious of their material interests and struggle to realise them.

The basis and the superstructure are the fundamental structural elements of any socioeconomic formation. They characterise its qualitative uniqueness, the difference between it and other formations. Besides the basis and superstructure, a socioeconomic formation includes other elements of social life (everyday affairs, sexual relations and so on), but it is the basis and the superstructure that determine the specific nature of the formation as a complete social organism.

Basis and superstructure are relative concepts, defining two distinct levels of social development. *The basis is the economic structure of society, the sum-total of the production relations of the given society*. The concept of the basis expresses the social function of the production relations as the economic basis of social phenomena that are outside the sphere of material production. While they are a form of the productive forces, the production relations at the same time determine the content of the superstructural forms. *The superstructure is the sum-total of "ideological" social relations that arise on the given economic basis*, i.e., the sum-total of social relations that are consciously created by people.*

In carrying on production and entering into production relations adapted to their forces of production, people require, first of all, what may be called institutions of regulation or management of their social relations. Insofar as production is managed

---

* This distinction between the social basis and the social superstructure was misrepresented by Nikolai Bukharin in his 1921 work *Historical Materialism: A System of Sociology*. Bukharin declared that the term "superstructure" included "any type of social phenomena erected on the economic base ... including social psychology ... as well as such phenomena as language and thought". Thus, social superstructure was equated by Bukharin with social consciousness. Later, Stalin enshrined this view as part of the canon of official Soviet "historical materialism". "The superstructure", Stalin declared, "consists of the political, legal, artistic and philosophical *views* of society and the political, legal, and other institutions corresponding to them" (J. V. Stalin, *Marxism and Linguistics*, New York, 1951, p. 9). Marx, however, made a clear distinction between the "political and legal superstructure" of society and the "definite forms of social consciousness" which corresponded to the superstructural institutions. Although superstructural institutions are consciously created by people, this does not mean that their ideas and aims are part of these institutions, any more than tools consist of both tools and people's ideas for making tools. Like tools, the social superstructure is the *material realisation* of people's ideas, not the ideas themselves. The Bukharin-Stalin conception of the superstructure as including people's political, legal, religious etc., ideas is a partial revival of the idealist conception espoused by Aleksandr Bogdanov that equates social being with social consciousness.

in the interests of a particular social class, with social regulation serving the purpose of maintaining a particular mode of exploitation, the institutions of social regulation become institutions of class rule or state institutions. There will also take shape forms of organised self-protection and resistance, or of revolutionary struggle, on the part of the non-ruling or exploited classes.

Political, legal and economic ideas, programs and modes of thought take shape in connection with the functions of management and class rule, either to promote or to resist the existing form of management and rule. This is the most immediate and direct way in which intellectual processes are connected with the economic structure of a given socioeconomic formation. Most remotely connected with the economic basis, and more directly related to the existing political conflicts, there arise further intellectual processes — religious, moral, philosophical, artistic and so on — and institutions associated with them.

Every socioeconomic formation has its basis and corresponding superstructure. The superstructure, like the basis, is therefore historically specific in character. Depending on what kind of economic basis, what classes a given society possesses, it will be dominated by the corresponding political, legal, religious and philosophical views and also institutions corresponding to these views. It is quite impossible for the economy of a country to be dominated by feudal lords or capitalists while in politics, in the legal system and in intellectual life, the predominant role is played by the working people. Such an incongruity could not possibly exist for any length of time. The relations of production in feudal or bourgeois society are class relations. And the class that holds the dominant position in the given economic structure naturally holds the dominant position in the ideological sphere, establishes its political domination, creates and passes laws preserving this economic and political domination, and therefore also holds the dominating position throughout the superstructure.

The distinction between basis and superstructure is a distinction between two social processes which are the most obvious and open to investigation, and most immediately affect the members of society and strike the attention of historians, and those which are less immediately obvious and the details of which can only be uncovered by patient researches. What is most obvious is the ideas which people are proclaiming, the speeches they are making and the epithets they are throwing at each other; the political, legal, religious, moral, philosophic, aesthetic battles they are fighting; and the organisations and institutions they have organised to wage these battles. Less obvious and, as it were, buried beneath all this but nevetheless sustaining it, are the economic processes and relations of the socioeconomic formation. All the hurly-burly on the surface is conditioned by the underlying economic relationships, and serves a social function relative to their development.

According to the idealist conceptions of history the primary, determining factor in social development is to be found in the ideas of society. According to the idealists, people first develop certain ideas, then they create organisations corresponding to those ideas, and on that basis they carry on their economic life.

"The whole previous view of history", wrote Engels, "was based on the conception that the ultimate causes of all historical changes are to be looked for in the changing ideas of human beings. . . But the question was not asked as to whence the ideas come into men's minds."[3]

On the other hand, the process of economic development is self-explanatory. If you ask "why did certain economic relations arise?" — why did private ownership come into being, why did products become commodities, why did wage-labour come into being and so on — then you do not have to look outside the sphere of economic development itself in order to find the explanation.

And then, having established the trend of economic development and the economic causes of it, it can be explained why, on the basis of that development, people grew dissatisfied with some ideas and developed other ones, rebelled against old political and legal institutions and set up new ones. Engels wrote: "... the economic structure of society always furnishes the real basis, starting from which we can alone work out the ultimate explanation of the whole superstructure of juridical and political institutions as well as of the religious, philosophical, and other ideas of a given historical period".[4]

We have considered the dependence of the superstructure on the basis, which is expressed in the fact that *the economic basis determines the content of intellectual processes of any given society and therefore the content of its superstructure*. Changes in the superstructure occur under the influence of changes in the basis, mediated through changes in social consciousness. The elimination of the old basis and emergence of a new one bring about the transformation of the whole enormous superstructure.

At the same time the superstructure possesses a *relative independence* in relation to its basis. A social system can never be so rigid and closely determined as a system of mechanical dependencies. The basis influences the superstructure through the interlocking economic and political interests of classes, the complex system of intermediate links between the economy and various forms of social consciousness. History is made by the people, by social classes. Responding to changes in the economic basis of society, to the rise of new productive forces, they create new ideas and conduct an ideological struggle against the old order, carry out a revolution, change the superstructure, sweep away the old, outmoded property relations — the legal expression of the old, outmoded production relations — and thus clear the way for the development of new production relations corresponding to the new productive forces. The dependence of the superstructure on the basis should not therefore be oversimplified, understood as a mechanism that operates automatically. It is wrong to attribute all changes in the superstructure to economic causes. Various interactions take place within the elements of the superstructure that lead to results which are sometimes not economically conditioned. It is only in the final analysis that the economy (the relations of production) determines the social superstructure.

The social function of the superstructure is to protect, fortify and develop its basis. In a class-divided society, the superstructure ensures the political and ideological supremacy of the class that holds the dominant position in the economy. It does this not only through ideological means, but also through other forms of social control. The state, for example, also employs coercion, includes such material factors as army, police force, courts and prisons. The superstructure is therefore always an *active force* influencing all aspects of social life, including its own basis. Thus, for example, from the economic processes of feudalism in Europe arose not only feudal ideas and a feudal superstructure, but also ideological controversies and institutional struggles which reflected the conflict between nascent capitalism and decaying feudalism; great ideological battles, political upheavals and religious wars took place — all of which played an indispensable part in the development of the feudal economy itself and in the economic change from feudal relations of production to capitalist ones.

3. The Unity and Diversity of the Historical Process

The development and replacement of socioeconomic formations determine the progressive course of history. One aspect of the material life of society — the productive forces — is the element that ensures continuity in the progressive development of society, determines the direction of this development from lower to higher stages. The other aspect of the economic development — the production relations — expresses the discontinuity in historical development. Obsolete production relations are abolished and replaced by a higher type of production relations and a higher socioeconomic formation. Consequently, the emergence and development of a socioeconomic formation, the transition to a higher formation, are due to the action of the law of correspondence of production relations to the character and level of development of the productive forces. This law manifests itself as a tendency in the development and replacement of socioeconomic formations.

As already noted, people have always lived and developed in society. At first this took place on the small scale of the primeval horde (which had developed out of the primate troop), based upon the cooperative making of tools for the gathering of small animals and vegetable matter. The horde consisted of a group of adult females, their children and a small number of adult males.

Later the primeval horde evolved into the clan, made up of equal numbers of adult women and men. The clan was a community of blood relations with a common ancestor, as well as common economic life, language, territory and culture, but only comprised about 30-100 people. The clan was headed by a council, which included all adult men and women and elected and replaced its military leaders (chieftains). Sexual relations between members of the same clan were prohibited. Several closely related clans were associated together into a tribe.

Joint activity (division of labour based merely on age and sex), equality in distribution, strict rules (taboos) and full compliance of the individual with them, and an elaborate system of conditioning of the younger generation for the daily rigorous struggle for survival, characterise the social relations of this period in the life of humanity, which lasted for tens of thousands of years. Here the dependence of the way of life and the whole system of relations on the level of production stands out clearly in all its primitive simplicity.

The primitive-communal formation based upon (male) hunting and (female) food gathering was universal. Nevertheless, slowly, the productive forces developed within its framework. Tribal women, who in the hunter-gatherer economy had worked in collective groups gathering wild fruits and nuts, and had used their digging sticks to dig up tubers and roots and capture small animals, gradually learned to harvest certain grass seeds (wild wheat and barley) and grind them to make flour. This development occurred first in Palestine around 10,000 BC.

By 9000 BC women in Palestine and northern Syria had learned to sow wild wheat and barley, modifying their digging sticks into primitive hoes. By 8500 BC permanent farming villages made up of mud-brick houses had sprung up throughout the "fertile crescent" (an arc of rain-watered uplands stretching from Palestine in the west to the northern end of the Persian Gulf in the east).

The development of agriculture, and shortly after it, the domestication of animal herds (goats and sheep at first, then cattle) brought about a new social division of labour within the primitive-communal system. At first the female food-gathering teams became agriculturalists, collectively tilling and harvesting the village fields with their primitive hoes, while the male hunting bands became herdsmen and livestock breeders.

Later, clans which occupied rich pastures gradually abandoned crop-growing and went over exclusively to livestock herding. Among the pastoral clans, the abandonment of crop- growing meant a radical decline of women's contribution to social production and the concentration of the control of the clan's means of subsistence in the hands of its male members. This led to a decline in women's status and authority within the clan and the replacement among the pastoralists of the previous matrilineal system of descent with patrilineal descent and thus the birth of patriarchal clans.

With the development of more sophisticated agricultural implements, particularly the plough, labour tended to become more productive. The use of the plough, drawn by cattle, occurred independently among farming villages in northern Iraq and in the Danube valley about 4500 BC, and later spread from there across western Asia and Europe. The oxen-drawn plough not only brought about the displacement of women from agricultural production (since men were responsible for cattle-breeding) and the emergence of patrilineal kinship among the agricultural clans. It also made it possible to do without collective tilling of the land; that is, the collective activity of teams of village women using primitive hoes was supplanted by individual men using a plough drawn by oxen. The clans began to fall apart into individual family units, in which the husband had possession over the means of subsistence (the livestock, plough and oxen). The house and adjacent land became the family's private possessions, while meadows, forests and other land remained the property of the village commune. Since arable lands were now cultivated by individual families, the resultant products no longer went into the common stock or were distributed among members of the village commune but became the private property of individual families. Later on, the land was also taken into the property of individual families, which became the basic economic units of society. Such were the origins of *private property*. Its emergence led to material inequality between people, to the division of society into classes.

Class society first appeared in the Nile river valley in Egypt around 3600 BC, and a few hundred years later in the valley of the Tigris and the Euphrates rivers in southern Iraq. The fertile and easily tillable soil of these river valleys yielded comparatively good harvests even with the use of only primitive implements of agriculture, and it was here that the primitive commune first began to disintegrate and be replaced by class-divided societies.

The system of relatively self-sufficient agricultural communes ruled over by a large centralised state which, besides its political functions, performed the economic functions of building and maintaining large-scale irrigation works, created a special type of society based on a mode of production that Karl Marx called the *Asiatic* (since he first became aware of it during his studies of India and China). This type of society first arose in ancient Egypt and ancient Iraq (Sumer) in the 4th millennium BC, in the Indus valley in modern-day Pakistan in the 3rd millennium BC, in the Yellow River valley in northern China in the 2nd millennium BC and in ancient Peru and Central America in the 1st millennium BC. The existence of this mode of production in ancient Egypt, Mexico and Peru, makes the use of the geographic adjective "Asiatic" anachronistic. Because exploitation within this mode of production was based on the forcible extraction of tribute (in material goods and labour services) from the village communes by a centralised bureaucratic state administered by a priestly and military nobility, headed by a single despotic ruler (the *lugal* in Sumer, the *pharoah* in Egypt, the "Son of Heaven" in China), latter-day Marxists have adopted different names to designate this mode of production, e.g. "hydraulic", "communal" or "tributary". The socio-political system based upon this mode of production has traditionally been designated as "Oriental despotism".

While states based upon this mode of production rose and fell over the millenia, change in the instruments and organisation of labour within the village communities was extremely slow. The tributary mode of production endured in the countries in which it arose until the rise of capitalism in Western Europe and its creation of international trading empires.

The slave-owning formation arose where slavery became the basis of social production. While the enslavement of prisoners of war was common throughout the period of the disintegration of the patriarchal clan system, slaves did not constitute the main labour force. This consisted of free kinsmen. However, in conditions where plough agriculture using animal traction was not dependent upon centralised irrigation projects, its introduction promoted the development of individual farming plots. Under these conditions, tribal chieftains were able to use prisoners of war to enrich themselves. The rich tribal elite eventually began to turn into slaves, alongside prisoners of war, their own improverished tribesmen who were taken into debt servitude. This was the basis upon which the slave-owning formation emerged in ancient Greece and ancient Rome.

As the social division of labour deepened and as production in agriculture and handicrafts increased, commodity-money relations developed accordingly. The owners of farms and workshops that used slave labour put part of the surplus produce created by slave labour on the market. Slaves themselves were also bought and sold on an ever increasing scale. To increase the amount of surplus produce, the slave-owners sought to increase the number of slave labourers. Wars of conquest were the main source of new slaves. Thus in the 2nd century BC, some wars provided the Roman slave owners with up to 200,000 slaves. The slave-owning mode of production reached its peak development with the creation of the large slave estates (the latifundia) following the Roman conquest of Italy, Spain and Gaul (France).

The slaves' subservient labour without any material or moral incentives to technical development or higher labour productivity eventually led to the stagnation and decay of the slave-owning system. The output of the large slave estates could be sold at lower prices than the output of small peasant and handicraft households. The consequent ruination of small producers led to the emergence in the Roman empire of a huge mass of dispossessed but free citizens who had been deprived of their means of production and lost contact with production altogether. In order to maintain social peace, the Roman state was obliged to maintain these people (the proletariat) at the expense of the surplus-labour of the slaves. In contrast to the modern proletariat, at the expense of whose labour capitalist society exists, the Roman proletariat lived at the expense of slave-owning society.

The ruin of free peasants and artisans undermined the economic, political and military might of the Roman empire, because the small producers had constituted the backbone of its military forces. Wars of conquest ever more frequently turned into defensive wars, and the source of cheap slaves began to run out. As the steady influx of cheap slaves to the big slave enterprises shrank to a trickle and the price of slaves went up, the surplus product produced by slave labour was reduced. The owners of the large slave estates began to put less and less of the declining surplus product on the market. The decline of trade led to a decline in urban populations as the towns fell into decay and lost their economic and political importance. Since large-scale slave production yielded less and less income, it became more profitable for the estate owners to divide their land into small plots and lease them on definite terms to free citizens or slaves. These agricultural labourers were bound to the plots of land and could be sold together with them. They made up a new stratum of producers who occupied an intermediate position between the slaves and the big landowners, known as *coloni*, the predecessors of the serfs in the feudal mode of production.

Feudal society developed out of the collision in the decaying western part of the Roman empire of two dissolving anterior modes of production — the slave-owning system of the Roman empire and the primitive-communal system of the invading Germanic tribes.

The word feudalism itself derives from the word "feud" (*fief*), which in Western

Europe meant the landed property transferred by the higher ranking lord (seigneur) first into life long and then into hereditary possession of a lower ranking lord (vassal) on condition that the latter perform definite services, usually of a military nature. Under the feudal system, the basic means of production — the land, grain-mills and wagons — were owned by the feudal lord. The peasants received land from the feudal lord, not to own but only to use. They were bound to the land and had to perform various labour services.

Unlike the slave-owning system, under the feudal system the producers were allowed possession of their own dwelling, tools, draught animals and livestock, seed, fodder and other means of production. By working their own plot of land, they produced the necessary product for themselves. So, the reproduction of the serfs' labour-power was their own concern. In working for the feudal lord, the serfs were not interested in the results their labour. But in cultivating their own plots, they were interested in raising labour productivity, for this was the source of their own means of subsistence. By creating a certain interest in labour among the direct producers and better conditions for the reproduction of the labour force in comparison with the slave-owning society, feudalism opened up wider possibilities for the development of the productive forces.

At the same time, feudalism was a relatively static society. The routine technology, local isolation and separateness, lack of communication and transport facilities, rigid ordering and control over all forms of activity, hierarchical divisions of the fiefs, heavy burden of traditions, strict regulation of intellectual life by the Catholic Church and domination of religion in the ideological sphere put a brake on all progressive changes. Life revolved in a circle, following a set and unchanging rhythm.

But slowly, over time within the feudal system there evolved the material preconditions for the breakthrough to new social forms of life. The development of the division of labour, the growth of commodity-money relations, the appearance of new markets, brought into being new productive forces, artisan cooperation and manufactory. The new productive forces demanded new social forms to provide them with scope for development. Thus feudalism was compelled to give way to a new socioeconomic formation — capitalist society.

Under capitalism history becomes world history in the full sense of the term: the former isolation of both peoples and territories disappears and for the first time a single world system of economy, a single world market, comes into being.

The source and foundation of the development of capitalism are the productive forces connected with wage labour. In this period the rate of economic and social development increases sharply, but the development itself proceeds in antagonistic forms because it is based on the capitalist's appropriation of surplus value — the unpaid labour of the workers. Competition, the scramble for profit, anarchy of production and periodic crises are the characteristic features of the development of capitalist economy.

In a comparatively short historical period, capitalism passes through a number of stages, beginning from the early capitalist accumulation and proceeding through the system of free enterprise to the age of monopoly capitalism. Continuing Marx's analysis of capitalism, Lenin showed that the transition from free competition to monopoly, to the omnipotence of finance capital, marks the beginning of a trend toward stagnation and decay and heralds the decline of capitalism as a socioeconomic system. But this trend towards stagnation must not be interpreted as a complete halt in the development of production. On the contrary, modern science and technology make it possible to achieve high rates of economic development. But under capitalism this development takes place very unevenly. Some capitalist countries or monopoly groups get ahead of others in the rat-race for profit, thus changing the balance of forces and intensifying contradictions. Imperialism in general brings about intensification of all the contradictions of capitalism — growth of militarism, political reaction, and the like. All this weakens the system of capitalism and creates preconditions for the socialist revolution, which opens the road to building of a classless society, but one based upon the generalisation of material abundance rather than, as was the case in the primitive commune, upon generalised poverty.

We have examined the general trend of historical development to the extent that it is determined by the laws of motion of material production. But this does not imply that we have explained social development at every point of the historical process. Concrete history is much richer, and is affected by a great number of factors that vary and modify that process. We cannot therefore regard this process as something that proceeds in a single line. Historical development springs from the interaction of many forces, and to understand it in its concrete forms we must take into consideration all the essential factors contributing to this interaction. Historical materialism provides the method for studying concrete history because it not only reveals the unity of history and its general direction, but also shows us how to perceive its diversity.

The founders of Marxism gave many a warning against vulgarisation of historical materialism and turning its general propositions into a formula to be imposed on concrete history and thus provide a substitute for studying the concrete facts. Thus Engels wrote:

> ... according to the materialist conception of history, the ultimately determining

element in history is the production and reproduction of real life. More than this neither Marx nor I have ever asserted. Hence if somebody twists this into saying that the economic element is the only determining one, he transforms that proposition into a meaningless, abstract, senseless phrase.[5]

Engels goes on to say that various elements in the superstructure, ideology and so on influence the course of development. If we disregard this historical interaction and fail to see the accidents through whose multitudes economic necessity forces its way, "... the application of the theory to any period of history would be easier than the solution of a simple equation of the first degree" [6]

All kinds of causes diversify the general course of world history. We have already mentioned the influence on society of geographical conditions, which, particularly in the earlier stages of social development, was one of the essential factors determining the uneven course of world history. Thanks to its geographical position, every people lives in a certain specific historical environment — and feels its effects. Nor must we disregard the influence on the course of history of such secondary factors, compared with economics, as the state, cultural originality, traditions, ideology and social psychology. Let us take culture, for example. The concept of the German philosopher Oswald Spengler and the British historian Arnold Toynbee of the existence of isolated and autonomous cultures, which implies a denial of the unity of world history, contradicts the historical facts. But it would be quite wrong to deny the originality not only of national cultures but also of whole regions and continents. Thus one may observe in the cultures of the peoples of Europe and Asia certain common features and a considerable originality which must not be disregarded when studying the history of these peoples.

The influence of one people on another is also an important factor in history. It has occurred in all kinds of forms, from wars and conquests to trade and cultural exchange. It may take place in all spheres of social life, from economics to ideology. Ideological influences have been of tremendous significance in history. The spread of Christianity played an important historical role in Europe and America, for instance, and in various countries of Asia and Africa a similar role was played by the spread of Buddhism and Islam.

The uniqueness of individual countries cannot be understood without taking into consideration the unevenness of world historical development. Some peoples forge ahead, others lag behind; for various concrete reasons some are able to leapfrog over whole socioeconomic formations. So, in every period throughout written history there existed not just one formation, but peoples at various stages of social development, and between them there were complex interrelations. This means that we do not find the same sequence of formations in the history of all peoples. Thus, among the Slavs and the Germanic peoples inhabiting central and eastern Europe the disintegration of the preclass system occurred in an age when the slave-owning formation (Roman empire) had exhausted itself and was in a state of decline; for this reason the slave structure that had begun to take shape did not develop into a formation and the peoples of central and eastern Europe passed straight from the tribal system to feudalism.

The character of the mutual influence exercised by peoples that are at different stages of historical development depends on the nature of their social systems. Thus it was in the nature of capitalism that capitalist Europe should have used its technical supremacy to enslave the peoples of other continents and subject them to colonial oppression. The development of these peoples was not only held up by colonialism; in many cases they were actually thrown back in both their economic and cultural development.

While recognising the progressive character of social development, the replacement of lower social formations by higher formations, historical materialism does not by any means regard this as a predetermined process. The diversity of history, the specific features in the development of continents and countries, are conditioned, as we have noted, by a whole set of diverse causes.

But diverse though the history of various peoples may be, there are in every historical period certain leading trends of social development. In defining a period of world history according to its leading trends, we use the concept of *historical epoch*. For example, we speak of the epoch of slave society or the epoch of feudalism, relating them to the time when these formations were the most advanced forms of social organisation existent. In our own day, vestiges of feudalism are still to be found in certain countries, but it would be absurd to speak of the present day as the "epoch of feudalism".

The concept of the epoch may be associated with definite stages of the leading formation. Thus, for example, we distinguish between the epoch of pre-monopoly capitalism and the epoch of imperialism (monopoly capitalism). To single out the leading trend in an epoch, we must, as Lenin taught, establish what class plays the central role in the epoch and determines its main content, the main direction of its development, its main features.

Unlike the concept of the socioeconomic formation, which characterises a certain stage in the development of society, the concept of the historical epoch is more concrete, expressing the diversity of processes occurring at a given time in a given stage of history. In one and the same epoch in various parts of the world, there have existed various formations. For example, alongside the peoples of ancient Greece and the Roman empire who lived in slave-owning society there lived other peoples who were still at the stage of the primitive-communal system or lived under the tributary mode of production; alongside the capitalism that had established itself in western Europe and North America by the early 19th century, there still remained feudal relations in certain parts of the world, the tributary and primitive-communal modes of production in others.

The concept of the historical epoch embraces both the typical and the non-typical for any given period of history. In each epoch, Lenin explained, there may be and will be separate, partial movements forward or backward, various deviations from the average type and rates of movement.

Finally, the concept of the epoch may be associated with the transition from one socioeconomic formation to another, when humanity is going through a transitional period, and tremendous changes are occurring in its social life. Thus the different periods of transition from feudalism to capitalism are characterised as the epoch of the Renaissance, or the epoch of bourgeois revolutions and feudal counter-revolutions.

Regarded from the standpoint of world history, our own time is also a transitional epoch — the epoch of transition from capitalism to socialism. This transition is the leading trend of contemporary social development, reflecting the profound crisis of the whole system of capitalism and the consequent appearance of proletarian revolutions and bourgeois counter-revolutions. ❦

Chapter 6
Social Revolution

In the development of society there occur both gradual evolutionary changes and leaps in various fields — science and technology, the means of production and communications, people's outlook. The most significant of these are termed "revolutions". But even significant changes in certain aspects of social life, taken by themselves, do not yet signify social revolution. Social revolution means a fundamental change in the whole socioeconomic system.

Qualitative transformations may also occur within one and the same socioeconomic system, during transition from one phase or stage of its development to another. Such, for example, is the transition from pre-monopoly capitalism to monopoly capitalism. But this is not a social revolution because the basic features of capitalism continue to exist. Social revolution, on the other hand, "is a change which breaks the old order to its very foundations".[1]

Social revolution implies a qualitative leap in the development of society, resulting in the replacement of one socioeconomic formation by another.

1. Social Revolution as the Law of the Replacement of Socioeconomic Formations

The replacement of socioeconomic formations is a complex and lengthy process involving changes in the material and technical base of society, in its economic system, political life, ideology and intellectual culture. These transformations do not occur simultaneously and not always in the same sequence. Many of them belong not to the revolution itself but to the process of its preparation or spontaneous maturing.

The appearance of new productive forces in the womb of the old society, changes in the economy and the disposition of the class forces, the aggravation of contradictions between new elements in social life and the obsolete socio-political system, the awareness of these contradictions among individuals and classes — all these are different aspects of the process that leads up to a social revolution. The revolution itself is a phase in the development of society when, as Lenin put it, "the numerous contradictions which slowly accumulate during periods of socalled peaceful development become resolved".[2]

What are these contradictions? First of all, the contradictions between the new productive forces and the obsolete production relations, and, secondly, between the new elements in the economic system of society (in its basis) and the old legal and political superstructure, and also between various sections of the superstructure.

The deepest cause of social revolutions lies in the contradictions between the new productive forces and the obsolete production relations. New production relations corresponding to the character of the new productive forces are usually conceived in the womb of the old system. Rudiments of feudal production relations, for instance, appeared within the framework of the decaying slave-owning society (the conversion of slaves on the estates into *coloni* — slaves who were granted use of small plots of land on the estate to provide for their own subsistence, and who could no longer be sold, but could only pass from one owner to another along with the land on which they lived and worked). Capitalist production relations emerged within the framework of feudal society, when commercial enterprises, banks and manufactories appeared.

The development of new economic relations undermines the obsolescent economic system from within. But the latter does not disappear of itself, because it has behind it the obsolescent ruling class, which makes every effort to retain its position. The feudal system in France, for example, at the end of the 18th century was riddled with decay, and yet the landlord class, which had huge holdings, privileges and political power, did everything it could to preserve the old system. There had to be a revolution to sweep away the old economic and political order, which was preventing the development of the new productive forces and capitalist production relations.

Thus *the conflict between the productive forces and the production relations manifests itself in a struggle between classes.* Some classes defend the obsolescent production relations and the socio-political system that is based upon them, while others seek to abolish them. The revolutionary classes destroy the outmoded legal and political superstructure and create a new one. They use the new state power they have created to complete the break-up of the old production relations and reinforce the new ones. Social revolution also involves more or less profound changes in the intellectual life of society, in its culture.

The main feature of the social revolution is the transfer of state power from one class to another in order to bring about a complete change in the relations of ownership of the means of production. Hence, every social revolution involves a political revolution, a radical change in the political system. But not every political revolution is a social revolution, that is, effects a change in the socioeconomic system.

Both social revolutions and political revolutions should be distinguished from *coups d'etat* and "palace revolutions". The latter do not bring about any fundamental change in either the socioeconomic order or the political system, but simply involve a forcible change in the composition of the governing groups and individuals within the existing political system.

Not every transfer of state power from one class to another, however, may be described as a social revolution. If an historically obsolete class again assumes state power, having temporarily regained the upper hand, this is not a social revolution, but a social *counter-revolution*, aimed at the restoration of the old order.

In bourgeois philosophy and sociology, this fundamental distinction is usually deliberately ignored. Revolution is usually described as a sudden, violent change in the existing political system — contrasted to gradual, peaceful change. Although revolution is indeed the opposite of gradual, evolutionary change, such a definition does not make any distinction between revolution and counter-revolution.

Another fault in this and similar definitions is that they equate revolution and "violent change". Of course, any social revolution involves the overthrow of the power of an obsolete class, which never relinquishes it voluntarily, and in this sense, as historical experience has shown, revolution is impossible without the use of armed force by the revolutionary classes. But whether the use of armed force by the revolutionary classes extends from the *threat* of violence to the *actual use* of violence, i.e., to civil war, depends on the specific conditions in which the revolution is carried out, on the relative strengths of the contending class forces.

Social revolution may be realised either relatively peacefully or through an armed uprising or civil war, but the manner in which it is realised is not its distinguishing characteristic as a social phenomenon, which is the destruction of the obsolete socioeconomic system and its replacement by a new system.

Social revolutions differ from one another in their *character* and *driving forces*. The *character* of a social revolution is determined by what social contradictions it resolves and what kind of socioeconomic system it establishes. Why, for example, was the Russian revolution of 1905-07 a bourgeois revolution even though the proletariat and not the bourgeoisie was its leader? Because the objective task of the revolution was to clear away the obstacles to the unhindered development of bourgeois socioeconomic relations through the overthrow of the autocratic political system and the vestiges of feudal production relations that the autocracy rested upon.

The *driving forces* of a revolution are the classes that carry it out, drive it forward and overcome the resistance of the obsolete classes. They depend not only on the character of the revolution but also on the specific historical conditions in which it occurs. Revolutions may be of the same character, but owing to differences of historical conditions may differ profoundly from one another in their driving forces. For example, the driving forces of the bourgeois revolutions of the 17th and 18th centuries in the west European countries included the peasantry and the plebeian sections of the urban population — the emerging working class and the urban petty bourgeoisie. The bourgeoisie was not only a driving force but was the ideological and political leader of these revolutions. But in the bourgeois revolution in Russia — the revolution of 1905-07, the February 1917 revolution and the first phase of the October Revolution (from November 1917 until the middle of 1918) — the bourgeoisie was not only not the ideological and political leader, it was not even one of the driving forces. The driving forces of the bourgeois revolution in Russia were the proletariat and the peasantry, led by the proletariat. Thus, as Lenin explained, the 1905 revolution and the first stage of the October Revolution were *bourgeois revolutions* in their social content but *proletarian revolutions* in their methods of struggle and political leadership.[3]

Social revolutions tremendously accelerate the development of history. In a few years, even a few months, of revolution the masses bring about more significant changes in social life than in the course of many decades of gradual, evolutionary development. Marx called them the locomotives of history.

Some bourgeois ideologists assert that revolutions are always carried out by a minority, by small groups of revolutionaries and not by the masses. These views coincide with the ideas of petty-bourgeois ultra-"left" revolutionaries, who reduce preparations for a revolution to conspiracy or heroic actions by a revolutionary-minded minority. The active revolutionary minority, of course, may be a catalyst of revolution, but without mass support and involvement, revolution inevitably turns into a *coup d'etat* or a reckless adventure.

In some bourgeois revolutions, the masses advance their own independent demands, and their struggle leaves a deep imprint upon the course of events; Marx and Lenin called such revolutions "real people's revolutions". Such, for example, were the American and French revolutions in the 18th century. At the same time, there have been bourgeois revolutions (for example the "Glorious Revolution" in England in 1688) in which the masses of the people took no active or independent part. Such revolutions do not leave a deep mark on history. But in some cases a revolution, beginning as an "upper-crust" revolution, may become in the course of its development a profound and historically significant event because it sets in motion the broad masses of the people. Such, for example, was the course of development of the Great French Revolution (1789-93).

For the masses to become involved in revolutionary struggle, they must appreciate the necessity of overthrowing the old system. So in periods of revolution new revolutionary ideas reflecting the historical problems that are ripe for solution acquire a special importance. These ideas help to mobilise the masses and weld them into a political army capable of breaking the resistance of the obsolescent classes. Consequently, a political upheaval is usually preceded by an *upheaval in social consciousness*—a profound change in the ideological outlook and political mood of the masses. The change in the sphere of intellectual culture, however, can only be completed on the soil of the new conditions of life that result from the triumph of the revolution and the establishment of a new socioeconomic order.

The question arises whether there must be a revolution in order to resolve social contradictions. Cannot they be resolved by means of reforms, partial concessions on the part of the ruling class, by means of gradual change? The opponents of revolution regard reforms as salvation from revolution. They deny the law-governed character of revolutions and see them merely as a result of the mistakes of the ruling circles, who failed to make the necessary concessions to the revolutionaries in time.

Reforms may temporarily soften social contradictions, but reforms cannot resolve them. Reforms may even eradicate particular manifestations or symptoms of fundamental social contradictions, but reforms cannot remove their source. Reforms do not resolve fundamental social contradictions, but only postpone their ultimate solution.

Liberals, including the reformist "socialists", counterpose reforms to revolution and regard reform as an end in itself, and thus try by means of reforms to divert the working people from taking the path of revolution. If reforms are used by the defenders of the old system to prevent its downfall, does this mean that revolutionaries must be opponents of all reform? Not at all. Marxist revolutionaries regard reforms, that is, concessions made by the ruling class to the working people, as a by-product of the class struggle, and seek to use the mass struggle for reforms to advance the revolutionary consciousness and organisation of the working people, to prepare them to carry out a social revolution.

2. HISTORICAL TYPES OF SOCIAL REVOLUTIONS

The transition from one socioeconomic formation to another always comes about in its own particular way, depending on what formation is dying and what formation is coming into being. The historical types of revolution differ accordingly.

The division of revolutions into different types is based, first, upon the character of the historical tasks that they are called upon to perform (which system they overthrow and which they establish) and, second, upon their class content. When discussing the question of the type of revolution Marxists always speak of what class it is made by and whose class interests it promotes. In their turn, revolutions differ in respect of their form, driving forces, degree of decisiveness etc.

The first replacement of one socioeconomic formation by another was the transition from the primitive-communal system to the socioeconomic formation based on the Asiatic (or tributary) mode of production in southern Iraq (Mesopotamia) and in the Nile River valley around 5500 years ago. The peculiar feature of this transition was that it supplanted pre-class society with a class society.

A number of social scientists, including the US anthropologist Lewis Henry Morgan, whose work was highly valued by Marx and Engels, believed that the change from pre-class to class society was evolutionary, i.e., did not involve a social revolution. But a different answer to the question was given by Engels in *The Origin of the Family, Private Property and the State*. While Engels based his conclusions on the transition from pre-class to class society in ancient Greece and Rome in the first millennium BC (which involved the replacement of the primitive-communal system by the slave-owning system), he showed that class division gradually formed in the womb of the primitive-communal system and finally led to a revolutionary upheaval which ended the remaining tribal relationships.

In slave-owning society, the basic antagonistic contradiction between the slave-owner and the slave was supplemented by the antagonism between the big landowners and money-lenders on the one hand and the small peasant farmers and artisans on the other. These contradictions engendered revolutionary movements of the peasants and other free citizens with a small amount of property. These movements quite often resulted in reforms, which the ruling classes were compelled to concede.

Another channel of revolutionary movement in the slave-owning societies was the struggle of the slaves against their oppressors. The biggest of these movements were usually combined with the struggle of the free poor. The greatest of these slave uprisings was the movement led by the gladiator Spartacus in 74-71 BC, in which more than 100,000 slaves participated.

The revolutionary movements of the slaves and the free poor undermined the slave-owning system but did not culminate in a victorious revolution that could sweep away this system and replace it with another, higher system. For this reason, the crisis in the slave-owning system in some states usually led to their being enslaved by other, more powerful states that subsequently themselves entered into a period of profound crisis and internal decay. The greatest of these states, the Roman empire, weakened internally by the rebellions of slaves and *coloni*, collapsed under the onslaught of its own mercenary armies, which were made up of the surrounding Germanic tribes, themselves undergoing a process of dissolution into classes.

Despite these individual features, however, the transition from slave-owning to feudal society confirms the general proposition that the replacement of one socioeconomic formation by another does not come about by evolution but demands a fundamental break-up of the obsolete order. In this particular case the demolition of the slave-owning system was carried out by the Germanic tribes supported from within by revolts by runaway slaves, army deserters, depressed *coloni* and free peasants (the Bacaudae insurrections of the years 407-17, 435-37 and 442-43).

The history of feudal society also recorded a number of revolutionary movements that did not culminate in victorious social revolutions. Such were nearly all the peasant wars and rebellions of the period when feudalism reached its zenith and entered a prolonged general crisis (a structural crisis between the productive forces and feudal relations of production). These included the peasant movement known as the "Grand Jacquerie" (1358) in France, the peasant revolt of Wat Tyler (1381) in England, the great rising of the Calabrian peasantry (1469-75) in Italy, the civil war between the serfs in Catalonia and their baronial lords in 1462 and again in 1484, and the Peasant War in Germany (1525).

The peasant movements achieved a higher stage of development than those of the slaves, but their weakness also lay in their spontaneity and lack of organisation. The material conditions for the replacement of feudalism by capitalism had not yet matured. This was reflected in the fact that there had not yet emerged a class that could lead the peasants to establish a new, more productive, socioeconomic system.

The most decisive rebellions against feudalism involved movements not only of the oppressed peasantry but also of the lower orders of the urban population — the apprentices, the poor. But the poor of the towns were too weak, disorganised and ignorant to provide leadership to the peasants.

While all of these peasant movements were defeated and politically repressed, with the exception of the Calabrian rising they forced the feudal landowners to grant concessions (relaxation of servile ties on the land, leasing of seigneurial lands to peasant tenants, substitution of money rent for rent in kind) that led to a rise in peasant incomes and the disintegration of serfdom. These changes in turn encouraged the feudal nobility to increasingly turn their lands to pasturage, particularly to supply the growing woollen industry in the towns.

The class that was needed to lead the peasants in demolishing feudalism came into being when capitalist relations began to take shape in the interstices of feudal society, in the first place within the medieval towns which supplied luxury goods to the feudal landowners. It was in this period (varying chronologically in different countries) that the preconditions for *bourgeois revolutions* began to mature.

The revolutions in the epoch of the crisis of feudalism and ascending development of capitalism occurred under the leadership of the urban bourgeoisie, which in some cases achieved victory through compromise with the feudal aristocracy, and in others fought on to accomplish its complete overthrow. The fighting force of these revolutions was the peasantry together with the poor people of the cities. Therefore, at the peak of their development such revolutions went much further than the goals set by the bourgeoisie.

A specific feature of the bourgeois revolutions was that they moved comparatively fast, their chief aim being to bring the political superstructure into accord with the capitalist system of economy already emergent in feudal society, and to secure the necessary conditions for its unhindered development. For this reason, bourgeois revolutions usually end with the conquest of political power by the bourgeoisie.

The *proletarian-socialist revolution*, which opens the road to the transition from capitalism to socialism, is a fundamentally new type of social revolution. Its aim is not to replace one form of class exploitation by another, but to sweep away exploitation and classes altogether.

The tasks of the socialist revolution are incomparably more complicated and profound that those of all previous revolutions. It is for this reason that it must set in motion the overwhelming majority of the population. Its driving forces are the wage-workers, the leader of the revolution, and other sections of the working people (most particularly, the oppressed and exploited sections of the middle classes).

In the political field, the socialist revolution puts the working class in power and establishes its class dictatorship (state power). This is accomplished by removing the bourgeoisie from its position of rule over society through the smashing of the old state machinery and its replacement with a fundamentally new state power, based on the mass organisations created by the working people.

The winning of political power by the working class, however, is not the completion of the socialist revolution, but only its beginning. Unlike all previous social revolutions, which were led by a rising new propertied class based upon new relations of production developing in the womb of the old society, the proletariat does not own any means of production. It must use its political power not simply to sweep away remnants of the old relations of production, but to demolish a still existent mode of production and to bring about a fundamental transformation of society, its economy and culture. The new state power must not only destroy the obsolete system as in previous revolutions; it must also build a new society.

"One of the fundamental differences between bourgeois revolution and socialist revolution", wrote Lenin, "is that for the bourgeois revolution, which arises out of feudalism, the new economic organisations are gradually created in the womb of the old order, gradually changing all the aspects of feudal society. The bourgeois revolution faced only one task — to sweep away, to cast aside, to destroy all the fetters of the preceding social order. By fulfilling this task every bourgeois revolution fulfills all that is required of it; it accelerates the growth of capitalism.

"The socialist revolution is in an altogether different position ... New incredibly difficult tasks, organisational tasks, are added to the tasks of destruction."[4]

3. Objective Conditions and the Subjective Factor of Revolution

A social revolution can succeed only when the maturity of its objective conditions coincides with the vigorous activity of driving forces, of the classes fighting for the realisation of their interests.

The existence of objective conditions for a revolution means that it must proceed according to certain laws. Social revolutions cannot be called into being at the will of small revolutionary-minded groups (as both the conservative and liberal opponents of revolutions, on the one hand, and the anarchist and other petty-bourgeois revolutionists on the other, allege or imagine).

One of the objective conditions for a social revolution is *a general crisis in the obsolete system*, an aggravation of all its contradictions to the point where it cannot continue to function according to its own laws, and is forced to introduce forms of organisation transitional to the new relations of production maturing within the womb of the old system.

The objective preconditions of revolution are not only economic. They also include socio-political conditions, and above all, the development of class contradictions, the alignment of class forces. Treating the objective preconditions of revolution as purely economic leads to opportunist inaction that is as false as the idealist views of the "ultra-lefts", to the wrong conclusion that the maturing of revolution is mechanistically determined by the degree of development of productive forces.

Revolution becomes possible when the contradictions between classes grow extremely acute. It is not therefore produced automatically by a conflict between the productive forces and production relations. Such a conflict has existed for decades in the developed capitalist countries (indeed, since the end of the 19th century), but this is not to say that all the objective conditions for social revolution have existed in these countries.

To make a revolution possible there must also be a *revolutionary situation*, which comes about in different countries according to specific national economic and political circumstances. A revolutionary situation is a build-up of socio-political conditions necessary for revolution. Its symptoms may change at various stages in history, but in all cases it presupposes a profound crisis of the old system. Lenin defined these symptoms as follows: (1) a crisis among the "upper classes", a crisis in the policy of the ruling class, when it is impossible for it to continue to rule in the old way, (2) the suffering and want of the oppressed classes have grown more acute than usual and they refuse to be ruled in the old way, (3) as a consequence of the above causes, there is a considerable increase in the socio-political activity of the masses, who uncomplainingly allow themselves to be robbed in "normal times", but, in turbulent times, are drawn by all the circumstances into independent historical action.[5]

Although the symptoms of a revolutionary situation may be connected with the level of revolutionary consciousness of the masses (heightening of their political activity), a revolutionary situation is an objective condition of revolution. This is because its occurrence does not depend upon the will of individual groups or parties or even of whole classes. The revolutionary workers' party, for example, cannot evoke at its own discretion a crisis of the old power, although its struggle may hamper the reactionary forces' scope for manoeuvre. A revolutionary situation may be brought about by various causes: economic shocks, failures of government policy such as the collapse of a military adventure, national conflicts leading to a sharp aggravation of class contradictions. In a number of cases revolutionary situations have grown out of wars (for example, the revolutions of 1905 and 1917 in Russia, the revolutions in eastern Europe and east Asia in the wake of World War II). However, as the revolutions in Cuba (1959) and Nicaragua (1979) and the revolutionary crises in Germany in 1923,

France and Spain in 1936 and France in 1968, have demonstrated, war is by no means a necessary condition of a revolutionary situation.

The revolutionary situation is an essential but not sufficient condition for a social revolution. For a revolution to take place, and particularly for it to be victorious, there must be not only objective conditions. There was a revolutionary situation in Russia in 1905, but the revolution was not victorious.

The defeat of a revolution may be due to several causes, including an internationally and/or nationally unfavourable alignment of class forces. But even with the alignment of class forces well in its favour, a revolution will not be victorious if there is not a sufficiently mature *subjective factor*. For a revolution to be victorious, the revolutionary class must be capable of sufficiently strong and resolute revolutionary action because the power of the obsolescent ruling class will never collapse of its own accord.

The elements of the subjective factor of revolution include: (1) revolutionary consciousness of the masses, their readiness and determination to carry through the struggle to the end (to the seizure of political power and the destruction of the power of the obsolete ruling class), (2) centralised organisation of the masses and their vanguard, which makes it possible to concentrate all the forces capable of fighting for victory of the revolution, and to act together and not in scattered, uncoordinated groups, (3) leadership of the masses by an organised vanguard sufficiently experienced and trained in battle and capable of evolving correct tactics of struggle and putting them into practice.

Thus, *social revolution demands unity of objective and subjective conditions.* This law of social revolution has been confirmed, as Lenin noted, by all revolutions and particularly by the three Russian revolutions of the 20th century (1905, February 1917, October 1917).

Although the objective conditions play a decisive role in history, the subjective factor may, under certain circumstances, determine the fate of a revolution. The subjective factor acquires this role whenever and wherever objective conditions for revolution have sufficiently matured. If the objective conditions for accomplishing historical tasks have not matured, no efforts on the part of progressive social forces can lead to a revolutionary transformation of society. But if the objective conditions are present, the results of social revolution depend on the subjective factor.

Opponents of Leninism sometimes oppose Marx's views on revolution to those of Lenin. They allege, for example, that Marx stressed the maturing of objective (particularly economic) conditions, while Lenin put the emphasis on the subjective factor, on revolutionary will, consciousness and action, and thus his views represent a "voluntarist" departure from "orthodox" Marxism. In reality, however, there is no contradiction between the views of Marx and those of Lenin. In principle they adopted one and the same solution to the question of the correlation of objective conditions and the subjective factor. The differences in their approach to this question are merely due to the different historical conditions in which they dealt with the question of socialist revolution.

In the lifetimes of Marx and Engels the objective conditions for a socialist revolution had not yet fully matured. The defeat of the Paris Commune testifies to this fact.[6]

In the epoch of monopoly capitalism, of the world imperialist system, the most developed capitalist nations become materially ripe for socialist revolution, which of course does not mean that *all* the objective conditions for the revolution mature in every country simultaneously, but that they will periodically mature in different countries. Thus, the role of the subjective factor increases; indeed, it becomes *the central question upon which the fate of humanity depends*.

In view of the changed historical conditions, Lenin enriched Marx's theory of proletarian revolution by producing a comprehensive study of the role of the subjective factor in the struggle for effecting a socialist revolution, including a profound deepening of the Marxist theory of the development of revolutionary consciousness within the working class and, flowing from that, of the tasks and character of the proletariat's revolutionary party. ❦

CHAPTER 7

SOCIAL CLASSES AND CLASS STRUGGLE

What are social classes? Why do classes exist at certain stages in the development of society? What place do class relations occupy in social life? The correct answering of these questions supplies the key to our understanding of the essence of such important social phenomena of the modern world as the state, political relations and idēological life. The class approach to the analysis of the life of any society divided into classes is one of the fundamental methodological principles of Marxism. Explaining the significance of this principle, Lenin wrote: "People always have been the foolish victims of deception and self-deception in politics, and they always will be until they have learnt to seek out the interests of some class or other behind all moral, religious, political and social phrases, declarations and promises".[1]

1. THE CONCEPT OF SOCIAL CLASSES

Social classes are large groups of people into which society is divided. But there are many other large groups in society, divided on different principles from those which divide classes. There are age groups, for instance (young and old generations), groups based on sex, race, nationality, occupation. Some of these divisions have a physical basis (age, sex), while others are purely social in origin (nationality, occupation). The physical differences between people do not in themselves cause social distinctions and only under certain social circumstances may be connected with social inequality. Thus, racial inequality is historical, not natural, in origin. Racial groups themselves are social categories, not biological categories. They arise through the social practice peculiar to capitalism of fetishising particular physical differences between people (usually skin colour) in order to ascribe social values of superiority and inferiority to these physical differences, and therefore justify the imposition of social inequality based upon racial categorisation. Similarly, the social inequality of the sexes is due not to natural but to historical causes. At the early stages of history, during the primitive-communal system, women played a leading role in society, which they subsequently lost owing to the division of society into separate family units based upon private property.

Class divisions in general usually have nothing to do with natural differences; they exist within one and the same racial or ethnic group, and cut across age and sex lines.

Some bourgeois sociologists seek the causes of the division of society into classes in political factors — in coercion, for instance, in the subjugation of some people or peoples by others. Of course, the transition from classless society to class society did not occur without coercion. But coercion only accelerated and deepened social inequality; it was not its cause. Violence does not explain the origin of classes any more than robbery explains the origin of private ownership of the means of production. Robbery may result in the passing of some property from one owner to another, but it cannot create private property as such.

The division of society into classes is due to economic causes; it existed, for example, in places such as ancient Egypt and ancient Athens, where no conquest had taken place. Its source is the division of labour within society, which presumes the isolation of producers engaged in various forms of production and the exchange between them of the products of their labour. First, agriculture and livestock breeding form special branches of labour, then handicrafts break away from agriculture, and finally mental work (e.g., the management of labour, record keeping, public administration) is separated from manual labour. The social division of labour and exchange of surplus products bring in their train private ownership of the means of production, which supersedes the previous communal form of property and gives rise to social groups that have unequal standing in social production — classes. Society is divided into rich and poor, exploiters and exploited, and a state of inequality reigns. As Engels put it, "... these warring classes of society are always the products of the modes of production and of exchange — in a word, of the economic conditions of their time".[2]

Classes were formed in two ways. The first was through the emergence out of the Neolithic village communes of the river valleys of the Tigris and Euphrates in southern Iraq and the Nile valley in Egypt of a stratum of specialists who developed and monopolised the knowledge and skills needed to direct large-scale public works.

Agriculture in these desert river valleys was dependent upon large-scale irrigation works, which required the cooperative efforts of many village communities. In Egypt, water was provided by the annual flooding of the Nile. However, it required the building and maintenance of large numbers of dykes and water basins to provide a regular source of water for irrigating crops. In southern Iraq (Sumer) the annual flood of the Tigris and Euphrates was insufficient, and water for irrigating farm land required the construction and maintenance of an extensive network of canals. The construction of these irrigation works necessitated specialised knowledge and the centralised direction of the labour of many village communities, knowledge and organising authority, which became concentrated in the hands of a minority made up of the village priests and clan chiefs who lived off the surplus product of the peasant farmers. At first this surplus product was voluntarily provided by the village communes to support the organisers of large-scale irrigation projects. However, as these organisers and administrators consolidated into a coherent group living together in a town (usually centred on a temple), the tribute made by the surrounding village communities was extracted through force, and the society became divided into an exploited class of peasant-craftsmen and an exploiter class of priest-officials — headed by a priest-king who, as the earthly representative of the temple deity, established his private ownership of the land. This was the general pattern out of which the first class-divided societies, based upon the tributary ("Asiatic") mode of production, arose in Sumeria and ancient Egypt around 5500 years ago.

The second way in which classes were formed was by means of the enslavement of the members of other tribes conquered in battle or of the impoverished members of one's own tribe who had fallen into debt. This was the general pattern out of which the slave-owning societies emerged in ancient Greece and, later, in ancient Rome, in the 1st millennium BC.

In summarising the experience of the development of classes, Marxism for the first time furnished an authentic scientific explanation of the essence of classes, the reasons for their emergence and the means to achieve their abolition. Karl Marx associated the existence of classes with specific historical phases in the development of social production, while bourgeois social scientists had never taken that into consideration. They regarded classes as an extra-historical and perpetual phenomenon ("there will always be rich and poor people"). Marx proved the historically transient nature of class-divided society and showed why and when class society would be abolished and replaced by a classless society. Marx proved that capitalist society is the last society in human history with antagonistic classes. The path leading to classless society, Marx maintained, lies through the proletariat's class struggle against all forms of oppression, aimed at establishing its class rule in society. In a letter written in March 1852 to Joseph Weydemeyer in New York, Marx noted: "no credit is due to me for discovering the existence of classes in modern society or the struggle between them. Long before me bourgeois historians had described the historical development of this class struggle and bourgeois economists the economic anatomy of the classes. What I did that was new was to prove: 1) that the *existence of classes* is only bound up with *particular historical phases in the development of production*, 2) that the class struggle necessarily leads to *the dictatorship of the proletariat*, 3) that this dictatorship itself only constitutes the transition to the *abolition of all classes* and to a *classless society*."[3]

In a work written earlier in 1852 — *The Eighteenth Brumaire of Louis Bonaparte* — Marx gave the following definition of what constitutes a class: "In so far as millions of families live under economic conditions of existence that separate their mode of life, their interests and their culture from those of other classes, and put them in hostile opposition to the latter, they form a class."[4] Here Marx defines classes as large numbers of families who, because of the production relations ("economic conditions of existence") they live under, have a common way of making a living, common interests and a common culture which are separate from those of the rest of society and which put them into an antagonistic relation with other such large numbers of families.

Marx later gave the following explanation of how class divisions were intrinsically connected to exploitative relations of production:

> The specific economic form in which unpaid surplus labour is pumped out of the direct producers, determines the relationship of domination and servitude, as this grows directly out of production itself and reacts back on it as a determinant. On this is based the entire configuration of the economic community arising from the actual relations of production, and hence also its specific political form. It is in each case the direct relationship of the owners of the conditions of production to the immediate producers — a relationship whose particular form naturally corresponds to a certain level of development of the type and manner of labour, and hence to its social productive power — in which we find the innermost secret, the hidden basis of the entire social edifice, and hence also the political form of the relationship of sovereignty and dependence, in short, the specific form of the state in each case.[5]

Here Marx located the category of social class in the relationship between the "owners of the conditions of production" and the "immediate producers", relations of production which allow the former to "pump" unpaid surplus labour out of the latter. The forms of extraction of surplus labour that are possible in any given class society are dependent upon the level of "social productive power" attained, since it is the latter that determines the actual or potential size of the social surplus product.

Synthesising the different aspects of Marx's description of classes, Lenin defined classes as "large groups of people differing from each other by the place they occupy in a historically determined system of social production, by their relation (in most cases fixed and formulated in law) to the means of production, by their role in the social organisation of labour, and, consequently, by the dimensions of the share of social wealth of which they dispose and the mode of acquiring it. Classes are groups of people one of which can appropriate the labour of another owing to the different places they occupy in a definite system of social economy".[6]

Let us examine this definition in more detail. Classes, says Lenin, are large groups of people that are distinguished primarily by their place in the historically determined system of production. This means that every class must be regarded in connection with the mode of production by which it is engendered, and that each antagonistic mode of production creates its own specific division of society into classes (e.g., landowning nobles and tribute-paying peasant villagers, slave-owners and slaves, feudal lords and serfs, capitalists and proletarians).

Within every system of production, classes occupy different or even diametrically opposed positions, this being determined by their relationship to the means of production. The relations of production in a class-divided society are relations of exploitation, of domination and subordination. This is due to the fact that the ruling class has a monopoly of the decisive means of production; that is, it possesses the most important means of production. Wherever one section of society monopolises the means of production, the producers must, in addition to the working time they expend providing for their own subsistence, spend additional working time on providing for the owner of the means of production.

The relationship of the classes to the means of production also depends on their role in the social organisation of labour. Classes perform various functions in social production: in class-divided society some of them manage production, control the economy and all social affairs and are engaged predominantly in mental work, while others bear the whole burden of compulsory, arduous physical labour.

As social production and the whole life of society grow more complex, various functions of control become necessary. In the agrarian societies of ancient Iraq, Egypt, China and India, for example, large-scale irrigation works demanded specialised knowledge and centralised organisation of labour that were not needed in either small individual or simple communal farming. The large-scale machine production of today would be unthinkable without organising activity, without management of production in all fields. In class society the management of social production is usually in the hands of the class that owns the means of production.

When certain production relations begin to hold up the development of the productive forces, the role of the ruling class in the social organisation of labour also changes; it loses its organising function in production and declines into a parasitic growth on the body of society. This happened with the slave-owners and the feudal aristocracy in their time, and the same thing has happened to the big bourgeoisie (it has relinquished its organising functions to the salaried managers and supervisors, even to teams of workers).

Classes also differ from one another according to the size and source of their social income. This distinction between classes is undoubtedly of great importance, but it is still not the defining factor. We can see this quite easily if we ask ourselves the question: Why do various sources of income exist and consequently various conditions for the existence of classes? The chief reason lies in their position in the system of social production. At first sight it may appear, as Marx said, that a class is formed by people having common sources of income. But this view does not go to the bottom of class relationships; what it assumes to be the main and determining relationships are, in fact, a form of distribution that depends on the relations of production. If we consider only the sources and sizes of income, we cannot correctly define classes and distinguish them from the multiple social strata and groups that also may receive their income from various sources. Under capitalism, for instance, workers in the same occupation have different sources of income: some clerical workers receive their wages from private employers, others from the state. Highly skilled workers are paid more than unskilled labourers. But does this give grounds for treating them as separate classes?

Class divisions run right through social life from top to bottom, affecting the whole system of social relations. These relations are divided into the "material" and the "ideological". But what kind of relations are established between classes — material or ideological? The answer is both. Classes are connected by certain economic relations which enable the exploiting classes to appropriate the labour of the exploited. The sum-total of these relations forms the class structure of society and constitutes the material, economic basis of the class struggle. The relations between classes, however, are not confined to the economic field; they acquire their most concentrated expression in political life. Finally, the relations between classes, the class struggle, are revealed in the sphere of ideology, in the intellectual life of society. As the founders of Marxism noted, the opposition between the proletariat and the bourgeoisie, which is rooted in the production relations of capitalism, affects the whole of social life, the living conditions of these classes, their domestic relations, and also the fact that the workers have different ideas and notions, morals and moral principles, and conduct different policies from those of the bourgeoisie. Such differences characterising the position of members of classes in everyday life, in education and culture, their ideas, beliefs and social psychology etc., are derived from economic relations.

Besides class distinctions in society, there are other social distinctions, for example, the distinction between town and country, that is, in the final analysis between the population engaged in industrial and agricultural work, and also distinctions between people engaged in physical or mental labour.

The division between town and country splits the whole population into two parts. This division has unique features in every class formation. For example, in feudal society the classes of peasants and the feudal lords were concentrated mainly in the countryside, whereas the towns were the centres of the artisans, the traders, the emerging bourgeoisie. In capitalist society all social classes are represented, although to a different degree, both in the town and in the country. Hence the division of the bourgeoisie and the petty bourgeoisie into urban and rural, the division of the working class into the urban and rural proletariat.

Group distinctions expressing the existence of smaller groups within classes are also considered social distinctions. For example, the bourgeoisie itself is divided into small, medium and big capitalists, depending on the amount of capital that they own.

There may also exist in society more or less significant groups of people that do not belong to any definite class (such, for example, are students who live off state grants, or police officers, who are salaried employees but whose role in the system of capitalist production is to protect the private property of the capitalists) and also the declassed people, who have lost their connection with their own class (for example, the lumpen-proletariat under capitalism, which consists of people who have no definite occupation and no desire to acquire one and who live by preying on the working class and the petty-bourgeoisie — pimps, swindlers, beggars, petty thieves, etc.).

Among diverse social distinctions, the main and definitive are class distinctions. First, they spring from the deepest foundations of society, that is, directly from the relations of people to the means of production, from the essence of the production relations, which determine all other social relations. Second, classes are the most powerful and usually the most numerous social groups, whose interrelations and struggle exert a decisive influence on the whole history of society, on its entire social, political and ideological life.

Bourgeois sociologists often attempt to dissolve the concept of "class" into the more general concept of the "socioeconomic group", defined by income level, and to replace the division of capitalist society into classes by a division into social layers, "strata" (such terms as "strata" and "stratification", borrowed from geology to denote the division of society into various layers, usually imply a certain hierarchy). All kinds of criteria are used to determine the composition of the various strata, such as occupation, wealth, education, place of residence and so on, but no emphasis is placed on the main and decisive factor — the place people occupy in the capitalist system of production, and therefore their relation to the means of production. It is this which determines their share of social wealth and the way they receive it. As Lenin wrote: "The fundamental criterion by which classes are distinguished is the place they occupy in social production, and, consequently, the relation in which they stand to the means of production".[7]

Bourgeois sociology analyses classes in terms of occupational categories and income statistics (and thus reaches the conclusion that the great majority of workers in the advanced capitalist countries are part of a white-collar occupational and middle-income socioeconomic group, and hence are "middle class".) By contrast with this superficial method, Marxism holds that *classes form in relation to one another and are fundamentally defined by the place they occupy in the system of social production and by their relationship to the means of production*. Thus, for example, the bourgeoisie is not simply a group of businessmen with a lot of money, nor is the proletariat just a mass of poor people with lousy jobs. Rather, these two classes are defined by their specific relation *to each other* in the capitalist system of social production. The capitalists own and control the means of production and subsistence, while the proletariat owns nothing but its labour-power, as a result of which the capitalists live by buying the commodity labour-power while the proletariat lives by selling this commodity to the capitalists.

The Marxist approach to classes is designed to uncover the actual exploitative and oppressive relations between classes which give rise to the *class struggle* between them that propels history forward. By contrast, bourgeois sociology determines classes in isolation from one another, by means of income size or occupation, and thus obscures the exploitative and oppressive content of the relations between classes in capitalist society, and therefore obscures the material basis for the struggle between them.

2. Social Structure and How It Changes

The sum-total of classes, social layers and groups — the system of their relationship — forms the social structure of society.

In analysing society's social structure, Marxism distinguishes between the basic and non-basic classes. The *basic classes* are those whose existence is engendered by the prevailing mode of production and without which it would be inconceivable. The basic contradiction of the given mode of production is expressed in the interrelationship and struggle between these classes. *Every antagonistic mode of production is characterised by two basic classes.*

Under the tributary ("Asiatic") mode of production, the basic classes were, on the one hand, the priestly and military nobility headed by a priest- or warrior-king and, on the other, the members of the village communes, i.e., the peasantry. All land and water resources — the decisive means of production — were owned by the king, who confronted the peasants as their landlord and sovereign. All nobles, from the king down to his local governors, lived on tribute from the village communes either in the form of surplus labour or in the form of surplus products.

In the countries dominated by the slave-owning mode of production (ancient Greece and the Roman empire) the two basic classes were the slave-owners and the slaves. The former possessed not only the means of production but also the labourer, who was regarded merely as an instrument of production. The Roman author Marcus Terentius Varro in his treatise on agriculture divided the implements for tilling the fields into three categories: "... implements possessed of speech, implements that emit inarticulate sounds and dumb implements; the speaking implements are slaves, those that emit inarticulate sounds are oxen, and the dumb implements are wagons".[8]

Under the feudal mode of production, the two basic classes were the feudal landowners (including the higher clergy) and the serfs. The serfs were entitled to the use of a small farm and certain instruments of production. But the feudal lords were the owners of the main means of production — the land, and it was this that allowed them to appropriate the peasant's surplus labour. The serfs were not regarded as completely the property of their feudal lord; the latter could not buy or sell them (unless the lord sold his lands). The feudal lord appropriated the peasant's surplus product either by means of corvée (payment in work), by means of quit-rent (payment in produce) or, in the period of the decay of feudalism, in the form of money rent.

Under the capitalist mode of production, the two basic classes are the bourgeoisie and the proletariat. The direct producers, the wage-workers, are legally free but are deprived of ownership of the means of production. Unlike the members of the village commune in the tributary mode of production or the serfs under feudalism, the wage-workers do not even have possession or use of the means of production. They can get access to the means of subsistence only by selling their labour-power to a capitalist. They are thus economically dependent upon the capitalists. For this reason, Marx and Engels called capitalist relations of exploitation a system of hired (or wage) slavery.

In the tributary, slave-owning and feudal societies, class distinctions were strengthened with the help of the state by dividing the population into hereditary castes or estates. In ancient India, for example, the population was divided into four castes: the Brahmans (noble priestly families), the Kshatriya (military nobility), the Vaisya (the members of the village communes) and the Sudra (the lowest section of society — people excluded from the commune). The caste division was hallowed by the Hindu religion (the latter believed that the god Brahma had created the Brahmans from his mouth, the Kshatriya from his arms, the Vaisya from his thighs and the Sudras from his feet).

In slave-owning societies and also in feudal society, the population was divided into castes, the law prescribing certain rights and obligations for each caste. The castes (or "estates") were formed on the basis of the class division but did not entirely correspond to it, since they introduced an element of the hierarchy of power and legal privilege. Thus, in ancient Rome the free population was divided into patricians (noble families) and plebeians (commoners).

Alongside the dominant relations of production, class-divided formations may still preserve survivals of previous modes of production or contain within them embryos of a new mode of production. This explains the existence of *non-basic or transitional classes*. Under the tributary mode of production, there existed slaves (employed mainly in non-productive household duties), minor officials (the scribes), private merchants and usurers, as well as craftsmen working for the nobility for wages in kind (rations). In addition, local nobles, who collected the tribute from the village communes, repeatedly sought to their assert legal title to the land under their jurisdiction, and therefore ownership of the tribute made by the village communities in their provinces. However, because the centralised despotic state had certain vital economic functions such as maintaining water control and irrigation projects, the development of private landlordship, by reducing the state's revenues, undermined the state's ability to perform these economic functions. When the central government could no longer finance these public works and they thus fell into disrepair, agricultural production sharply declined, making the tribute that peasants paid to local private landlords unbearable.

The result was usually a political crisis which ended with the overthrow of the reigning dynasty, usually by way of a peasant uprising, and the emergence of a new dynasty which brought the local governors to heel or replaced them with new governors. (This, for example, was the cause of the periodic peasant wars in China, which resulted in the replacement of one dynasty by another, the military commander of the peasant armies installing himself as the new "Son of Heaven", i.e., emperor.)

In slave-owning societies there existed merchants, moneylenders, small free peasant farmers, free craftsmen, wage-workers (principally as merchant seamen), as well as a great number of declassed elements living off state handouts. In feudal society, there existed in the towns social classes comprising craftsmen organised in guilds and corporations, merchants and so on. The guild craftsmen became exploiters, and their apprentices — the exploited mass of workers. Big landowners employing both capitalist and pre-capitalist forms of exploiting the peasants continued to exist for a long time in capitalist society.

In most capitalist countries there is the non-basic class of the petty bourgeoisie, comprising peasants, craftsmen, small traders and small property owners — a numerically significant section of society who play a considerable part in the political struggle. Economically they hold an intermediate position between the bourgeoisie and the proletariat. The fact that they are owners of private property brings them closer to the bourgeoisie (although, unlike the unearned private capitalist property, theirs is usually earned property, based on personal labour); but they are also linked with the proletariat by being toilers themselves and experiencing the oppression of capital.

The basic and non-basic classes are closely interdependent since, in the course of their historical development, the basic classes become non-basic, and vice versa. The basic classes degenerate into non-basic classes when the dominant relations of production which lie at the foundation of a given mode of production are supplanted by new dominant relations of production. The rise of new relations of production transforms non-basic classes into basic classes once those new relations of production have been consolidated as a distinct mode of production.

The capitalist mode of production is unique in that, over time, it simplifies the class structure of society, polarising it between a numerically smaller and smaller ruling class and a growing mass of proletarians. In the middle of the 19th century the bourgeoisie was rather numerous because the instruments of labour were owned mainly by individual capitalists. In England this class constituted 8% of the able-bodied population; in other countries the proportion was even larger, while the army of hired labour did not account for more than half of the able-bodied population.

The development of monopoly capitalism brought with it an unprecedented concentration of production and centralisation of capital, particularly since the second world war. The numbers of the bourgeoisie in relation to the population have decreased owing to the monopolies' crushing many small and medium-size capitalists. It now numbers between 1% and 4% of the population of the highly developed capitalist countries. At the same time, the power and wealth of the monopoly bourgeoisie in these countries have multiplied. Thus just 1% of families in the US own about 80% of all industrial stock.

Under pre-monopoly capitalism, the bourgeoisie consisted primarily of individual owners of enterprises, while in the 20th century joint-stock companies became the dominant form of capitalist property. Initially, company shares were a means of attracting capital and the savings of the well-to-do sections of the petty bourgeoisie in order to concentrate and invest these funds in the interests of the major shareholders. In time, however, the stock market became flooded with numerous securities, and thus many workers became minor shareholders. Bourgeois economists immediately interpreted this fact as a transformation of capitalist corporations into "public property" and as the advent of "people's capitalism". In reality, by becoming a shareholder a person did not turn into a capitalist and, moreover, had absolutely no say in running the corporation whose stock he or she possessed. The actual purpose of companies going "public" was to attract workers' savings so that they could then be used in the interests of the major shareholders.

The emergence of monopoly capitalism led to a separation of the ownership of capital from managerial functions. In the wake of this development, some bourgeois sociologists asserted that a "managerial class" was depriving the capitalists of the actual power and control of their companies, and that therefore the question of ownership had become irrelevant. These allegations, however, do not reflect the actual situation. Firstly, the monopoly bourgeoisie exercises its power by taking a direct part in the managing of banks and industrial companies. Members of the richest families sit on the boards of directors of industrial and commercial companies and banks. Besides, they have promoted their cronies to the corporations' high administrative positions. Secondly, the top managers of major corporations and banks (the business executives, chief executive officers), where they are not recruited from bourgeois families, are drawn into the bourgeoisie. While company presidents, vice-presidents, CEOs and other senior executives are salaried employees, unlike lower and middle managers, their salaries and bonuses far exceed the market value of the qualified work they perform, and hence are a specific form of their participation in the appropriation of the surplus value created by other people's labour. Their salaries and bonuses enable them to accumulate capital, including through large share purchases (which are, in any case, often part of their "salary package").

The army of hired labour confronting capital has grown considerably over the last two centuries, its ranks having been swelled mainly by numerical reduction of the petty bourgeoisie in both town and country who have been driven out of business.

As capitalism develops, the petty bourgeoisie disintegrates; a small portion of it adds to its wealth and joins the capitalists, while the larger part goes bankrupt and assumes the position of either economically dependent property-owners or semi-proletarians and proletarians. This is a regular process based on the advantages of large-scale production over small-scale production, on the law of the concentration and centralisation of capital discovered by Marx.

But Marxists have never claimed that the trend towards proletarianisation of the middle classes must lead to their complete disappearance. As Lenin observed, the development of capitalist production follows a contradictory course: "A number of new 'middle strata' are inevitably brought into existence again and again by capitalism (appendages to the factory, work at home, small workshops scattered all over the country to meet the requirement of big industries, such as the bicycle and automobile industries, etc.). These new small producers are just as inevitably being cast again into the ranks of the proletariat."[9]

Monopoly capitalism undermines the "old" middle class consisting of small farmers, shopkeepers, artisans, petty manufacturers and self-employed professionals (doctors, lawyers, teachers etc.), pushing part of them into the ranks of the proletariat. At the same time, it produces a "new" middle class that works directly for capital, consisting principally of salaried technical, marketing, managerial, financial, medical, scientific and legal experts whose intermediary position between the bourgeoisie and the proletariat rests upon their monopoly over advanced educational training. However, monopoly capitalism also has a long-term tendency to proletarianise these occupations by commodifying the product of their labour and by undermining their monopoly of skills.

The army of hired labour, "liberated" by capital from any, even small, ownership of the means of production, constitutes in the developed capitalist countries the overwhelming majority of the population — more than 75% of the economically active population. On a world scale, wage-earners number more than one billion.

Bourgeois ideologists often assert that in the context of the development of semi-automated, computerised production the proletariat is destined to disappear, first, because of the decrease in the numbers of people engaged in industrial production and the increase in those employed in the service industries and, secondly, because of the increase in non-manual labour ("white-collar" employees in general).

It must be noted first of all, however, that bourgeois sociologists and economists wrongly associate the concept of the "proletarian" exclusively with the manual worker. Marx himself introduced the concept of the collective labourer, comprising manual and brain workers.

In defining the working class, one has to proceed from determining *its place in the system of social production*, its *relationship to the means of production* and its *role in the social organisation of labour*. For Marxism, the working class consists of all those people (as well as their dependents) who, firstly, are economically compelled by their lack of ownership of the means of production to sell their labour-power for a wage or salary and, secondly, if they are hired, create surplus value by their labour or enable their employer to appropriate surplus value created by other producers.

The white-collar employees are not a separate class; most of them are simply wage-workers employed in non-industrial occupations. The increase in their numbers since the 19th century was enhanced by the development of the sphere of services (transport, communications, trade, credit, banks and insurance, cultural institutions, public administration and so on). This sphere also reproduces the structure of capitalist society. People employed in services do not stand outside the class division of society; they become part of those classes into which people engaged in industry and agriculture are divided.

The rapid growth of white-collar employees, which considerably exceeds that of the able-bodied population as a whole, does not testify to the "deproletarianisation" of the population or to the emergence of a new intellectual "middle class" absorbing the proletariat, but to capital's increased need for that type of labour-power.

The term "intellectuals" is generally used to denote the section of people professionally engaged in work of an intellectual nature. It may also include a considerable number of white-collar workers, but not all of them, of course, because most are not employed in intellectual work as such but perform various purely technical functions. Moreover, computerisation has mechanised much clerical and sales work, thereby converting many white-collar workers into machine operators with conditions of work that are similar to those of growing numbers of industrial workers.

Thus we see that the class structure of capitalist society comprises various non-basic classes and intermediate layers besides the basic classes. What is more, the classes are not closed groups of people like the hierarchical estates of feudal times. Individuals are constantly moving from some groups or social strata to others.

Bourgeois sociologists try to present this fluidity in capitalist society as the disappearance of class divisions. Some of them maintain that classes are in constant movement with people entering them and going up and down inside them, like lifts in a large building. Of course, there is far greater social mobility in capitalist conditions than under feudalism with its numerous hierarchical barriers. But class barriers do not disappear under capitalism, and class contradictions increase. Whereas in the early stages of the development of capitalism some members of the landed nobility, rich peasants etc. were able to penetrate the ranks of the bourgeoisie, today it is no easier to enter the circle of the monopolists than it was in the age of feudal absolutism for a petty-bourgeois to gain admission to the nobility. The US economist Ferdinand Lundberg in his book *The Rich and the Super-Rich* calculated that in the 1960s there were 200,000 very rich people in the United States, most of whom belong to the 500 richest families. More than 60% of them had inherited their wealth.

Although the class status of certain individuals may change, this does not eliminate the distinctions between classes, which form the social structure of society. Moreover, the changes occurring in the social status of the masses under capitalism — the ruining of small business operators, the proletarianisation of intellectual labour, the growth of unemployment among the workers — only broaden the gap between the basic classes of capitalist society.

3. Class Interests and Class Struggle

Class struggle has persisted throughout the history of society, ever since the collapse of the primitive commune. The age of capitalism brought further intensification of the class struggle.

What is it that causes the conflict between classes? Is it historically inevitable? Bourgeois historians and sociologists maintain that it is the result of a "misunderstanding", a "mutual failure of communication" between classes, the misguided policies of the ruling sections of society, "incitement by evil-minded elements" and so on. Many of them make an appeal for social and moral values capable of uniting the warring classes. But to express hopes that it is possible to unite classes with irreconcilable, antagonistic interests with the help of even the "best" ideas or moral values implies a false, idealist approach to the question. In reality there can be no stable social, political and moral unity in a society where classes are thrown into opposition by the conditions of their economic existence.

The class struggle is evoked by the diametrically opposed social position and contradictory interests of the different classes. What are class interests? What is behind them? It is sometimes asserted that class interest is determined by the consciousness of the members of the given class. This is incorrect. The working class of any given capitalist country may not be aware of its fundamental interests and may restrict itself to fighting for certain reforms that do not challenge the position and basic interests of the capitalist class (increased wages, reduction of working hours). But this does not mean that its fundamental class interests do not exist.

Class interest is determined, not by the consciousness of the class, but by its position and role in the system of social production. The proletariat's fundamental class interest is to abolish private property since the proletariat is a propertyless class and private property is the root source of its exploitation and oppression.

The bourgeoisie and the proletariat are antagonistic classes because their interests are diametrically opposed and irreconcilable. The same was true of the basic classes in the societies that preceded capitalism: tribute-collecting nobles and peasant farmers, slave-owners and slaves, feudal lords and serfs.

There may be antagonistic relations not only between the opposed classes of one socioeconomic formation but also between the classes of different formations, one of which is superseding the other. Such, for example, were the relations between the bourgeoisie and the feudal aristocracy in the period when bourgeois methods of exploitation came into conflict with those of feudalism. But because both classes were exploiters, they were able to unite. Feudal methods of exploitation merged with bourgeois methods in the economies of several countries, and in the political field the bourgeoisie and the landowners often formed a common front, particularly when faced with a common enemy — the mass of the people led by the proletariat.

Whereas the opposition or divergence of class interests forms the basis of the struggle between classes, coincidence of the interests of different classes creates a possibility of their working together. In the situation created by contemporary capitalism, there are objective conditions for combined action on the part of the proletariat and the bulk of the rural and urban middle classes against the monopolies. As the most revolutionary, organised and united class, the proletariat is the natural leader of any alliance of these groups.

In the class struggle, even radically different social classes, when faced by a common enemy, may find that their interests temporarily coincide. Thus, the struggle for national independence in the colonies, for example, may provide grounds for combined action on the part of the mass of the working people (working class, peasantry, urban petty bourgeoisie) and the national bourgeoisie. But in such a situation each class acts according to its own class interests. This is why Lenin demanded "... a precise analysis of those varied interests of different classes that coincide in certain definite, limited common aims".[10]

Bourgeois sociologists and the advocates of class-collaborationist reformism deny the necessity of the class struggle. They assert that the driving force of progress is "class cooperation". But in point of fact, the driving force of development of class-divided societies is the struggle between the classes. Materialist dialectics tells us that the source of all development lies in the conflict of opposing forces and trends. In class society, this law of dialectics manifests itself in the class struggle.

The class struggle, for example, exerts a profound influence on the development of the productive forces. One of the incitements to introduce machinery was the desire of the capitalists to break the resistance of the workers, to force them to submit to the compulsory rhythm of factory production. Marx observed that in Britain, "... since 1825, the invention and application of machinery has been simply the result of the war between workers and employers".[11] The workers' resistance prevented the capitalists from multiplying their profits mainly by increasing working hours and forced them to concentrate their efforts on reducing the amount of necessary working time by increasing labour productivity, by employing more efficient machinery. But the Marxist proposition that the class struggle is the driving force of development of class-divided societies does not imply that it is the prime cause of development of the productive forces. The class structure of society and the class struggle it produces are themselves determined by the development of the productive forces and production relations.

The class struggle acts as the driving force of historical development primarily because it is the means by which an obsolete social system is transformed into a new and higher system. The conflict between the new productive forces and the obsolete relations of production finds its expression in an antagonism between classes. This conflict is resolved by a social revolution, which is the highest manifestation of the class struggle.

The class struggle acts as the motivator of historical events not only in an epoch of social revolution but also in so-called peaceful epochs. The reforms, the minor improvements lauded by the liberal and social-democratic reformists are, in fact, a by-product of the class struggle. Lenin contrasted the socialist theory of the class struggle as the only real mover of history to the bourgeois theory of cooperation between classes as the driving force of social progress. He wrote:

According to the theory of socialism, i.e., of Marxism ... the real driving force of history is the revolutionary class struggle. According to the theory of bourgeois philosophers, the driving force of progress is the unity of all elements in society who realise the "imperfections" of certain of its institutions. The first theory is materialist; the second is idealist. The first is revolutionary; the second is reformist. The first serves as the basis for the tactics of the proletariat in modern capitalist countries. The second serves as the basis of the tactics of the bourgeoisie.[12]

4. Forms of Class Struggle and Organisation

The class struggle may vary greatly in character and form. It occurs in various spheres of social life — in economic relations, in politicsand ideology; it may have different degrees of intensity, from passive opposition to a hostile class to active attack on its positions and drastic clashes; it may be hidden or open, spontaneous or conscious. The substitution of some forms of class struggle for others depends on changes in the situation, on the degree of intensity of the contradictions between the interests of the various classes, on the development of each class.

The forms of the class struggle are connected with the forms of class organisation. This comes out very clearly in the example of the class struggle of the proletariat. The working class conducts its struggle against the capitalist exploiters in three main forms: economic, political and ideological.

The economic struggle is, historically, the first form of the proletariat's struggle against the capitalists. In all countries the workers' struggle began by their defending their immediate daily economic interests. They fought for higher wages, reduced working hours, improved of working conditions. It was in this struggle that the proletariat's first organisations arose — the trade unions that were to become its school of class struggle. Strikes, partial or general, are a vitally important means of economic struggle.

Contemporary bourgeois ideologists argue that today the working class of the developed capitalist countries is "integrated" in capitalist society and "has a stake" in that society because it receives from it some of the good things of life. However, they conceal the fact that all these good things have been produced by the working class itself and that only its persistent struggle has restored to it a part of what was created by its own labour. As in the old days, the workers, whose productivity has now grown so much, still do not receive a considerable part of the wealth they create, are still cheated of the surplus value.

The economic struggle not only counteracts the process of impoverishment of the proletariat; it also gives it the organisation to deal with wider revolutionary tasks. If the workers did not fight the rapacity of capital, they would be degraded, as Marx put it, to one level mass of broken wretches past salvation. "By cowardly giving way in their everyday conflict with capital, they would certainly disqualify themselves for the initiating of any larger movement."[13]

Significant though it may be, the economic struggle is not in itself enough to do away with capitalist exploitation and oppression, because it leaves intact the capitalists' ownership of the means of production and their political power. It can achieve only occasional concessions from the bourgeoisie. Consequently, any attempt to give pre-eminence to the economic struggle, and hence to confine the proletariat's struggle to efforts to secure reforms within the capitalist system, is essentially detrimental for the interests of the working class because it blocks the proletariat from attaining a revolutionary consciousness. To achieve this there must be *political struggle* on the part of the proletariat.

In contrast to the economic struggle, the final objectives of which never go beyond satisfying the workers' daily socioeconomic needs, the political struggle is waged to promote the proletariat's fundamental class interests, since these can be fulfilled only by way of a radical political transformation.

Political struggle takes many forms, ranging from participation in elections to parliaments, local councils and other state organisations to mass demonstrations and political strikes (strikes to force a change in government policy or to force a change of government), from the peaceful use of the parliamentary platform to the revolutionary struggle for power. The chief objective of the proletariat's political struggle is to overthrow the political power of the capitalist class and establish its own power, the dictatorship of the working class, and, once this power has been won, to consolidate it as the instrument for building socialist society.

Historically, political struggle developed after the economic struggle, but it ranks first in importance. The reasons for this are:

1. Economic struggle implies that the exploiters can be defeated by individual detachments of the working class (such as the workers of a particular enterprise or industry), whereas in the political struggle workers are ranged against the collective representative of the capitalist class — its state power.

2. In the economic struggle, the workers defend their own immediate, daily interests, sometimes the interests of separate groups of the working class, but in the political struggle they are defending their class interests.

3. In the economic struggle, if it is conducted separately from the political struggle, the workers acquire only a trade-union consciousness, that is, an understanding of

their own narrow occupational interests, and seek only to achieve reforms within the system of capitalist rule and exploitation; in the political struggle, led by a Marxist party, the working class can acquire a truly class, proletarian, socialist, consciousness, an understanding of its fundamental class interests, of its historical mission and revolutionary objectives.

4. The economic struggle provides the proletariat with the broad organisations such as trade unions, which devote their attention to one issue or a small number of issues; the political struggle demands that the proletariat create its own political party, consisting of those who have an understanding of the proletariat's fundamental class interests and a clear program for how to realise them.

From what has been said, it will be clear that the economic struggle of the workers is only a weak, embryonic, form of their class struggle against the capitalist exploiters. The fully developed form of the proletarian class struggle is the political struggle. As Marx noted:

> The political movement of the working class has as its ultimate object, of course, the conquest of political power for this class, and this naturally requires previous organisation of the working class developed up to a certain point and arising precisely from its economic struggle.
>
> On the other hand, however, every movement in which the working class comes out as a class against the ruling classes and tries to coerce them by pressure from without is a political movement. For instance, the attempt in a particular factory or even in a particular trade to force a shorter working day out of individual capitalists by strikes, etc., is a purely economic movement. On the other hand, the movement to force through an eight-hour, etc., law, is a political movement ...
>
> Where the working class is not yet far enough advanced in its organisation to undertake a decisive campaign against the collective power, i.e., the political power of the ruling classes, it must at any rate be trained for this by continual agitation against this power and by a hostile attitude toward the policies of the ruling classes. Otherwise it will remain a plaything in their hands ...[14]

To rouse the working class for a political struggle, it must be made aware of its fundamental class interests. The theory of scientific socialism gives the working class this awareness. It reveals the laws of social development and the laws of the development of capitalism and shows the working class the ways and means of struggle for freedom from exploitation and oppression, for socialism. The theoretical, ideological struggle of the working class, of its parties, is aimed at freeing the workers' minds from bourgeois ideas and prejudices. The introduction of Marxist ideology into the spontaneous working-class movement raises it to a higher level of development. So the ideological form of a class struggle is just as essential for final victory of the proletariat as other forms of the class struggle.

In the course of this struggle, classes acquire political and ideological shape. Their complex path of development transforms them from a passive object of history into its conscious and active subject, its makers. From being classes "in themselves" they become classes "for themselves".

"Economic conditions", wrote Marx, "had first transformed the mass of the people of the country into workers. The combination of capital has created for this mass a common situation, common interests. This mass is thus already a class as against capital, but not yet for itself. In the struggle ... this mass becomes united and constitutes itself as a class for itself".[15]

In the formation of a class as an actively operating subject, as a class "for itself", an important role is played by the emergence of the corresponding political organisations, particularly *political parties*. The class struggle finds its most definite form of expression in the struggle of political parties. Political parties express the interests of classes and lead their struggle.

Parties differ from classes in that they (1) never embrace the whole of a class but only part of it; and (2) they are the result of the conscious joining together of the advanced, most politically active representatives of the given class in the name of definite political ideas and aims, whereas classes themselves arise spontaneously as a result of the economic development of society. The party therefore arises after the class has taken shape.

Bourgeois ideologists, and also reformists and revisionists, try to obscure the connection between parties and classes. Many bourgeois sociologists follow the German sociologist Max Weber in dividing society into three independent orders: economic, social and political. Classes are placed in the economic order. The so-called status groups, which are distinguished by the degree of respect they command in society, make up the social order, while parties are assigned to the political order. This approach to the question offers the possibility of conceiving parties as isolated from classes. Of course, the division of society into parties does not usually coincide with the division into classes. A class is quite often represented not by one but by several parties expressing, along with the general class interests, the interests of separate groups within the class.

The proletarian party is the advanced, politically organised and active part of the working class, its political vanguard. The majority of workers are too physically and mentally crushed by their conditions of work to be able to rise to the level of class consciousness that distinguishes the vanguard; even a trade union, a simpler kind of organisation more easily understood by the less developed sections of the workers, cannot take in the whole proletariat. No-one, therefore, should cherish the illusion that under capitalism (or even in the conditions of the transition from capitalism to socialism) the dividing line between the vanguard of the working class and the whole class can automatically disappear. This line will be erased only with the achievement of a socialist society.

All other organisations of the proletariat — trade unions, cultural and educational associations — serve as necessary means in the class struggle, but they cannot solve the fundamental problem, the problem of abolishing the capitalist system and carrying out a socialist revolution. Only a Marxist party, which is the *highest form of class political organisation of the proletariat*, is capable of uniting the activities of all proletarian organisations and guiding them to the one goal of socialist revolution.

But there are reformist parties as well as revolutionary parties of the working class in many capitalist countries. Reformism is not an accidental phenomena in the working-class movement. It is an inevitable product of the spontaneous workers' movement. However, two different forms of reformism need to be distinguished.

One form recognises the antagonism of interests between the workers and their employers and that the workers will never get anything from the capitalists without a struggle. However, its horizon is limited to the attainment of improvements in the workers' wages, working conditions and democratic freedoms within the framework of the capitalist system. This form of reformism — "class-struggle reformism" — arises spontaneously out of the direct and immediate experience of the majority of the working class.

The other form of reformism within the working-class movement arises out of monopoly capitalism's granting, from its super-profits, of more secure conditions of employment to a minority of workers (usually the skilled, male, unionised workers), thus cushioning them from the shocks of the capitalist boom-bust cycle and providing them with material advantages in the competition between workers. The privileges accorded to the "protected" upper strata of the working class — the labour aristocracy — tend to spontaneously generate a perspective of *class-collaborationist* reformism among these workers, i.e., the view that the interests of capitalists and wage-workers are fundamentally harmonious, not antagonistic, and that workers can improve their living standards by collaborating with the capitalists to make their businesses more profitable. This spontaneous class-collaborationist outlook provides a stable basis for the domination of the leadership of the mass workers' organisations (the trade unions) by petty-bourgeois careerists, the labour bureaucracy. The latter act as merchants, haggling with the capitalists over the terms of sale of the commodity labour-power. Their privileges and possibilities for social advancement are dependent on the continued existence of their ability to function as intermediaries between the wage-workers and the capitalist employers. They *consciously* promote class-collaborationist views within the working-class movement as a whole, actively subordinating it to the bourgeoisie in both politics and ideology.

The heterogeneous nature of the working class leads inevitably to divergence of views and aspirations among its different sections, and every turn in the development of the class struggle intensifies these divergences, evoking both ultraleft and opportunist deviations and trends. The dialectics of the revolutionary movement are such that its very growth, the involvement of the wider sections of the working class and particularly other (for example, petty bourgeois) social strata, which is in itself a positive phenomenon, may at the same time help to cultivate both ultraleft sectarianism and opportunism in the socialist movement.

Opportunism in the socialist movement is the adaptation of the ideology and politics of the movement to the reformist consciousness and politics of the spontaneous workers' movement, the tendency to efface the qualitative differences in ideology, politics and organisation between the two. Ultraleft sectarianism involves attempts by small groups of leftists to substitute their own actions and dogmatic preconceptions in place of the difficult and painstaking task of winning the mass of workers to revolutionary politics.

Opportunist tendencies and ultraleft sectarianism have the same class roots. They arise from the impatience, inconsistency and vacillation of radicalised petty-bourgeois intellectuals and workers under their influence. The psychology of petty-bourgeois radicalism leads people to adopt super-revolutionary catchwords and adventurist actions and thus to abstain from involvement in the mass struggle because it does not measure up to their romantic ideals and dogmatic preconceptions. When such super-radicalism does not work, the petty-bourgeois revolutionists capitulate to the reformist consciousness and politics of the spontaneous workers' movement.

Internal stratification within the working class and the class-collaborationist politics of the labour bureaucracy are used by the bourgeoisie as a chief means of weakening the working-class movement. But although the bourgeoisie in certain countries may temporarily be able to slow down the development of the class struggle of the proletariat, it has no power to stop it.

The class struggle is the basic law of development of class societies, and its driving force. This law discovered by Marx and Engels consists in the fact that "... all historical struggles, whether they proceed in the political, religious, philosophical or some other ideological domain, are in fact only the more or less clear expression of struggles of social classes, and that the existence of these classes and thereby the collisions, too, between them are in turn conditioned by the degree of development of their economic position, by the mode of their production and of their exchange determined by it".[16] This law, as Engels put it, is as important to historical science, to understanding of the development of class society, as the law of the conversion of energy is to natural science. ❦

CHAPTER 8

THE POLITICAL ORGANISATION OF SOCIETY

Classes and class antagonisms complicates the structure of social life. New forms of social relations, political and legal, arise. Political activity comprises a number of organisations and institutions that were unknown in pre-class societies. The most important of them is the state, which is the organisation of political power of the ruling class. In class society, political parties and other public organisations arise that are designed to win or maintain political power, to fight for the interests of this or that class. All these organisations and institutions, taken together, constitute the *political organisation of society*. The political organisation of any class society may thus be defined as *a system of institutions and organisations regulating the political relations between human communities (e.g., nations), classes and states*. The political life of society embraces political institutions and relations, political consciousness and activities.

1. TRANSITION FROM THE NON-POLITICAL (COLLECTIVIST) ORGANISATION OF SOCIETY TO ITS POLITICAL ORGANISATION

In primitive collectivist society, social relations were regulated by the force of habit, custom and tradition embodying thousands of years of life and work in common within the clans and tribes that constituted the form of human community of this stage of social development.

The appearance of more developed forms of social division of labour and private ownership of the means of production rendered the tribal organs of administration unfit for the new conditions. As Engels observed, the tribal system of administration "was burst asunder by the division of labour and by its result, the division of society into classes. Its place was taken by the *state*."[1]

Whereas the tribal organs of power rested on social ownership of the means of production of the primary human groups — clans and tribes — the state was to serve the interests that had arisen out of relations based on private ownership of the decisive means of production. Inasmuch as the means of production had become concentrated in the hands of a small group who used it to bend the direct producers to their will, the state represented and defended the interests of the exploiters against the labouring classes. Its appearance was a result of and objective indication of the splitting of society into large groups of people with different relations to the means of production in which one group exploited the labour of others. The irreconcilable nature of the class contradictions made it necessary for there to be an organisation of power which was no longer identified with the community as a whole. In place of the public power that represented the community of interests of the tribe, the state emerges as a public power that seems to "stand above society" and increasingly "alienates itself from society".

The state is characterised by three basic features or attributes.

First, it is a *special organisation of power to coerce*, in contrast to the direct organisation of the armed people which existed in tribal society. A feature of the state, as Lenin explained, is not its power to forcibly compel in general, which is to be found in some form or other in the organs of administration in any society, but the fact that it is a power that does not coincide with the armed organisation of the mass of population and is exercised by a special category of people. A permanent stratum of privileged officials (the civil and military bureaucracy), special contingents of armed people (army, police, secret police), and their corresponding physical appendages, e.g., prisons and other places of confinement — such are the essential components and instruments of state power.

Second, the state organisation of society presupposes the levying of *taxes* that are needed for the upkeep of the apparatus of power. As internal and external contradictions become more intense and the state apparatus grows, its maintenance swallows up more and more of the resources of society.

Third, the subjects of the state are divided not according to kinship relationships but on the basis of *territory*. The coercive power of the state is exercised directly over the inhabitants of a certain territory. The territorial division of people promotes the development of economic ties and the creation of political conditions for their regulation. The state protects the interests of the dominant class, the class that owns the decisive means of production, primarily within the boundaries of a given territory, keeping the labouring classes there in subjection. This is its main task inside the country. But it also protects the interests of the economically dominant class beyond the state frontiers, guarding its territory, wealth and population from incursions of the states of other exploiting classes or attempting to extend the territories under its control at the expense of neighbouring states or countries further afield that lack sufficient strength to resist. This is the external function of the state, which is subordinate to the main internal function.

The state is thus a *political superstructure on an economic basis*. It is the special organisation of power, of force, thanks to which a class (or, temporarily, an alliance of classes) becomes the ruling class, imposing its interests and will upon society as a whole. In normal times, i.e., outside of a social revolution or counterrevolution, the ruling class is the economically dominant class, the class that owns the decisive means of production. The essence of the state is thus determined by the relationship of the ruling class to the other classes. The state is *the organisation of the ruling class for the protection of its fundamental interests* and, above all, the relations of production through which this class appropriates the social surplus product. The basic function of the state within the social organism is to hold down the exploited classes, for which purpose it relies ultimately on force, on organs of coercion and violence (police, army, prison guards etc.). Every state is therefore a *class dictatorship*. "Dictatorship", Lenin pointed out, "is rule based directly upon force and unrestricted by any laws".[2] Whenever the fundamental interests of the ruling class are threatened by the oppressed classes, the ruling class defends its position through the use of organised violence (civil war), through rule unrestricted by any laws.

The internal activity of the state is not limited to this main function, however. As an organisation of the ruling class, it seeks to regulate also the relations between members of that class, in order to promote its unity in the struggle with the opposing classes. In some cases the state also regulates interrelations between the exploiting classes inasmuch as it defends their common interests (thus the feudal absolutist state, while expressing the interests of the serf-owning feudal landlords, also gave some protection to the merchants, to the emergent bourgeoisie). The state also has means (mainly legal) of regulating the whole system of social relations — ethnic (if the state exercises its power over ethnically diverse groups of people), family and so on, thus promoting the consolidation of a certain socioeconomic order. Finally, the state deals with a number of economic and cultural problems in the interests of the ruling class, or its politically dominant fraction.

The emergence and development of private property, of course, shifted the centre of gravity in the leadership of economic activity on to the property owners themselves and their private representatives. But in almost any society that has passed the primitive communal stage, there are certain needs of development of production and intellectual culture that the individual exploiter cannot and does not wish to deal with.

In capitalist society, particularly at the imperialist stage of its development, the activity of the state becomes ever more extensive. The capitalist state acts as a major property-owner and investor. It levies a third or more of the national income from the population in the form of taxes and redistributes it in favour of the owners of the big corporations and the banks (the financial oloigarchy) by means of a system of state subsidies, credits, state contracts and so on. As the process of material production becomes more and more complex, involving the use of increasingly sophisticated equipment, higher demands are placed on the cultural level of the work force and, consequently, on the system of public education which is partly, or even largely, financed and organised by the state.

Bourgeois ideologists cite the diversity of state activities as an argument for denying its class essence. They regard the origin of the state as mainly due to intellectual factors — mutual consent, the growing moral maturity of people who have "become aware" that social life cannot be organised without a public power. This approach implies that the "natural" condition of human existence is as atomised individuals and that without the state there could be no social life. It further implies that, having once arisen, the state must exist foreever.

Historical materialism, on the contrary, argues the historical character of the state, which is concerned with the class essence of state power.

The functions of the state, though diverse, are all subordinated to its main function, which expresses its class essence. No matter how we approach the state's activities, it turns out that these serve the interests of the ruling class. Thus, in building irrigation works the first states, the despotisms of ancient Egypt, India, China and the Near East were mainly concerned with the development of production in the interests of the extraction of tribute from the peasant-farmers for the benefit of an exploiting class of military and priestly nobles.

In contemporary bourgeois society the state, by using funds obtained from the population through taxation for subsidising "industry" and placing orders with it, by paying for researtch and development, enables the bourgeoisie to exploit the working people not only directly at their own enterprises but also indirectly, throughout the system of social production. By the same token, state expenditure on public education, which is met out of the taxes paid by working people, is mainly designed to prepare a sufficiently skilled labour force for the employers.

The state protects the property of the ruling class and its privileges through the *law*. In primitive communal society human relations were regulated by custom, tradition and morality (generally accepted norms of behaviour any violation of which evoked social condemnation). The appearance of private property and the divisdion of society into classes complicated social life and created a demand for standards of behaviour that could be forcibly imposed on the exploited classes.

Law is the sum total of standards of behaviour laid down in legal acts enforced by the state. Any violation of these standards evokes the intervention of the punitive organs, which apply forcible sanctions (execution, imprisonment, confiscation of possessions and income) on the offender. The state lays down in its legal acts the standards of conduct that are of vital importance to the ruling class and which secure the functioning of the social organism without any serious disturbances that might threaten the supremacy of the exploiters.

Law is the will of the ruling class embodied in legal acts. Therefore, like the state, law has a class character and is an instrument in the hands of the ruling class.

Law legitimises also the standards that regulate relations between property-owners themselves and provides the judicial sanction necessary for the "normal" functioning of economic relations. Every property-owner in dealing with other property-owners wants to safeguard his or her own interests, whether in the field of commerce, finance or anything else. The transfer of his or her property to his or her heir or another person also demand judicial regulation.

All these factors gave rise to the need to strengthen and supplement the objective relations of production that constitute the economic structure of society with legal acts. Law formulates the economic relations and the social relations dependent upon them, that is, the relations between classes (for example, no rights — legally recognised freedoms and immunities — for some and privileges for others, formal equality before the law), between families and the relationships among family members, between ethnic groups within the country, between citizens of the state and citizens of states etc. It also defines the legal status of all social institutions and organisations and legally specifies the position, rights and duties of individual citizens. Law embraces in some degree all aspects of the life of society, all forms of people's activities and all forms of social relations within class-divided society.

Just as the state cannot manage without law, so the law cannot function without the state, which enforces the legal norms. Law originated together with state and together with it will wither away when the causes that engendered it have disappeared.

With the emergence of the state and the law there came into being new forms of relations between people that had not been known in primitive communal society — *political* and *legal* relations, a political and legal superstructure upon the economic basis of exploitative relations of production. Political relations are, at bottom, relations between classes. But not all relations between classes may be regarded as political. When the workers sell their labour-power to the capitalist or even when they fight for increased wages or shorter working ours, these relations and this struggle are economic and not by any means political. But if the workers at even one workplace present demands to the collective representative of the capitalist class, to the bourgeois state, this is a political struggle, a demand for a change in the relationship between the classes.

Political relations between classes express in a concentrated form their fundamental economic interests. These relations, like all superstructural relations, take shape through the medium of people's consciousness. They are built up in accordance with political ideas and goals, with the ideas and views of political movements and parties. The policy of a class is the more or less conscious line of conduct of this class (or, at least, its class-conscious vanguard, i.e., that section of the class that is conscious of the class's fundamental interests) in relation to other classes and the state.

This line of conduct is pursued in the economic and cultural spheres, although in themselves these spheres may lie beyond the bounds of politics. Thus we can speak of the economic (trade and financial) policy of the bourgeoisie, which it pursues mainly though the medium of the state, of the policy of the bourgeoisie in the sphere of national relations, the sphere of public education, and so on. Of course, education is a sphere of culture, not of politics. But under capitalism, education is subordinated to the needs of capitalist production. This is, in fact, the essence of bourgeois policy in the sphere of public education.

It follows, then, that political relations in class society not only constitute a special sphere but also accompany all other relations in one form or another. In the broad sense of the term, political relations between classes, states and nations include legal relations. Every law passed by the state, every law enforcement measure is a political measure.

How does politics, and specifically its organised social form, affect the whole of society? How does politics influence economics?

Above all, the whole system of political relations expresses the economic relations of class society and is the only form in which these relations can function. It is because the economy cannot function and develop at a certain stage outside this form that it gives rise to politics.

Politics has a direct influence on economics through the economic policy of the ruling class, which is pursued mainly through the state's domestic policies (e.g., state subsidies and financial support of the major private property-owners, labour legislation); through its foreign policy (e.g., forcible seizure of new sources of labour, raw materials and markets); and finally through the "non-military" aspects of its foreign policy which are aimed at obtaining more favourable economic conditions for business activity, for investment of capital in other countries and for the export of commodities to foreign markets. Politics also influences the economy indirectly. It does so by supporting the socioeconomic system that engendered a given type of state or (in the case of the politics of revolutionary classes) by creating new political organisations that play a decisive role in the victory of new progressive economic relations over those that have become obsolete.

The active role of politics in relation to economics may, as Engels observed, proceed in three basic directions: either political factors operate in the same direction as economic development, in which case they accelerate it; or else they operate against the trend of economic development and retard it; or, finally, they slow down economic development in some directions and push it forward in others (the commonest, mixed type of influence).

For instance, the policy of the young revolutionary bourgeoisie in the epoch of the establishment of capitalism on the whole stimulated the development of the productive forces, although in most cases it sought compromises with the former ruling classes and thus to a certain extent held up economic development. The influence of the policy of the imperialist bourgeoisie on the economy can be ranked in the second category (the accelerated development of certain branches of the economy is mainly connected with war preparations).

"On the whole, the economic movement gets its way", wrote Engels, "but it has also to suffer reactions from the political movement which it itself established and endowed with relative independence".[3]

We must also note the undeniable increase of the role of politics, and particularly political organisation, in the life of society and its economic development today. There are many reasons for this: the development of social production and increased need for state regulation of economic activities and state support for finance capital; the increase in the number of conscious elements in social life, despite the spontaneous character of the development of bourgeois economy as a whole; the growth in the social weight of the working class and of the need of the imperialist bourgeioisie for political mechanisms to deceive it and to flatter and bribe its better organised sections.

2. Development of Political Organisation and Its Role in Social Life

In the course of history private property has changed its forms, and the types of class structure and modes of exploitation have changed with it, bringing in their train different political beliefs and relations — in short, different political organisations of society.

The limited division of labour within the village communities of river valleys of the ancient East and, at the same time, their dependence upon extensive irrigation works requiring extremely centralised state authority, gave rise in the countries of the Near East, India, China and Java to despotisms (states in which all the inhabitants, of whatever class, were completely subordinate to an absolute ruler). The state was the instrument through which the ruling class (consisting of a military-priestly nobility headed by the despotic ruler — the "god-king", the "divine emperor") kept the village communities in subjection and expropriated their social surplus product.

In the slave-owning societies that arose in Mediterranean Europe, the rightless position of the slaves and the division of the free members of society into castes and exclusive groups, some of which enjoyed a privileged position, were established in law and legal relationships. The state was, in essence, the dictatorship of the slave-owners: it guarded their property and privileges, and kept the slaves and other opposing sections of society in subjection.

There were various forms of administration in slave-owning society. "At that time there was already a difference between monarchy and republic, between aristocracy and democracy. A monarchy is the power of a single person, a republic is the absence of any non-elected authority; an aristocracy is the power of a relatively small minority, a democracy is the power of the people ... All these differences arose in the epoch of slavery. Despite these differences, the state of the slave-owning epoch was a slave-owning state, irrespective of whether it was a monarchy or a republic, aristocratic or democratic."[4]

Other political organisations had scarcely evolved, although there did exist certain political groupings and associations of slave-owners (e.g., the "party" struggles in Greece and Rome), and secret organisations were not uncommon among the slaves. In the political life of nearly all slave-owning societies, religious organisation played a prominent part.

The feudal mode of production brought into being a new type of political organisation and new legal and political relations. Here, too, economic compulsion was supplemented with other forms, although the exploiter did not have the legal right of life and death over the exploited. Feudal law granted privileges to some estates and deprived others of almost all rights.

A characteristioc feature of the feudal state was the hierarchical system and vassal relationships. For a long time, while its various provinces were economically isolated, the feudal state remained politically diffuse. Dukes, princes and barons were essentially independent rulers with their own armies, sometimes even their own coinage. But with the growth of the bourgeoisie and the development of market relations, the central power began to combat this feudal isolation with the help of the expanding towns, and it was then that the transition to absolute monarchy began. Republican forms of government were far less frequent in the epoch of feudalism and existed mainly in the medieval towns inhabited by rich merchants and bankers.

A distinctive feature of European feudal society was the tremendous role played by the Roman Catholic Church in the system of state power; it was a political as well as an ideological force. The Catholic Church was a mighty centralised force with its own military formations (orders); the feudal lords had to share their power with the Church (which was also the largest landowner and exploiter of serfs) and were quite often subordinate to the higher clergy.

Besides the state, legal institutions and the Church, the political organisation of feudal society comprised various hierarchical organisations and associations. Political organisations and parties in the modern sense were almost non-existent. The organisations created by the oppressed masses, when taking part in peasant wars and urban uprisings to defend their freedoms from the incursions of the feudal lords, were often religious in form.

The political organisation of class-divided society achieves its peak development under capitalism. The legal and political relations of capitalist society reflect the peculiarities of its production relations. In contrast to the hierarchical inequality of feudal estates, formal equality before the law is a characteristic feature of the legal standard of bourgeois society. The law ceases to be localised and is enforced throughout the country. The complexity and diversity of the economic and other social relations are paralleled by the complexity and diversity of legal standards, which regulate not only the relations between classes but also all forms of economic relations in the field of production and distribution, particularly commodity-money relations, the status of social organisations, political parties and the press; the norms of the civil and criminal law, the personal rights of citizens and so on, are worked out in great detail. Despite all this, however, just as in previous epochs, the law mainly expresses the interests and will of the ruling class — the capitalists — and protects bourgeois property.

The process of the centralisation of state power that began with the rise of the bourgeoisie under late feudalism is completed under capitalism; national centralised states arise. The feudal monarchy yields place to the republic or constitutional monarchy (a monarchy subordinate to bourgeois law enacted by a bourgeois parliament). The legislative, executive and judicial powers are separated. Instead of a mercenary army there is a professional army supplemented by mass conscription. The main organs of state power — civil service, army, police, intelligence and prisons — become larger and more bureaucratic (directed by privileged, specialised functionaries).

Political relations, political forms and methods of struggle acquire added weight and importance as the class struggle gains wider scope and becomes more open. The political parties, along with the state, occupy an extremely important place in the system of political organisation. The press, radio and television become instruments of enormous power in the political struggle.

The abolition of medieval relations, of serfdom and the privileges of the feudal estates, was a tremendous step forward in human progress. It was an important gain for the working people, who for the first time acquired the right to have their own political organisations and press organs. Capitalist relations of production, based upon generalised commodity production, require the legal recognition of equality between all commodity owners, including the formal equality between buyers and sellers of the commodity labour-power (between capitalist employers and wage-workers). This formal equality in the sphere of the capitalist market (which includes the labour market) is the basis for political democracy under capitalism — the recognition of the formal, legal, right of all citizens to participate equally in influencing state policy.

But despite this advance from the system of feudal monarchy, democracy under capitalism remains restricted and formal. This is because there is no real equality between those who produce social wealth (the working people) and those who own the means of production of social wealth (the bourgeoisie). The possibility for the working people — the working class and the petty bourgeois farmers, shopkeepers, etc. — to actually influence state policy is restricted by the limited access they have to the material means of influencing state policy — which requires the ability to fund political parties, hire venues for political meetings and own printing presses and radio and televsion stations.

These real material limitations that private property places upon the working people's ability to exercise their formal political rights, expose the falsity of the bourgeois ideologists' assertion that, with the emergence of the universal electoral franchise in parliamentary democracies, the state loses it class character and becomes representative of the whole of society. This is also the argument of the petty-bourgeois reformists who call themselves socialists and Marxists.

Thus, Eduard Bernstein and Karl Kautsky in their day acknowledged, though with some reservations, the class nature of the state, but only in relation to the past. In their view, the parliamentary democratic state can serve whichever class is able to secure a majority of representatives in the legislature and therefore in the government accountable to it. It offers the opportunity to the working class to win the electoral struggle and place the state at its service. So the task of the working class is allegedly not to destroy the bourgeois state but to take it over and to use it in its own class interests. The petty-bourgeois reformist "socialists" regard the whole system of parliamentarism — the system of periodic elections to parliament, separation of powers and the existence of several political parties — as "pure" democracy.

In reality, however, the parliamentary system does not in itself change the class essence of the bourgeois state or make it an instrument of majority rule. The capitalist minority ensures the protection of its class interests through the machinery of the executive power, which is virtually independent of the parliament elected by popular vote. The executive power is in the hands of officials (civil service bureaucrats, army officers, police chiefs etc.) who are not accountable to the electorate and who form a privileged caste associated with the bourgeoisie in every respect. It is this caste of privileged unelected officials who run the affairs of state.

Furthermore, the system of parliamentary representation itself restricts the majority, the working people's influence on the affairs of state to placing a voting paper in a ballot box every few years. Because of the large size of electoral consistuencies under the parliamentary system, it is impossible for the vast majority of voters in any constituency to meet together to discuss state policy, and to hold their elected representatives accountable, including immediately replacing them if they are dissatisfied with their performance. The activities of these parliamentary representatives are limited to discussion and voting on legislative proposals which originate from the executive power. Moreover, they are accorded all sorts of privileges similar to those of the state bureaucracy, particularly high salaries, which ensure that their interests are aligned with those of the bourgeoisie and not with those of the majority of the voters.

There is the possibility that in a situation of revolutionary mobilisation of the masses, the revolutionary working-class party may be victorious in a bourgeois parliamentary election. This, however, would not testify to the "merits" of parliamentary democracy, but to the force of the revolutionary mass mobilisation. Moreover, even such a victory of the revolutionary proletarian forces in parliament would change nothing. Such a parliament would in short order be confronted with the counter-revolutionary revolt of the executive apparatus of the bourgeois state (the military and police commanded by bourgeois officers). Without *revolutionary organs of state power* to crush this counter-revolutionary revolt, the left-wing forces would suffer defeat. And these revolutionary organs of state power, which organise the involvement of the working masses in political life *far more fully* than any parliament, would make the parliamentary system *redundant*.

The transition to monopoly capitalism at the end of the 19th century enhanced the economic role of the bourgeois state. The accumulation of state property, militarisation, allocation of increasing tax revenues for economic development, state subsidies to the monopolies — all this has enlarged the bourgeois state's role in production and in social relations.

The "state" economy, however, does not replace the "private sector", but coexists with it and supplements it. It develops on the basis of capitalist private property and strengthens its positions by adapting them to the growing socialisation of the process of production in the interests of the owners of the big corporations and banks.

The Marxist view of the state is distorted not only by the petty-bourgeois reformist "socialists" but also by the anarchists. Taking their cue from the petty-bourgeois, socialist-tinged criticism of capitalism, the anarchists find themselves incapable of pointing out any practical way of abolishing capitalism. Anarchism as a petty-bourgeois trend in the age of pre-monopoly capitalism was characterised by inability to distinguish the working class as the progressive organising force of the revolutionary movement of the masses, by worshipping "spontaneity", by neglect or underestimation of political work and by the counterposing of the "revolutionary instinct" of the masses to the tasks of conscious ideological and organisational preparation for social revolution, above all for the seizure of state power.

Contemporary anarchists usually do not deny the significance of the political struggle. But they still ignore the painstaking work that has to be done to prepare the working-class masses for social revolution. Instead, they constantly urge rebellion, neglect or downplay the importance of the proletariat's struggle for democracy, remain hostile to the proletarian state (which they consider an inevitable vehicle of bureaucratic rule) and completely deny the importance of centralism, which they contrast to autonomism.

After the demonstrated success of Marxism in providing leadership to the working class in carrying out a revolutionary struggle for power in Russia and other countries in the 20th century, anarchism today does not usually appear in its "pure" form. It usually manifests itself as "Marxists" who deny in practice the significance of taking into account the balance of class forces in deciding revolutionary tactics and the importance of organisational and educational work among the masses, and who consequently substitute the actions of small minorities for mass action. Such pseudo-Marxist petty-bourgeois radicals also rule out the possibility of specific tactical compromises and agreements for common action by the working class with liberal bourgeois political forces and the use by the revolutionary movement of bourgeois-democratic state institutions such as parliament at a certain stage of the struggle.

When confronted by the tasks of socialist construction, they belittle the role of the revolutionary party and the role of the proletarian state in economic life. They regard centralism as such as an evil and, like the anarchists, contrast it to "workers'" self-administration in autonomous economic units. While paying lip service to the concept of the dictatorship of the proletariat, in practice they oppose its essence, sharing with the anarchists a hostility to the use of coercive political measures by the victorious proletariat to suppress the bourgeoisie. At the same time, they have a belief in the omnipotence of the use of force to bring about the transformation of the economy, i.e., that a socialist economy can be achieved simply or largely through the confiscation of bourgeois property, rather than through the organisation of the working class to take over and centralise the direction of all economic activities. "The difference between socialisation and simple confiscation is that confiscation can be carried out by 'determination' alone, without the ability to calculate and distribute properly, *whereas socialisation cannot be brought about without this ability* ... It is typical of the petty-bourgeois revolutionary not to notice that routing, putting down, etc., is not enough for socialism. It is sufficient for a small proprietor enraged against a big proprietor. But no proletarian revolutionary would ever fall into such error."[5]

3. The Political Organisation of Post-Capitalist Society

The winning of political power by the working class through the overthrow and destruction of the bourgeois state power creates the new type of political organisation of society essential for building the classless, socialist (or communist) society. The basis for this political organisation of society in the transition period between capitalism and socialism is the proletarian state, the *proletariat organised as the ruling class*. "Between capitalist and communist society lies the period of the revolutionary transformation of the one into the other. Corresponding to this is also a political transition period in which the state can be nothing but the *revolutionary dictatorship of the proletariat.*"[6]

Like all other states, the proletarian state is a class dictatorship, i.e., it is rule based directly on force unrestricted by any laws. However, unlike all previous states, the proletarian state is dictatorial in a new way: because this state represents the interests of the majority (the working people) and suppresses a minority (the bourgeoisie), it does not require a *special force* to suppress the resistance of the bourgeoisie, but instead utilises the *general force* of the majority — the armed working class, organised into a popular militia under the command of officers selected from its own ranks by a government chosen by a central congress of local councils of working people's delegates. The state, as a special organisation of power over society, begins to "wither away". "Instead of the special institutions of a privileged minority (privileged officialdom, the chiefs of the standing army), the majority itself can directly fulfil all these functions, and the more the functions of state power are performed by the people as a whole, the less need there is for the existence of this power."[7]

In the *Communist Manifesto* of 1848, Marx and Engels pointed out that the "first step in the revolution of the working class, is to raise the proletariat to the position of ruling class, to win the battle of democracy".[8] True to the materialist approach to the solution of social problems, Marx and Engels did not seek to lay down any preconceived blueprint as to specific forms through which the proletariat could be organised as the ruling class or the exact manner in which this would be combined with the winning of the most complete, consistent democracy. They expected the experience of the mass movement to provide an answer to this question.

The experiences of the 1848-49 revolutionary mass movement enabled Marx to be more concrete about how the working class could "win the battle of democracy". The state organisations of the bourgeoisie — its army, police, courts and civil bureaucracy — would have to be *broken up and destroyed.* New organisations of state power would have to be created by the working class in the very course of its revolutionary struggle for power. In their March 1850 address to the Communist League, Marx and Engels pointed out that in any new democratic revolution the workers must not subordinate themselves to the "new official governments" created by the bourgeois democrats, but "must establish simulatenously their own revolutionary workers' governments, whether in the form of municipal committees and muncipal councils or in the form of workers' clubs or workers' committees, so that the bourgeois-democratic governments not only immediately lose the support of the workers but from the outset see themselves threatened by authorities which are backed by the whole mass of the workers". Furthermore, "the workers must attempt to organise themselves independently as a proletarian guard with commanders elected by themselves and with a general staff of their own choosing, and to put themselves at the command not of the state authority but of the revolutionary community councils which the workers will have managed to get adopted".[9]

The workers' clubs or committees should seek to overthrow the bourgeois state authorities and, centralised through a national congress of delegates from the local workers' committees, organise an "election for a national representative assembly" in which revolutionary "workers' candidates are put up alongside the bourgeois-democratic candidates". Within the "national representative assembly", Marx and Engels believed the workers' representatives should fight for the establishment of a centralised democratic republic.[10]

The specific forms through which this centralised democratic republic could organise the proletariat to be the ruling class were not answered by the two pioneers of scientific socialism. It was only through studying the experience of the Paris Commune of 1871, in which the "proletariat for the first time held political power"[11], that Marx and Engels were finally able to specify how a proletarian democracy would be institutionally different from a bourgeois democracy. The Commune, Marx observed, was "the political form at last discovered under which to work out the economic emancipation of labour".[12]

The revolutionary uprising in Paris in March 1871 came in the wake of the defeat of the bourgeois French army during the 1870-71 Franco-Prussian war. During the war the working people of Paris had been organised into a militia, the National Guard. In March 1871 the French army and almost the entirety of the Parisian bourgeoisie abandoned Paris to the advancing Prussian forces. The Central Committee of the National Guard, elected by the armed working people of Paris, took over not only the defence of the city. Through a newly elected municipal government, the Paris Commune, they were also drawn into the tasks of deciding and implementing all affairs of state.

"The first decree of the Commune", Marx noted, "was the suppression of the standing army, and the substitution for it of the armed people".[13] In place of a special coercive force for the suppression of the majority, the armed population was organised by the Commune government and became the guarantor of majority rule. For this reason, Engels declared that the Commune was "no longer a state in the proper sense of word".[14]

In his 1891 introduction to Marx's 1871 study of the Paris Commune, *The Civil War in France*, Engels singled out three measures taken by the Commune for particular attention. First was the Commune's decision to "do away with all the old repressive machinery previously used" by the exploiter minority to suppress the exploited majority. Second, the Commune "filled all posts — administrative, judicial and educational — by election on the basis of universal suffrage of all concerned, subject to the right of recall at any time by the same electors". Third, "all officials, high or low, were paid only the wages received by other workers".[15]

The Paris Commune, Lenin wrote in April 1917, was — like the soviets of workers' and soldiers' (and, later, peasants') deputies that had emerged in Russia — a "revolutionary dictatorship, i.e., a power directly based on revolutionary seizure, on the direct initiative of the people from below". This is "an entirely different kind of power from the one that generally exists in the parliamentary bourgeois-democratic republics of the usual type still prevailing in the advanced countries of Europe and America". The fundamental characteristics of this type of state power, Lenin explained, are "(1) the source of power is not a law previously discussed and enacted by parliament, but the direct initiative of the people from below in their local areas — direct 'seizure', to use a current expression; (2) the replacement of the police and army, which are institutions divorced from the people and set against the people, by the direct arming of the whole people; order in the state under such a power is maintained by the armed workers and peasants *themselves*, by the armed people *themselves*; (3) officialdom, the bureaucracy, are either similarly replaced by the direct rule of the people themselves or at least placed under special control; they not only become elected officials, but are also *subject to recall* at the people's first demand; they are reduced to the position of simple agents; from a privileged group holding 'jobs' remunerated on a high, bourgeois scale, they become workers of a special 'arm of the service', whose remuneration *does not exceed* the ordinary pay of a competent worker". This, "and this *alone*", Lenin insisted, "constitutes the *essence* of the Paris Commune as a special type of state".[16]

Lenin sought to emphasise that what distinguished the Commune-type state, the revolutionary dictatorship of the proletariat and the other exploited producers, from the bourgeois-democratic parliamentary state was not that it had carried out the socialist expropriation of capital, but that it was the most *consistent form of democracy*. Lenin highlighted this point because many of the Bolshevik leaders, like Lev Kamenev, thought that in advocating a transfer of state power from the bourgeois Provisional Government to the soviets, Lenin was abandoning the perspective of carrying through a democratic revolution as the necessary bridge to the *socialist* dictatorship of the proletariat, in favour of a perspective of proceeding directly to the socialist revolution, to the expropriation of bourgeois property in city and village. In reply, Lenin pointed out that Kamenev and those who shared his view had "repeated the bourgeois prejudice about the Paris Commune having wanted to introduce socialism 'immediately'", whereas the "real essence of the Commune is not where the bourgeois usually looks for it, but in the creation of a *state* of a special type", and that the soviets in Russia represented a state of the same type — a more *democratic* type of state for dealing with immediate social problems such as distribution of food rations to the working masses.[17]

In his 1917 work *The State and Revolution,* Lenin drew out the connection between the political measures carried out by the Paris Commune and the socialist reorganisation of society. Firstly, the Commune appeared "to have replaced the smashed state machine 'only' by fuller democracy ... But as a matter of fact this 'only' signifies a gigantic replacement of certain institutions by other institutions of a fundamentally different type. This is exactly a case of 'quantity being transformed into quality': democracy, introduced as fully and consistently as is at all conceivable, is transformed from bourgeois into proletarian democracy; from the state (= a special force for the suppression of a particular class) into something which is no longer the state proper."[18]

Secondly, this qualitatively new, fuller democracy serves to unite the interests of the exploited producers, "the workers and the majority of the peasants" who are "oppressed by the government and long for its overthrow, long for 'cheap' government"[19]. By replacing the standing army with a popular militia, and administration by a bureaucracy (privileged officials) with administration by officials paid ordinary "workmen's wages", the proletarian state provides "cheap" government. The abolition of remunerative privileges for all state officials, Lenin emphasised, "shows more clearly than anything else the *turn* from bourgeois to proletarian democracy".[20]

Thirdly, the political measures taken by the Commune in organising qualitatively new state institutions are measures *transitional* to the socialist organisation of society. "While completely uniting the interests of the workers and the majority of peasants, at the same time" these political measures "serve as a bridge leading from capitalism to socialism". While the measures carried out by the Paris Commune concerned "the purely political reorganisation of society", Lenin pointed out that "they acquire their full meaning and significance only in connection with the 'expropriation of the expropriators' either being accomplished or in preparation, i.e., with the transformation of capitalist private ownership of the means of production into social ownership".[21] This is because, as Marx observed, "the political rule of the producer cannot coexist with the perpetuation of his social slavery".[22] The Commune-type state, Marx explained, provided the proletariat with the political "lever for uprooting the economical foundations upon which rests the existence of classes, and therefore, of class rule".[23] How this lever was to be used for this purpose had already been foreshadowed by Marx and Engels in the *Communist Manifesto*:

> The proletariat will use its political supremacy to wrest, by degrees, all capital from the bourgeoisie, to centralise all instruments of production in the hands of the State, i.e., of the proletariat organised as the ruling class …
>
> Of course, in the beginning, this cannot be effected except by means of despotic inroads on the rights of property, and on the conditions of bourgeois production; by means of measures, therefore, which appear economically insufficient and untenable, but which, in the course of the movement, outstrip themselves, necessitate further inroads upon the old social order, and are unavoidable as a means of entirely revolutionising the mode of production.[24]

Dialectically conceived, the dictatorship of the proletariat is the *realisation of democracy* for the proletariat. It is *that* precisely because, and to the extent that, it is the *negation of democracy* for the bourgeoisie. For the proletarians, their dictatorship collectively over their class enemy is simply the logical carrying out to its ultimate conclusion of their revolutionary class struggle. Since its dictatorial, i.e., coercive, aspect expresses only the quantity and quality of the bourgeois resistance to be suppressed, the dictatorship of the proletariat ceases progressively to be a dictatorship as the objective fact of bourgeois resistance, actual or potential, ceases to exist. Furthermore, as the conditions and relations of bourgeois society are progressively abolished, the proletarian state progressively loses its character as an instrument of social coercion. The dictatorship of the proletariat will wither away as all classes, including the proletariat, are dissolved into the classless, socialist society of freely associated collective owners of the means of production. The public power will lose its political character, i.e., will cease to be an instrument of class rule, and become a voluntary association for the management of the collective welfare of *associated humanity*.

In summary, the dictatorship of the proletariat can less than any historical epoch be understood other than *dialectically*. Since capitalist society is the final antagonistic social form in the development of human society — antagonistic in the twofold sense that it is based, objectively, upon class divisions, and based subjectively upon ignorance of the true relation between nature and human society — its revolutionary transmutation into a socialist society involves *the most radical break with the past* it is possible to conceive. But this is because it is the most complete *return*, on an enormously higher level of development of productive forces, to the spontaneous

solidarity of the most primitive human societies. The *form* of this process can be none other than the dictatorship of the proletariat, of the propertyless mass of humans objectively associated through socialised labour on a world scale, precisely because its *content* is the negation of that negation from which all previous historical movement has sprung, namely, the negation of social solidarity by class division, exploitation and oppression. ❦

CHAPTER 9
THE HISTORICAL FORMS OF HUMAN COMMUNITY

The way in which people are organised to produce the material goods they need for their survival is the basis of all social relations. It determines the structure of society, the types of social groups and the more or less stable historical forms of *human community*.

1. THE CLAN AND TRIBE AS HISTORICAL FORMS OF HUMAN COMMUNITY IN PRE-CLASS SOCIETY

In the pre-class period of social development, the main forms of human community were the *clan* and *tribe*. The data gathered by anthropology, ethnology and archaeology tell us that the clan or *gens* superseded the primitive horde form of life during the upper Palaeolithic period, when modern humans first appeared.

The clan may be defined as a primary productive, social and ethnic group of pre-class society, possessing common origin, language, customs and beliefs, and common features of everyday life and culture; a group in which kinship ("blood") ties as well as production relations play a primary role in the performance of all its activities.

The economic basis of the clan was primitive communal property in its settlements and hunting and gathering grounds. The tools used by the clan members for hunting, gathering and food processing were, in the main, personal possessions, but the productive power of these tools was too primitive to allow individuals either to make tools on their own or to secure food supplies through individual labour activities. The group of people forming the clan had to cooperate to make their tools and to use them to produce the material goods needed for survival. Collective labour activities on communally owned hunting and gathering grounds and egalitarian distribution of the results of these labour activities were essential to the survival of the social group.

The tribe was a larger community than the clan, usually comprising several hundred or several thousand (perhaps even tens of thousands) of people. If well developed, it would comprise many clans. Every clan remained an independent unit of social production within the tribe, but the tribe brought into being a new form of social property and a new form of social organisation. There was now tribal as well as clan property. For the most part, this was territory (the areas settled by the clans that were associated within the tribe, the hunting grounds, pastures and other lands). This meant that there was a need for government of the tribe as a whole, particularly in its relations with neighbouring tribes, and hence there appeared cheftains and administrative bodies such as the tribal council and the general assembly of warriors or elders of the tribe.

In its day, the clan or tribal form of community was the only possible form in which production, or, for that matter, primitive communal society as a whole, could function and develop. Hence the existence of such a form among all peoples at the stage of the primitive communal system, and also its survival for tens of thousands of years.

The clan and tribe offered scope for the development of economic activity and culture on the basis of the hunter-gatherer system of material production and, later, of the system of hoe agriculture and early pastoralism. It created favourable conditions for the preservation and accumulation of production experience and the rudiments of intellectual culture, and for the improvement and perfection of language. At the same time, kinship relationships limited the numerical growth of the social groups and hindered communication, particularly individual people's movements.

The force of tradition and custom that facilitated the functioning of the social organism was so great that it prevented any substantial change in the life of the tribe. The growth of contradictions in the clan-tribe organisation ultimately led to the supplanting of old forms of community by other forms under the pressure of changes in the productive forces and the relations of production which they engendered. Strictly speaking, the formation of tribes had already initiated the splitting up of the united multi-functional community. Inasmuch as the tribe performed only some of the social functions, this was the beginning of the breakaway of the ethnic community from its immediate economic functions. Then came the pair-based couple and the tendency to separate marital-sexual relationships from common ethnic relations.

2. The Emergence of Classes and the Development of New Forms of Human Community

With the beginning of the social division of labour (separation of handicrafts from agriculture and animal herding, or administration of the construction and maintenance of extensive irrigation works from farming/handicraft production), and with the appearance of barter relations, the clan-tribe organisation was forced to yield to new forms of human community. These new forms were based not on kinship relations but on certain *territorial links* between people belonging to different clans and tribes who were, however, closely connected with one another by the character of their economic activity, their trade or other economic relations.

On the basis of the tributary ("Asiatic") mode of production, combination of farming and handicrafts in the village acted to preserve elements of the clan organisation among the peasant-farmers. But the tribal chieftains and witch-doctors increasingly servered their ties with the individual village communities, constituting themselves into an exploiting class of military and priestly nobles living in temple-based towns, with their retinues of specialised scribes, household servants, craftsmen and soldiers, from which they politically controlled and exacted tribute from the inhabitants of large territories in which they administered trade and irrigation works.

Early slave-owning societies such as Athens and Rome also gave rise to new forms of human community in which people lived on one terrority and were bound together by a common system of law and political administration centred on a city-state, and in which petty commodity production and trade fostered a common language and intellectual culture, as expressed in their customs, morals and traditions.

With the replacement of the slave mode of production by feudalism, the manor or fief of the seigneurial lord became the dominant form of human community in western Europe, though clan and tribal forms of association were partially reintroduced by the Germanic tribes that had conquered the western Roman empire and out of which the feudal ruling class had emerged.

But in the course of time, as commodity production and trade revived in western Europe the economic isolation of the feudal manors began to break down, and wider forms of human community began to emerge associating people over large territories, and giving them a common language and common cultural features — *nations*.

The capitalist origin of nations was expounded by Marx and Engels in the *Communist Manifesto*:

> The bourgeoisie keeps more and more doing away with the scattered state of the

population, of the means of production, and of property. It has agglomerated population, centralised means of production, and has concentrated property in a few hands. The necessary consequence of this was political centralisation. Independent, or but loosely connected provinces, with separate interests, laws, governments and systems of taxation, became lumped together into one nation, with one government, one code of laws, one national class-interest, one frontier and one customs-tariff.[1]

Marx and Engels had in mind the process of formation of nations in the birthplace of capitalism, i.e., western Europe, where the maturing of capitalist relations simultaneously abolished economic and political isolation. The fact that these two processes were simultaneous usually led to the formation of one-nation-states, although even in these states internal differences found expression in local dialects and customs.

Sometimes, for various reasons, the bourgeois state was formed before all the ethnic groups living on the given territory were absorbed into one nation. In such cases a multinational state was formed, with a privileged position for one or several nations which, having evolved before the others, became the driving force in the creation of the bourgeois state. Mutinational states also arose when one of the old feudal principalities, in alliance with an emerging commercial and manufacturing bourgeoisie, absorbed neighbouring principalities and consolidated itself as an absolute monarchy ruling over a large and ethnically diverse empire. In the course of the further development of capitalist economic relations, several nations were formed on the territories ruled over by this imperial semi-feudal state power.

In a polemic with the Russian populists, who followed the bourgeois sociologists in regarding national ties as the "continuation and generalisation" of tribal ties, Lenin showed that the actual merging of the inhabitants of separate provinces, lands and principalities into the Russian nation had taken place on the basis of commodity-capitalist relations, which had led to the formation of a market embracing the whole of Russia: "Since the leaders and masters of this process were the merchant capitalists, the creation of these national ties was nothing else than the creation of bourgeois ties".[2]

Thus, Marxists maintain that *nations are the product of the rise of capitalist economic relations* and of the struggle of the bourgeoisie against pre-capitalist social relations and classes. Lenin pointed out that capitalism's "broad and rapid development of the productive forces *calls* for large, politically compact and united territories, since only here can the bourgeois class — together with its inevitable antipode, the proletarian class — unite and sweep away all the old, medieval, caste, parochial, petty-national, religious and other barriers" to the development of capitalist economic relations.[3]

Consequently, the nation as a specific historical form of human community is the product of a *specific stage of historical development*, i.e., the rise and consolidation of commodity-capitalist relations. Lenin explained the process of formation of nations as follows:

> For the complete victory of commodity production, the bourgeoisie must capture the home market, and there must be politically united territories whose population speaks a single language, with all obstacles to the development of that language and its consolidation in literature eliminated. Therein is the economic foundation of national movements. Language is the most important means of human intercourse. Unity and unimpeded development of language are the most important conditions for genuinely free and extensive commerce on a scale commensurate with modern capitalism, for a free and broad grouping of the population in all its various classes and, lastly, for the establishment of a close connection between the market and each and every proprietor, big or little, and between seller and buyer.[4]

For Marxists *the nation is an historically constituted, relatively stable community of people formed on the basis of a unified system of commodity-capitalist relations*. Sustained life within a single capitalist socioeconomic formation is what forges diverse pre-capitalist communities into a nation. Nations are therefore not "imaginary communities", as some contemporary bourgeois sociologists argue, but objective realities defined by four features — a *common economic life based on commodity-capitalist relations*, a *common territory* upon which that economic life is conducted, a *common language* that facilities commodity production and exchange, and a *common social psychology manifested in a specific, common intellectual culture resulting from sustained life within a specific capitalist socioeconomic formation*.

Nations are the product of distinct and historically definite capitalist socioeconomic formations. This is true even for nations that develop as by-products of capitalist colonialism, as have many of the nations of the Americas, Asia and Africa. Where such an integrated and unified system of commodity-capitalist relations has not emerged, a colony or semi-colony may never develop into a nation, but instead will remain a conglomeration of diverse ethnic groups held together by the rule of a colonial power or by the bureaucratic-military machine of the post-colonial state.

To hasten the process of formation and consolidation of its own distinct capitalist socioeconomic formation, every national bourgeoisie seeks to forge a nation-state to bring its political power to bear on the situation. But nations and states are qualitatively different social formations. A nation is the form of human community that accords with the capitalist socioeconomic formation, while the state is the centralised organisation of force of a ruling class. Sometimes the nation and the nation-state coincide, e.g., the French nation and the French nation-state. But often they do not. Sometimes different nations are politically unified under a state that represents the centralised organisation of force of one nation's ruling class — e.g., the United Kingdom of Great Britain and Northern Ireland, which politically unifies the English, Scottish and Welsh nations, plus a part of the Irish nation, under the English ruling class's state power.

The nation was the form of human community corresponding to *the rise of capitalism*. It helped promote the development of the productive forces of this society and played an important part in overcoming political separateness. The formation of nations and national movements helped to abolish pre-capitalist social relations and establish the dominance of the capitalist mode of production.

But in the course of time, even the national framework proves too narrow for the capitalist mode of production. Capitalism creates a national and also a world market, which not only consolidates the nation as an economic community but also establishes economic ties between all nations, ultimately turning capitalism into a world economic system.

This leads to profound contradictions, to the emergence of *two tendencies in the development of nations under capitalism*. The first tendency is that of the formation of nations, the emergence of national life and movements for national unity and national independence; the second tendency intensifies economic intercourse between nations and breaks down national differences by means of capital's internationalisation of economic activity. "Both tendencies", wrote Lenin, "are a universal law of capitalism. The former predominates in the beginning of its development, the latter characterises a mature capitalism that is moving towards its transformation into socialism."[5]

The contradiction between these tendencies assumes antagonistic forms. The bourgeoisie of the developed nations seeks national privileges over less developed nations and seeks to extort monopoly super-profits from the latter by exploiting the uneven level of development of the productive forces in the world economy. Conversely, the progress of indigenous productive forces in the less developed nations, colonies and semi-colonies is impeded by their exploitation at the hands of the bourgeoisie of the developed nations; in opposition to this, the peoples of the less developed nations, colonies and semi-colonies fight against the colonial rule and imperialist exploitation.

The type of human community which corresponds to socialism, to a socioeconomic formation based on social ownership of socialised productive forces, is *socialised humanity*, i.e., the worldwide community of all people in which national distinctions have disappeared. The first step on this road involves the seizure of state power by the proletariat in each separate country. "The proletariat of each country must, of course, first of all settle matters with its own bourgeoisie", Marx and Engels pointed out in the *Communist Manifesto*. But while the proletarian revolution is in form a "national struggle", in substance it is a world struggle, since the obstacle to the proletariat's liberation is capitalism, a world system of exploitation.

Voluntary cooperation by the workers of the world is essential to the process of building a classless, socialist society, to utilising and further developing the worldwide socialisation of the productive forces initiated by capitalism. Through this voluntary cooperation of proletarian states, the inequalities between nations will be consciously done away with. Only by overcoming the actual inequality of nations, by arranging things so that the more developed nations help the peoples who had been exploited and oppressed by the bourgeoisie of the developed nations, and only by consistently practising international cooperation and mutual assistance can the proletariat ruling in the developed nations draw all nations into a *single, multi-national proletarian state*. The advance toward socialism, toward a classless free association of humanity based on the social ownership of the means of production and the withering away of class divisions, creates the necessary material and intellectual basis for the *gradual withering away of national differences* and the merging of nations. A worldwide socialist economy developing according to a single, socially determined plan and securing a degree of economic integration never known before, will gradually be formed throughout the world. There will emerge a common intellectual culture which will fully absorb all that is best in the intellectual culture of each nation. There will emerge a common language, a common means of communication for all people. Humanity will become *one united, cooperative community* completely free of class and national antagonisms.

Each specific mode of production gives rise to a corresponding type of human community; these historically supersede one another in the progressive development of human society. Their supplanting of one another shows that the development of social production and the social progress that it brings demand wider forms of human community with greater stability and stronger social ties.

The different types of human community correspond only basically to certain modes of production and the socioeconomic formations based upon them. Situations seldem occur in history when these types appear in their "pure" form. Owing to the unevenness of economic development, one can find on our planet all types of human community existing at one time, from the tribal community to the developed nation. Genetically the clan and tribe precede the administrative temple-town and village association of the tributary mode of production (in the ancient Near East, India, China and the Americas) and the *polis* and slave estate of the slave mode of production (in ancient Greece and the Roman state), and the feudal manor and other pre-capitalist forms of community precede the nation. But in actual history on a world scale, and very often within the framework of any existing socioeconomic formation and state, elements of the older types of human community are to be found alongside those that have superseded them. This is particularly true among those peoples subjected to capitalist colonialism. Colonial rule and imperialist exploitation of the peoples of Latin America, Africa and Asia played a decisive role in holding back the development of indigeous capitalist economies among these peoples and in retarding the process of their formation into nations.

3. National Relations Under Capitalism

The formation of nations gave rise to the national question, whose development under capitalism may be considered in two major stages.

The first stage was the epoch of the establishment of capitalism and the decay and decline of feudalism, the epoch of the transformation of fragmented feudal communities into nations, when this process was, as a rule, led by the bourgeoisie. In this period, which began approximately in the 16th century, humanity (in Europe and North America) experienced the first round of national-liberation wars and revolutions.

The second stage is the epoch of imperialist, monopoly capitalism which began approximately at the beginning of the 20th century. During this period, the principal content of the national question is the struggle against the system of colonial rule and imperialist exploitation of the newly emerging nations of Asia, Africa and Latin America.

Objectively, in their character and role, the national movements of emergent capitalism were anti-feudal. They formed one of the conditions for the assertion of capitalism in the struggle of the bourgeoisie and the mass of the people against feudal economic and political relations. In the age of imperialism, the bourgeoisie of the developed nations oppresses the peoples of the colonies and semi-colonies, and the latter fight for their political and economic independence. While the demands of the oppressed peoples of the colonies and semi-colonies for political and economic independence are a reflection of the needs of capitalist development of these peoples, the chief obstacle to the achievement of these demands is not the survivals of pre-capitalist relations but the domination of the world economic and political system by imperialist bourgeoisies of the developed nations.

In the first period of the national question, national oppression was the product of the contradiction between the survivals of feudal socio-political relations and emergent capitalism. In the second period, national oppression arises out of the contradiction between the monopoly finance capitalism of the developed nations and the world imperialist system created by it and the emergent capitalism of the colonised peoples.

National oppression under capitalism is the product of the uneven development of capitalism on a world scale, though uneven development in itself does not give rise to national oppression under capitalism. The driving force of national oppression under capitalism is the *capital relation*, which is both exploitative (surplus-value producing) and expansive (accumulation of capital). The bourgeoisies of the more developed nations seek to exploit the labour and markets of the less developed countries.

Under capitalism all social movements directly or indirectly acquire a political character and become socio-political movements and trends. Political activity itself, however, inevitably develops in *national forms*. This can be seen not only in the case of the bourgeoisie fighting for political supremacy under the banner of nationalism, but also in the case of the working class. This class becomes a political force when its movement assumes a *nationwide* scale, or, as Marx and Engels put it, when its "numerous local struggles" merge "into one national struggle between classes. But every class struggle is a political struggle."[6] The working class fights mainly against the bourgeoisie that exercises political rule over it.

The national question is a political one also because, in a situation in which social relations are regulated by state and law, it is bound to involve both the country's constitution and state organisation, the policy conducted by the ruling class. To this should be added the fact that inter-state relations, which inevitably have a political character, usually assume the character of relations between nations.

National relations under capitalism play a tremendous part also in the intellectual life of nations. All kinds of mental activity assume a national form. Ideological life itself develops, if regarded from the national standpoint, on the basis of the struggle of two trends "... that correspond to the two great class camps throughout the capitalist world and express the *two* policies (nay, the two world outlooks) in the national question".[7] These two trends are *bourgeois nationalism* and *proletarian internationalism*.

The *nationalist* does not simply proceed from the recognition of nations and support for struggles against national oppression. The nationalist regards all other social interests from the standpoint of "national interests", either ignoring them or subordinating them to the "national interest". This finds expression in denial of the irreconcilable opposition of class interests between the exploiting class and the exploited classes, in the denial that the class struggle is the driving force of social development. It also finds expression in the adulation of everything that is particular to the nationalist's own nation, regardless of its socio-political content, including adulation of reactionary social and political institutions, customs and traditions.

In its extreme form, nationalism becomes *national chauvinism* — contempt for the pecularities and interests of people of other nationalities, and in the overt assumption of the inferiority of other nationalities and the superiority of the nationalist's own nation.

National chauvinism very often seeks justification in the *racialisation* of nations, i.e., ascribing racial characteristics to national differences. Racism became particularly widespread in the age of imperialism, when the bourgeoisie of the developed capitalist countries, which were mainly populated by people of European origin, subjugated numerous "coloured" peoples, and in some cases conducted a policy of physical extermination toward them.

Racism assumes that separate "races" of people — with clearly definable sets of social and physical characteristics — exist, have always existed and will always exist. In reality, racial groups are socially constructed categories based on the fetishisation of superficial, external physical characteristics — usually skin colour. Racism is the ideology and social psychology which overtly or covertly ascribes social value to these fetishised superficial physical differences — dividing people into "inferior" and "superior" racial groups in order to justify an institutionalised system of social inequality based on racial categorisation. By dividing people into racial groups, the bourgeoisie is able to proclaim its recognition of the formal equality of all people while superexploiting a particular section of the working people (working people categorised as members of one racial group) and winning support for the maintenance of capitalism from those working people not subject to racial oppression, who are thereby granted relative priveleges in terms of access to employment, better paid and more secure jobs, social services etc.

A nation is *not a racial group*, since it is not historically formed on the basis of the social fetishism of physical features. But national chauvinists often seek to ascribe racial characteristics to nations, to portray the members of other nationalities as racially, i.e., biologically, different and inferior to members of the national chauvinists' own nationality and thus to rationalise national rivalry and national oppression as a product of "inherent", "biological" differences between peoples of different nationalities.

Nationalism is closely bound up with *cosmopolitanism*. Outwardly, they stand in opposition to each other. Nationalism exaggerates national peculiarities while cosmopolitanism denies their significance. Nationalism and cosmopolitanism are idelogical expressions of the two basic tendencies in the national question under capitalism. Cosmopolitanism expresses the tendency towards the internationalisation of economic relations as capitalism develops into a worldwide system of production. But by isolating this tendency and opposing it to the second tendency, the tendency toward the formation of new nations among the peoples dominated by the imperialist bourgeoisie of the developed nations, cosmopolitanism justifies the economic (and, frequently, political) enslavement of these newly emerging nations. Cosmopolitanism serves the imperialist policies of the developed capitalist nations, which, under the flag of abandoning national differences, seek to impose their domination, their language, their culture on the less developed nations. It is the reverse side of the nationalism of the imperialist "great" powers.

From what has been said, it follows that the concepts "national" and "nationalist" by no means coincide. The *national* embraces the field of relations between all ethnic communities under capitalism. No class can ignore national peculiarities; they are all involved in national relations, which are a historically transient feature of social relations; they must all define their position on the national question. *Nationalism*, on the other hand, expresses the ideological outlook and policy of the bourgeoisie on the national question. It seeks to *unite* all members of a given nation and to *separate* them from people of other nationalities. The nationalist seeks to blunt recognition of class distinctions and antagonisms within any given nation, while sharpening the distinctions between nations. The nationalist outlook and policy are therefore an obstacle to the development of the international solidarity of the working class. This corresponds exactly to the interests of the bourgeoisie, and is why Marxists are opponents of nationalism. As Lenin explained:

> The [class-conscious] proletariat cannot support any consecration of nationalism; on the contrary, it supports everything that helps to obliterate national distinctions and remove national barriers; it supports everything that makes the ties between nationalities closer and closer, or tends to merge nations. To act differently means siding with reactionary nationalist philistinism.[8]

In opposition to bourgeois nationalism, Marxists advocate the outlook and policy of *proletarian internationalism*, the recognition of the identity of class interests of the workers of all nations and the policy of international solidarity, equality and mutual assistance between workers of all nations in their common struggle against capitalist exploitation and oppression.

Any departure from internationalism towards nationalism implies a shift from proletarian class positions toward bourgeois positions and harms the liberation struggle of the working class.

At the same time, the working class cannot take a nihilistic approach to the national question, mainly because national relations constitute an important element in the social and political environment in which every national contingent of the working class has to fight. In particular, the working class cannot ignore *national oppression* because "nothing holds up the development and strengthening of proletarian class consciousness so much as national injustice".[9]

Proletarian internationalism therefore demands opposition to national oppression and support for equality between nations, so as to break down the mistrust that national injustices introduce into the relations between workers of oppressor and oppressed nations. Marxists therefore support the struggles of oppressed nations for an end to national inequality. They advocate the *fullest and most consistent democracy in the relations between nations*.

As part of this policy Marxists uphold the democratic political demand for the recognition of the *right of nations to self-determination*, i.e., the right of oppressed nations to freely decide what their political relationship will be to the oppressor nation, up to and including the right to political secession, to constitute an independent nation-state of their own. This does not mean that Marxists advocate the splitting up of multinational states and the formation of an independent nation-state by every nation. To the contrary, Marxists are for the creation of larger multinational states and, ultimately, the integration of all nations into a single, worldwide multinational state. But we recognise that such multinational political unity can be achieved only *voluntarily*, on the basis of the fullest democracy. Speaking of the national question in the multi-national state of tsarist Russia during the first world war, Lenin explained that the Russian Marxists, the Bolsheviks, supported "freedom of self-determination, *i.e.*, independence, *i.e.*, freedom of secession for the oppressed nations, not because we have dreamt of splitting up the country economically, or of the ideal of small states, but on the contrary, because we want large states and the closer unity and even fusion of nations, only on a democratic, truly internationalist basis, which is *inconceivable* without freedom to secede".[10]

Lenin also explained that the abolition of capitalism and the creation by the victorious revolutionary proletariat of a socialised economy, created only the economic preconditions for the elimination of the legacy of national oppression, which could not be fully uprooted without the fullest democracy in all spheres of social life. It was therefore necessary for the class-conscious vanguard of the working class in a multinational proletarian state to continue to recognise and defend the right of national self-determination, the right to political secession of formerly oppressed nations within that state:

> By transforming capitalism into socialism the proletariat creates the *possibility* of abolishing national oppression; the possibility becomes a *reality* "only" — "only"! — with the establishment of full democracy in all spheres, including in the delineation of state frontiers in accordance with the "sympathies" of the population, including complete freedom to secede. And this, in turn, will serve as a *practical* elimination of even the slightest national friction and the least national mistrust, for an accelerated drawing together and fusion of nations that will be completed when the state *withers* away.[11]

But this cannot be achieved if the democracy, the equality of people to participate in the administration of state policy, is simply formal. As Lenin explained:

> That is why internationalism on the part of the oppressors or "great" nations, as they are called (though they are great only in their violence, only great as bullies), must consist not only in the observance of the formal equality of nations but even in the observance of an inequality of the oppressor nation, the great nation, which must make up for the inequality which obtains in actual practice. Anybody who does not understand this has not grasped the real proletarian attitude to the national question, he is still essentially petty-bourgeois in his point of view and is, therefore, sure to descend to the bourgeois point of view.[12]

The bourgeoisie of every nation strives for national privileges in relation to other nations; the petty-bourgeois democrat assumes that national inequality can be eliminated simply by recognising the formal equality of nations, by the achievement of the democratic political demand for national self-determination. But as we have noted, national oppression does not stem simply from formal political inequality between nations, but from the exploitation of less developed nations by the finance capital of the developed capitalist nations. "The domination of finance capital and of capital in general", Lenin pointed out, "is not to be abolished by *any* reform in the sphere of political democracy; and self-determination belongs wholely and exclusively to this sphere".[13] Consequently, proletarian internationalism demands not simply formal equality, formal democracy between nations, but *real* democracy, real equality, which cannot be achieved without active measures to eradicate the legacy of past oppression, including preferential treatment toward the oppressed nation in all areas where its real conditions of life are unequal with those of the former oppressor nation.

Proletarian internationalism on the part of members of an oppressor nation therefore demands that they distinguish between the nationalism of an *oppressor* nation and the nationalism of an *oppressed* nation. *In relation to the oppressed nation*, the nationalism of the oppressor nation is a reactionary ideological weapon justifying national privileges. *In relation to the oppressor nation*, the nationalism of the oppressed nation has a general democratic content that is directed against national oppression. This does *not* mean that Marxists endorse and support the nationalism of oppressed nations. As Lenin pointed out:

> ... the proletarians, opposed as they are to nationalism of every kind, demand ... as a matter of principle that there should be no [national] privileges, however slight ... *Insofar as* the bourgeoisie of the oppressed nation fights the oppressor, we are always, in every case, and more strongly than anyone else, *in favour*, for we are the staunchest and the most consistent enemies of oppression. But insofar as the bourgeoisie of the oppressed nation stands for *its own* bourgeois nationalism, we stand against. We fight against the privileges and violence of the oppressor nation, and do not in any way condone the strivings for privileges on the part of the oppressed nation ...
>
> The bourgeois nationalism of *any* oppressed nation has a general democratic content that is directed *against* oppression, and it is this content that we *unconditionally* support.[14]

That is, while Marxists oppose *all* nationalism, including the nationalist outlook of oppressed nations, they recognise that the nationalism of oppressed nations must be combated *in a different way* than the nationalism of oppressor nations. The nationalism of oppressed nations can be combated effectively only by championing the democratic aspirations and sentiments that are expressed in a distorted way by this nationalism, by demanding an end to all national privileges and inequalities. Marxists support the *national liberation struggles* of oppressed nations, not to reinforce nationalism among the working people of these nations but, on the contrary, to assist in liquidating its influence over them and to win them to the *anti-nationalist* outlook and policy of proletarian internationalism. ❦

Chapter 10

The Marxist Conception of History and Revolutionary Optimism

In the preface to his 1859 *Contribution to the Critique of Political Economy,* Marx gives the fullest formal statement he ever made of his "materialist conception of history". Innumerable misinterpretations and misrepresentations have been made, not only by critics of Marxism but by many of its erstwhile adherents, concerning this statement. A brief review of the general aspects of the statement will therefore not go amiss as a conclusion to this exposition of the fundamentals of historical materialism.

1. A Scientific Guide to Revolutionary Practice

Marx explains that in the course of his studies for his university diploma, and particularly as a result of his examination of Hegel's *Philosophy of Law,* he came to the conclusion in 1844 that "neither legal relations nor political forms could be comprehended whether by themselves or on the basis of a so-called general development of the human mind, but that on the contrary they originate in the material conditions of life, the totality of which Hegel, following the example of English and French thinkers of the eighteenth century, embraces within the term 'civil society'; that the anatomy of civil society, however, has to be sought in political economy".[1]

He goes on to explain that "the study of this" which he began in Paris and continued in Brussels led to a "general conclusion" which "Frederick Engels, with whom I maintained a constant exchange of ideas by correspondence ... arrived at by another road". This "general conclusion", Marx explains, "became the guiding principle" for all his studies in political economy, and is set out as he gives it below (the paragraphs have been numbered for convenience of reference):

(1) "In the social production of their existence, [people] inevitably enter into definite relations, which are independent of their will, namely relations of production appropriate

to a given stage in the development of their material forces of production.

(2) "The totality of these relations of production constitutes the economic structure of society, the real foundation, on which arises a legal and political superstructure and to which correspond definite forms of social consciousness.

(3) "The mode of production of material life conditions the general process of social, political and intellectual life. It is not the consciousness of [human beings] that determines their existence, but their social existence that determines their consciousness.

(4) "At a certain stage of development, the material productive forces of society come into conflict with the existing relations of production or — this merely expresses the same thing in legal terms — with the property relations within the framework of which they have operated hitherto. From forms of development of the productive forces these relations turn into their fetters. Then begins an era of social revolution.

(5) "The changes in the economic foundation lead sooner or later to the transformation of the whole immense superstructure. In studying such transformations it is always necessary to distinguish between the material transformation of the economic conditions of production, which can be determined with the precision of natural science, and the legal, political, religious, artistic or philosophic — in short, ideological forms in which [people] become conscious of this conflict and fight it out.

(6) "Just as one does not judge individual by what he thinks about himself, so one cannot judge such a period of transformation by its consciousness, but, on the contrary, this consciousness must be explained from the contradictions of material life, from the conflict existing between the social forces of production and the relations of production.

(7) "No social order is ever destroyed before all the productive forces for which it is sufficient have been developed, and new superior relations of production never replace older ones before the material conditions for their existence have matured within the framework of the old society. [Humankind] thus inevitably sets itself only such tasks as it is able to solve, since closer examination will always show that the problem itself arises only when the material conditions for its solution are already present or at least in the course of formation.

(8) "In broad outline, the Asiatic, ancient, feudal, and modern bourgeois modes of production may be designated as epochs marking progress in the economic development of society.

(9) "The bourgeois mode of production is the last antagonistic form of the social process of production — antagonistic not in the sense of individual antagonisms but of an antagonism that emanates from the individuals' social conditions of existence

— but the productive forces developing within bourgeois society create also the material conditions for a solution of this antagonism.

(10) "The prehistory of human society accordingly closes with this social formation."[2]

In considering this, the fullest formal statement by Marx of his and Engels' materialist conception of history, the first fact to notice is its date. It was, Marx says, the "general conclusion" he and Engels reached in 1844, and which when Engels "too came to live in Brussels, we decided to set forth together" in opposition to "the ideological one of German philosophy", i.e., in *The German Ideology* of 1845-46. This work, Marx says, they were unable to get published, but in writing it they had nevertheless "achieved our main purpose — self-clarification".

To gain a more complete view of the "general conclusions" which Marx and Engels had reached at that time, it is therefore necessary to read the results derived from their "self-clarification". Here is what they wrote in *The German Ideology*:

> Finally, from the conception of history we have sketched we obtain these further conclusions: (1) In the development of productive forces there comes a stage when productive forces and means of intercourse are brought into being, which, under the existing relationships, only cause mischief, and are no longer productive but destructive forces (machinery and money); and connected with this a class is called forth, which has to bear all the burdens of society without enjoying its advantages, which, ousted from society, is forced into the most decided antagonism to all other classes; a class which forms the majority of all members of society, and from which emanates the consciousness of the necessity of a fundamental revolution, the communist consciousness, which may, of course, arise among the other classes too through the contemplation of the situation of this class. (2) The conditions under which definite productive forces can be applied, are the conditions of the rule of a definite class of society, whose social power, deriving from its property, has its *practical*-idealistic expression in each case in the form of the State; and, therefore, every revolutionary struggle is directed against a class, which till then has been in power. (3) In all revolutions up till now the mode of activity always remained unscathed and it was only a question of a different distribution of this activity, a new distribution of labour to other persons, whilst the communist revolution is directed against the preceding *mode* of activity, does away with *labour*, and abolishes the rule of all classes with the classes themselves, because it is carried through by the class which no longer counts as a class in society, is not recognised as a class, and is in itself the expression of the dissolution of all classes, nationalities, etc., within present society; and (4) Both for the production on a mass

scale of this communist consciousness, and for the success of the cause itself, the alteration of [people] on a mass scale is necessary, an alteration which can only take place in a practical movement, a *revolution*; this revolution is necessary, therefore, not only because the *ruling* class cannot be overthrown in any other way, but also because the class *overthrowing* it can only in a revolution succeed in ridding itself of all the muck of ages and become fitted to found society anew.[3]

The above quoted passage from *The German Ideology* makes it clear that Marx and Engels' conception of history was formulated not, as is commonly supposed by critics and simplifiers, to provide historians with a consistently materialist *interpretation* of history, but to provide socialists with an understanding of the laws of motion of human society so that they could *change* it. It was to provide them with a scientific guide to *revolutionary social practice*. The final two clauses from Marx's 1859 preface, which are usually omitted in quotation, reveal that the standpoint of the author is not that of a historian, but of a *revolutionist*.

The fact of the practical origin and purpose of Marx and Engels' materialist conception of history gives an entirely different perspective to Marx's famous statement itself. Its *dialectical movement* leaps at once to comprehension. The whole period of human history, recorded and unrecorded, is treated as a *process of transition* from the natural animal *Homo sapiens* to the fully developed socialised human being of the classless, socialist society of the future; a society which *because* it has eliminated the internal "antagonism that emanates from the individuals' social conditions of existence" (the social compulsion to labour for others in order to live), will be able to take conscious, collective command of its fate. Unless this basic *dialectical movement* is grasped, the whole conception is falsified.

Moreover, once Marx's statement is viewed in this light, its rigorous *scientific* method becomes clear: Marx deals with the *past* only so far as it is under a variety of historically developed disguises *active* in the present. He indicates "in broad outline" the various "epochs marking progress in the economic development of society" — progress because they have given rise to a mode of production that is the "last antagonistic form of the social process of production", a society which develops the productive forces to a point where they create "the material conditions for a solution to this antagonism".

Marx's analysis begins with the concrete facts of present-day society. It finds in existence a fact of class antagonism, and a body of revolutionary hopes and aspirations faced by a body of conservative and counter-revolutionary resistance. These phenomena he traces to their common root in the existing form of the *social process of production*. This, in turn, is traced to its historical causation in the previous forms of the social process of production — feudal society, and this in turn is seen to have likewise been an historical product (of ancient Roman slave-owner society).

The earliest period cited — the "Asiatic" — is included since, even in 1859, there was historical evidence sufficient to indicate that the rise of the "ancient" slave-owning societies of Mediterranean Europe had come into existence after the emergence of a previous form of social process of production in Asia (the oriental despotisms of Mesopotamia). Marx left out of his "broad outline" any reference to what might have existed before the "Asiatic" form, since there were no data available to him at the time about the period in the "economic development of society" that preceded this form. It was later, *much* later, in the 19th century that the researches of Darwin and the pioneer anthropologists Bachofen, Morgan, Tylor and Frazer provided evidence to subtantiate the Marxist thesis by proving that there had been a series of "epochs" in the historical progression of human society from its most primitive beginnings up to the stage of "civilisation".

It is self-evident that history as a *record* is a record of what people have done; of what has been done by human beings to human beings. It is also, so far as the facts are available, a record of what they have tried to accomplish — only too often without success. But if that is all history is, the ironical legend told by Anatole France becomes a most undeniable, as well as most melancholy, truth. Anatole France told how an eastern potentate caused his "wise men" to write the history of the world in 10,000 volumes. Then, as he neared death, he ordered its compression successively into 1000, 100, then 10 volumes, and then into one volume. Finally, on his deathbed, he ordered its compression into one sentence, and received this for his answer: "They were born; they suffered; they died."

And, indeed, if the dialectical materialist conception of the potential *positive outcome* of the historical process is rejected, that is all that human history has to teach us. In bourgeois hands, history is truly a "dismal science" —- at best a chronicle of scandals, at worst a nightmare of ghastly failures.

Historical materialism lifts the whole subject above this pessimism and futility. In the first place, it gives a *reason* for the hopes and strivings of human beings. It faces the facts of oppression, but in doing so it gives a courage that enables observers to see also their causes and above all, their consequences, and in these their cure — the foundation fact upon which a larger, saner, scientific optimism may be held.

The Marxist conception of history is notable, too, in that it is the first to give the mass of humanity the centre of the stage as the chief protagonist in the drama. All other conceptions bring in the "mob" merely as does a melodrama: to provide an animated chorus of approval for, and a doltish, uncouth background to, the airs, graces, deeds and posturings of the "star" performers — the "great men". For Marxism, history is what the *whole* of the human race has done, *not* only a few of them.

2. The General Law of Social Revolution

Examined carefully, it will be seen that the Marxist conception of history pointedly discriminates *two active sides* in the structure of society — the unconsciously formed social relations of production (the "economic foundation" or "basis") and the consciously created relations of social regulation (the "legal and political superstructure"). These in turn have *opposite* modes of movement, of advance. The economic foundation develops by simple accretion, by the gradual addition of detailed alterations, which, infinitesimal in themselves, nonetheless, over time, become apparent as a *qualitative* change in the basis of society.

To take an illustration from the technological side of the development of the economic foundation of capitalism: Watt's steam engine was not so great an alteration of Newcomen's engine, or Trevithick's, as to call for any great excitement. Yet, at the time, and in the then existing circumstances, it made all the difference. The factory system was becoming more and more widespread in Britain. Machines driven by wind, water, horse and human power were coming more and more into use, and to make those machines, coal was increasingly in demand. Coal mining presented the problem of water in the pit and of its extraction. Watt's steam engine was first invented as an *improved* variety of pumping engine. It needed little alteration to become a new source of motive power which qualitatively transformed a creeping advance into a breakneck "industrial revolution".

With regard to legal and political changes quite a different process is to be observed. Here it is not a question of what one individual may change — as is the case with changes in technology, in the material forces of production. Here it is a question of changing the codes and rules to which *all* must submit. Put thus, it becomes obvious that questions of social change involving alterations in the *basic accepted* principles of law and government cannot help but be fought out in the end as partisan struggles.

For instance, in Europe at the end of the Middle Ages there arose the question of what, if any, were the proper limits of the authority of the papacy. This in the then prevailing political conditions in Europe involved the practical question as to which of *two* governing powers — that of the Catholic Church and that of the kings and princes — had the prior claim to the obedience of the individual. And, since this raised the further question — whose authority could decide between the rival claimants? — there arose, in practice, though in disguised form, the claim of the individual to judge, not only between church authority and secular state authority, but between all public authority and the authority of the *individual* conscience.

It is a matter of history that this "Reformation" struggle was fought out as a revolutionary struggle — with fierce warfare, bloodshed and savage coercion on both sides. It is also a matter of historical fact that it did not end until the whole "legal and political superstructure" of society had been changed. Nor can it be denied that as the struggle was actually fought out, the text of the Bible and its interpretation became an immediate point of contention. But *why* did the text of a Bible whose canon was closed in the fourth century become suddenly a source of contention on an all-European scale in the 15th and 16th centuries? Where had the problem been in the intervening centuries?

The questions raised by the Reformation struggle had been raised, all of them, by different individuals as speculative questions long before. Some of them had been raised by heretical sects which had been crushed. Why did these questions raised in the Reformation suddenly flare up into great partisan issues? Why were they not only fought out through a whole epoch of revolution and counter-revolution, but so raised that they culminated in the irony of the "Counter-Reformation" — the Catholic Church saving itself from destruction, in those lands where it retained its political dominance and temporal power, by a voluntary self-criticism and purgation?

No answer is possible except the one supplied by the Marxist conception of history, which is revolutionary and epoch-making precisely because it explains (what all alternative conceptions fail to explain) not only the continuity of history, but its discontinuity. Its dialectical quality lies in just this pivotal fact — *it explains the continuity from the discontinuity, and the discontinuity from the continuity*.

It is here more than anywhere else that professorial "explainers" of Marxism in the Anglo-Saxon world have worked their worst mischief and given excuses for the whole brood of revisers, re-interpreters and bringers-up-to-date. They have purged the Marxist conception of history of its *dialectical* approach, and have turned it into either a simple continuation of the mechanical materialism of the 18th century or a dogmatic supplement to the eclectic nature-materialism of the 19th century.

The formulation of his and Engels' conception of history given by Marx in his 1859 preface is, in fact, their complete refutation in advance. It is nothing less than *classic* in its importance as a demonstration of the materialism in Marx's *dialectics*, and the dialectics in Marx's *materialism*.

All materialism *begins* with the fact that our ideas are *reflections* — are derived from objective material reality. That Marx's conception *includes* this elementary and basic form of materialism is as obvious as is the fact that he gives a prominence never previously given to economic facts as the salient feature in that material reality. But Marx's conception goes far beyond that elementary beginning. The "explainers" who see in it nothing but the fact that every aspect of life is tied to economics thereby reveal that they have completely failed to grasp the real Marxism in the conception.

Marx's revolution in the *materialist doctrine* consisted in nothing less than immense quantitative extension of (with its concomitant qualitative change in) the *material reality* from which he explained people's ideas, and thought activity generally. The 18th century materialists had taken into account only the phenomena of external and internal nature, and those of personal association. The nature-materialists of the 19th century merely added on (without integrating) the abstract conception of "evolution". Marx saw that *social relations* were positive *material facts* which, developing in accordance with their *own special laws of motion*, not only operated as determinants in themselves, but *radically transformed* and retransformed the operative significance of the phenomena of nature and of human association.

This not only revolutionises the doctrine of materialism: it provides a basis for the complete and final refutation of all idealism. Most of all, in making materialism *dialectical* it not only reduced the phenomena of social revolution to terms of a general law of social evolution, but also in providing an objective basis for the unification of theory and practice, it showed how the practice of revolutionary struggle could be rationally justified and scientifically guided. It is, in fact, here, in the classic formulation of his conception of history, that Marx's whole theory and practice are shown in their inseparable *unity*. Implicit in its compact formulation is the whole of *dialectical materialism*, objective and subjective.

To realise its liberating force, it must be viewed from a whole series of angles.

Firstly, in its most general aspect, it completely revolutionises the conception of the relation between the individual and society. All previous materialists had conceived human society as a simple aggregation of human beings and had, accordingly, seen in history nothing beyond a multitude of individual behaviours and their consequences. On this view, which is substantially the view of all non-Marxist historians and social theorists, society is the product of the aggregation of independently originating individuals. On Marx's view, the individual is the *product* of society, and not its raw material.

If the formulation quoted from the 1859 preface (clause 1) is examined, it will be perceived that Marx takes as his starting point in his conception of history production *relations*. People *enter* into these relations "independent of their will", and it is these *relations* which in their totality, constitute the *real* foundation of society. It takes, perhaps, an effort to grasp the seeming paradox that relations *between* people must be conceived as logically and historically antecedent to the people themselves. But once it is seen that Marx is analysing *that which exists here and now*, and is reaching his conception of the *past* by means of this analysis of the *present*, it becomes obvious that to every person now living, the social relations of production into which he or she enters in the course of "making a living" are most obviously material realities which pre-existed him or her. If this analysis is carried back to its logical conclusion, we reach the obvious "poser": what about the *first* people? The Marxist answer is a dialectical one: *the first people were not people!* Nature-evolved anthropoid primates in their nature-begotten struggle with nature *transformed themselves into people*, into humans, and their interrelation into a social one by *production activity*. And this production activity — this transformative, antagonistic interrelation between humanity and nature — is the general source and origin of the whole movement of human history, as it is also, in specific stages of social development, the *basis* of each and every historical epoch.

But Marx's conception is not limited to formulating the basic law of motion of human society in general — though, if his critics and simplifiers had perceived that what Marx formulated was a law of *motion,* students of Marxism would have been spared many intellectual follies. Marx discriminated this law not only into its basic dialectical determinants, but also into its whole series of determinated phases. Not the abstract law in general, but the specific, concrete, law of the *transformation* of this motion, of the transition from epoch to epoch in history — the law of motion in detail, the specific law of social revolution — is the outstanding feature of Marx's conception of history.

With the aid of this conception, it becomes possible to unravel all the "mysteries" — of the rise and fall of kingdoms, empires etc. — which have baffled historical speculation. Each historical epoch, each mode of production, is relatively stable within itself. While its potentialities are being developed, history in the *real* sense seems to have come to a stop. Yet this very stability is the chief promoting cause of the economic development which in the end breaks up the society and brings into existence a new historical epoch in the economic development of society.

The static view which conceived society as totally disintegrated by a social revolution and restarted afterwards, and the purely abstract "evolutionary" view, which affirmed solely that the new society was only the old society in a new shape, were both refuted by the Marxist conception of history. And they were refuted by being *synthesised*. The old society was broken up (as to its superstructure and its social *relations* of production), the old society was continued unbroken (as to its *forces* of production) in the new society. By discriminating the "unity" of the abstract concept "society" into the specific antagonism of productive forces and the production relations (upon whose basis there arises a specific legal and political superstructure), Marx was able to formulate the laws of social *movement*, transformation and revolution. If the quotation from his 1859 preface is examined it will be seen that out of 10 clauses, all but three deal with the revolutionary transformation of society.

Before Marx and Engels, revolutions could be explained materialistically only as *interruptions* of the normal course of social development (or, alternatively, as returns to normality compelled by a deviation from "natural law"). Only idealistically could revolutions be brought within the compass of a general law — by treating them as products of the evolution of ideas. Marx and Engels were the first, and stand out as the only, materialist thinkers who have adequately comprehended both the "normal" evolution of human society and its periodical revolutionary transformation within the compass of a general law.

The consequences of this law for practice are enormous. On the one hand, the need to treat society as a *process* (and not simply as a "structure") cuts the ground from under the feet of all conservatism and all dogmatism. It also becomes impossible to treat society as a closed mechanism whose outcome is foreordained in the nature of its structural interrelations. And it is no less impossible to treat society as a purely relative fact — a *mere* expression of private consciousness and will. Society — that which moves in history — is an objective material fact, and it has structure, which must be understood before the individuals making up society can be understood. But this structure is both the product of a dialectical process and the starting point for a fresh development. That society "evolves" from social revolution to social revolution is the first and most basic conclusion to be derived from the Marxist general law of motion of society.

3. Historical Materialism and the Proletarian-Socialist Revolution

Precisely because the Marxist conception destroys conservatism (the view that society cannot fundamentally be altered) on the one side and utopianism (the view that society can be revolutionised at will) on the other, it is the conception which vindicates a scientifically based revolutionary optimism to the full. Since society (see clause 7) is never broken up by social revolution until "the material conditions for the existence" of new, superior relations of production "have matured within the framework of the old society", i.e., until the productive forces to which these new, superior production relations are appropriate "are already present or at least in the course of formation", it follows that any general movement to revolutionise society is in itself evidence that the change *can be made* — that objective realities exist corresponding to the aspirations and hopes of the revolutionary class and its party.

It is not Marx and Engels' notion that, for instance, the *idea of socialism* will arise *spontaneously* in the heads of each and every individual proletarian. Ideas are engendered and develop necessarily in social interaction, and therefore follow within limits their own law of development. But for the idea to arise in the first place, and to become general in the second place, an objective social reality must exist from which the idea has arisen. There must exist, and be felt to exist, a *social problem* for which a solution must be found — and it is under the promptings of the urgency of the problem as well as their cogency and applicability to the *needs* viewed in the light of practical everyday reality that ideas spread and develop into "forms of public opinion".

It was, in point of fact, as Marx and Engels themselves noted, *not* the proletariat, but the intellectuals of the aristocracy and the bourgeoisie, who first formulated the general idea of socialism as an alternative to the bourgeois order. It was only *after* capitalist society had reached maturity and had, therefore, begun to reveal its inner contradictions in full force — that is, during the emergence of its highest stage, the stage of monopoly capitalism, in the last decade of the 19th century — that the idea of socialism as an alternative to capitalist society began to spread on a mass scale among the proletariat as a result of the propaganda work of socialist parties made up of intellectuals and politically advanced workers.

Conversely, although the idea of socialism is by no means *spontaneously* engendered in the heads of the mass of proletarians by the class struggle, there is spontaneously born among the proletarians the *need* to struggle, first for immediate betterment of their conditions of existence, then ultimately for liberation from capitalist oppression and exploitation. Capitalism thus, while it does not spontaneously put the idea of a proletarian socialist revolution into the heads of the proletariat, does, and with ever growing urgency, create a series of *social problems* for which a proletarian socialist revolution is objectively the *only* ultimate solution. And when the recognition of this fact (however vague and imperfectly as to details) becomes widespread among the proletariat, it may be taken as proved that the objective possibility exists for bringing the new social order into being.

Marx also makes it clear (see clause 4) that he envisages the proletarian-socialist revolution as an historical epoch of *prolonged struggles*. That in the course of such an epoch there should be changes of fortune for the contending classes necessarily follows from the nature of the concept of an "era of social revolution". It should not be surprising then that the proletarian revolution tends to follow the line of least resistance — to first overthrow capitalist rule where it is *weakest*, rather than where it is strongest. Nor should it be surprising if the first proletarian revolutions — precisely because they succeed where capitalist rule is weakest — also inherit the material basis of that weakness and, as a result of that circumstance, suffer defeat at the hands of bourgeois counter-revolutions backed by the *strongest* capitalist powers. Indeed, Marx expected as much. Commenting on the defeat of the first attempted revolutionary uprising of the proletariat — in Paris in June 1848 — he wrote:

> Bourgeois revolutions, like those of the eighteenth century, storm swiftly from success to success; their dramatic effects outdo each other; men and things seem set in sparkling brilliants; ecstasy is the everyday spirit; but they are short-lived; soon they have attained their zenith, and a crapulent depression lays hold of society before it learns soberly to assimilate the results of its storm-and-stress period. On the other hand, proletarian revolutions ... criticise themselves constantly, interrupt themselves continually in their own course, come back to the apparently accomplished in order to begin it afresh, deride with unmerciful thoroughness the inadequacies, weaknesses and paltriness of their first attempts, seem to throw down their adversary only in order that he may draw new strength from the earth and rise again, more gigantic, before them, recoil ever and anon, until a situation has been created which makes all turning back impossible, and the conditions themselves cry out:
>
> *Hic Rhodus, hic salta!* [Here is the obstacle, now jump!][5]

Marx's revolutionary optimism, his confidence in the eventual victory of the proletarian revolution, was based upon the fact that capitalism creates not only the material *conditions* but also the *social agency* for its own overthrow. But it is only through a series of prolonged struggles, of proletarian revolutions and bourgeois counterrevolutions, that this social agency — the proletarian class — can, with the aid of the advanced theory brought to it by its class-conscious vanguard, come to *understand* that there can not be a *positive outcome* to the historical process other than through the victory, on a world scale, of the proletarian-socialist revolution. ❦

Notes

References to the works of Marx and Engels and Lenin in the most frequently quoted editions have been abbreviated as follows:

LCW V.I. Lenin, *Collected Works*, Progress Publishers, Moscow, 1964-1970
LSW V.I.Lenin, *Selected Works* [in three volumes], Progress Publishers, Moscow, 1975
MECW K. Marx and F. Engels, *Collected Works*, Vols. 1-47, Lawrence and Wishart, London, 1975-1995
MESC K. Marx and F. Engels, *Selected Correspondence*, Progress Publishers, Moscow, 1975
MESW K. Marx and F. Engels, *Selected Works* [in three volumes], Progress Publishers, Moscow, 1969-1970

Introduction

1 *MESW*, Vol. 1, p. 20
2 *The Macquarie Dictionary* (Macquarie Library: Sydney, 1989), p. 381
3 F. Engels, *The Condition of the Working Class in England* (Progress Publishers: Moscow, 1973), p. 64
4 *ibid.*, pp. 64-65
5 K. Marx, *Capital*, Vol. 1 (Penguin Books: Harmondsworth, 1976), p. 283
6 *MESW*, Vol. 1, p. 14

Chapter 1. Historical Materialism as a Science

1 Cited in D. Gribanov et al, *Einstein and the Philosophical Problems of 20th Century Physics* (Progress Publishers: Moscow, 1979), p. 18.
2 Philosophical *materialism* is the view that outside of our consciousness there exists an external world that is independent of any consciousness, but which may be reflected in our consciousness; that the totality of objects in this external world constitute matter and that consciousness is a product of particular material systems, i.e., living organisms with nervous

systems and brains. Philosophical materialism stands in opposition to philosophical *idealism*, which holds that consciousness, either human or supernatural, is the sole or primary feature of reality and that matter is a product of our own individual consciousness (subjective idealism) or of a disembodied supernatural consciousness (objective idealism).

3 *G.W.F. Hegel* (1770-1831) was the culminating figure of the German idealist school of philosophy that began with Immanuel Kant. Hegel sought to resolve the traditional philosophical distinction between mind and matter by postulating a unified, monistic reality in which matter is the "alienated" expression of its inner organising force — reason or the Absolute Spirit. While Hegel's theory of being was idealist, he viewed reality as undergoing a process of dialectical development. In his afterward to the second edition of *Capital* Vol. 1, Marx observed that the "mystification which the dialectic suffers in Hegel's hands by no means prevents him from being the first to present its general forms of motion in a comprehensive and conscious manner. With him it is standing on its head. It must be inverted, in order to discover the rational kernel within the mystical shell".

4 *LCW*, Vol. 19, p. 25

5 *Positivism* is the bourgeois philosophical trend initiated by Augustus Comte (1798-1857), an offshoot of empricism, which holds that the only valid knowledge is "positive", i.e., immediately empirically verifiable. Comte envisaged the discovery of laws of social development based on projecting existing social trends mechanistically into the future. His followers, the neo-positivists, reject any general social theories or "value judgements" beyond the simple description of actual events and social institutions.

6 *LCW*, Vol. 1, p. 142

7 *Epistemology* is the study of the sources, development, limits and validity of knowledge.

8 *LSW*, Vol. 1, p. 44

9 *MESW*, Vol. 1, pp. 503-04

10 *LSW*, Vol. 1, p. 25

11 *MESC*, p. 172

12 F. Engels, *Anti-Dühring* (Progress Publishers: Moscow, 1969), pp. 136-37

Chapter 2. Social Being and Social Consciousness

1 *Aleksandr Bogdanov* (1878-1928) was a leading member of the Russian Social-Democratic Labour Party. After the defeat of the 1905-07 revolution he led an ultraleft current within the Bolshevik faction. A doctor by profession, between 1904 and 1906 he wrote a three-volume philosophical work, *Empiriomonism*, in which he sought to "fuse" Marxism with the subjective idealist philosophy of "empiriocriticism" developed by the Austrian physicist Ernst Mach (1838-1916). Lenin's 1908 work *Materialism and Empiriocriticism* refuted

the views of the Machists by assessing the new discoveries in physics (the electron, radioactivity) from the standpoint of the dialectical materialist theory of knowledge.

2 *MESW*, Vol. 3, p. 488

3 *LCW*, Vol. 20. p. 24

4 *LCW*, Vol. 29, p. 70

5 *MESW*, Vol. 3, p. 48

6 *LCW*, Vol. 7, p. 45

7 K. Marx and F. Engels, *The Communist Manifesto and Its Relevance For Today* (Resistance Books: Sydney, 1998), p. 56

8 A. Bonnard, *Civilisation grecque. De l'lliade au Parthénon* (Lausanne, 1954), p. 183

9 F. Engels, *Anti-Dühring*, p. 105

10 *MECW*, Vol. 3, p. 181

CHAPTER 3. FORMS OF SOCIAL CONSCIOUSNESS AND THEIR FUNCTION

1 *MESW*, Vol. 1, pp. 24-25

2 *ibid.*, p. 33

3 K. Marx and F. Engels, *The Communist Manifesto and Its Relevance for Today*, p. 59

4 J. Davis, *Capitalism and Its Culture* (New York, 1935), p. 400

5 F. Engels, *Anti-Dühring*, p. 115

6 K. Marx, *Capital*, Vol. 1, p. 173

7 *MECW*, Vol. 3, p. 174

8 F. Engels, *Anti-Dühring*, p. 374

9 *MECW*, Vol. 3, p. 174

10 *MESW*, Vol. 3, p. 373

11 *ibid.*, p. 373

12 F. Engels, *Dialectics of Nature* (Progress Publishers: Moscow, 1972), p. 184-85

13 Quoted from "The Heritage of K. Marx", *Kommunist*, No. 7, 1958, p. 23.

14 F. Engels, *Dialectics of Nature*, p. 231

15 Aristotle, *The Works of Aristotle* (Oxford University Press: Oxford, 1908), Vol. 8, p. 1031b7f

16 *Neo-Thomism* is the official philosophical doctrine of the Roman Catholic Church based on the teachings of Thomas Aquinas (1225-1274).

17 *MESW*, Vol. 3, p. 375

Chapter 4. Material Production the Basis of Social Life

1 K. Marx, *Capital*, Vol. 1, p. 283

2 According to Benjamin Franklin's definition, which Marx quotes in *Capital*, humanity is a "tool-making animal" (*ibid.*, p. 286).

3 *MESW*, p. 20

4 See K. Marx, *Capital*, Vol. 1, p. 285.

5 See *ibid.*, p. 103 where Marx explicitly endorsed the view that his purpose in writing *Capital* was to disclose "the special laws that regulate the origin, existence, development and death of a given social organism and its replacement by another, higher one".

6 See *MESC*, p. 244.

7 Marx and Engels noted that the first prerequisite of history is the "existence of living human individuals. Thus the first fact to be established is the physical organisation of these individuals and their consequent relations to the rest of nature" (*MESW*, Vol. 1, p. 20).

8 K. Marx, *Capital*, Vol. 1, p. 784

9 *ibid.*, p. 286

10 "A development in the productive forces that would reduce the absolute number of workers, and actually enable the whole nation to accomplish its entire production in a shorter period of time, would produce a revolution, since it would put the majority of the population out of action. Here we have once again the characteristic barrier to capitalist production, and we see how this is in no way an absolute form for the development of the productive forces and the creation of wealth, but rather comes into conflict with this at a certain point in its development." (K. Marx, *Capital*, Vol. 3 [Penguin Books: London, 1981], p. 372)

11 K. Marx, *Grundisse* (Penguin Books: Harmondsworth, 1977), p. 703-04 (emphasis added)

12 K. Marx, *Capital*, Vol. 1, p. 325

13 K. Marx., *Capital* (Penguin Books: London, 1981), Vol. 3, p. 927

14 *MESW*, Vol. 1, p. 504

15 *ibid.*, p. 519

16 K. Marx, *Grundisse*, p. 541

17 F. Engels, *Anti-Dühring*, p. 330

18 K. Marx, *Capital*, Vol. 3, pp. 1023-24

19 *ibid.*, p. 568 (emphasis added)

Chapter 5. The Socioeconomic Formation

1 *LCW*, Vol. 1, p. 140

2 *MESW*, Vol. 1, p. 503

3 *MESW*, Vol. 3, p. 84
4 F. Engels, *Anti-Dühring*, p. 37
5 *MESW*, Vol. 3, p. 487
6 *ibid.*, p. 487

CHAPTER 6. SOCIAL REVOLUTION

1 *LCW*, Vol. 33. p. 110
2 *LCW*, Vol. 13, p. 37
3 *LCW*, Vol. 23, pp. 238-239; Vol. 29, pp. 157, 203
4 *LCW*, Vol. 27, p. 89
5 *LCW*, Vol. 21, pp. 213-14
6 *MESW*, Vol. 1, p. 193

CHAPTER 7. SOCIAL CLASSES AND CLASS STRUGGLE

1 *LCW*, Vol. 19, p. 28
2 F. Engels, *Anti-Dühring*, p. 37
3 *MESW*, Vol. 1, pp. 528
4 *ibid.*, p. 479
5 K. Marx, *Capital,* Vol 3, p. 927
6 *LCW*, Vol. 29, p. 421
7 *LCW*, Vol. 6, pp. 262-63
8 Quoted from *Ancient Modes of Production. Original Sources* (Leningrad, 1933), p. 20 (in Russian).
9 *LCW*, Vol. 15, p. 39
10 LCW, Vol. 12, p. 404
11 *MESW*, Vol. 1, p. 521
12 *LCW*, Vol. 11, p. 71
13 *MESW*, Vol. 2, p. 75
14 *ibid.*, pp. 423-24
15 K. Marx, *The Poverty of Philosophy* (Progress Publishers: Moscow, 1973), p. 150
16 *MESW*, Vol. 1, pp. 396-97

CHAPTER 8. THE POLITICAL ORGANISATION OF SOCIETY

1 *MESW*, Vol. 3, p. 326
2 *LCW*, Vol. 28, p. 236
3 *MESW*, Vol. 3, p. 491

4 *LCW*, Vol. 29, p. 479
5 *LCW*, Vol. 27, p. 334
6 *MESW*, Vol. 3, p. 26
7 *LCW*, Vol. 25, pp. 425-426
8 *MESW*, Vol. 1, p. 126
9 *ibid.*, p. 181
10 *ibid.*, p. 182
11 *ibid.*, p. 98
12 *MESW*, Vol. 2, p. 223
13 *ibid.*, p. 220
14 *MESC*, p. 275
15 *MESW*, Vol. 2, pp. 187-188
16 *LCW*, Vol. 24, pp. 38-39
17 *ibid.*, p. 53
18 *LSW*, Vol. 2, pp. 267-68
19 *ibid.*, p. 269
20 *ibid.*, p. 268
21 *ibid.*, p. 269
22 *MESW*, Vol. 2, p. 223
23 *ibid.*, p. 223
24 *MESW*, Vol. 1, p. 126

Chapter 9. The Historical Forms of Human Community

1 *MESW*, Vol. 1, pp. 112-13
2 *LCW*, Vol. 1, p. 155
3 *LCW*, Vol. 20, p. 45
4 *ibid.*, p. 396
5 *ibid.*, p. 27
6 *MESW*, Vol. 1, p. 116
7 *LCW*, Vol. 20, p. 26
8 *ibid.*, pp. 35-36
9 *LCW*, Vol. 36, p. 608
10 *LCW*, Vol. 21, pp. 413-14
11 *LCW*, Vol. 22, p. 325
12 *LCW*, Vol. 36, p. 608
13 *LCW*, Vol. 22, p. 145

14 *LCW*, Vol. 20, pp. 411-12

CHAPTER 10. THE MARXIST CONCEPTION OF HISTORY AND REVOLUTIONARY OPTIMISM

1 K. Marx, *A Contribution to the Critique of Political Economy* (Progress Publishers: Moscow, 1977), p. 20

2 *ibid.*, pp. 20-22

3 *MESW*, Vol. 1, pp. 40-41

4 *LSW*, Vol. 1, p. 25

5 *MESW*, Vol. 1, p. 401